Drawing & Rendering for Theatre

DUBLIN

Donated to

**Visual Art Degree
Sherkin Island**

Drawing & Rendering for Theatre

A PRACTICAL COURSE FOR SCENIC, COSTUME, AND LIGHTING DESIGNERS

Clare P. Rowe

Amsterdam   Boston   Heidelberg   London   New York   Oxford
Paris   San Diego   San Francisco   Singapore   Sydney   Tokyo

Focal Press is an imprint of Elsevier

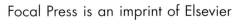

Acquisitions Editor: Cara Anderson
Publishing Services Manager: George Morrison
Project Manager: Mónica González de Mendoza
Assistant Editor: Robin Weston
Marketing Manager: Christine Degon Veroulis
Cover Design: Pamela Poll

Focal Press is an imprint of Elsevier
30 Corporate Drive, Suite 400, Burlington, MA 01803, USA
Linacre House, Jordan Hill, Oxford OX2 8DP, UK

Library of Congress Cataloging-in-Publication Data
Rowe, Clare P.
    Drawing and rendering for theatre : a practical course for scenic, costume,
and lighting designers / Clare P. Rowe.
        p. cm.
    Includes index.
    ISBN 978-0-240-80554-2 (pbk. : alk. paper)   1. Theaters–Stage-setting and
scenery.   2. Costume design.   3. Stage lighting.   4. Drawing.   I. Title.
    PN2091.S8R62 2006
    792.02′5–dc22
                                                                2007011641

British Library Cataloguing-in-Publication Data
A catalogue record for this book is available from the British Library.

ISBN: 978-0-240-80554-2

For information on all Focal Press publications
visit our website at www.books.elsevier.com

07 08 09 10 11 12   10 9 8 7 6 5 4 3 2 1

Printed in China

Table of Contents

Introduction

DRAWING

To those with little experience in drawing, the ability to accurately draw can seem like a magical gift. Certainly there are those few who are born with exceptional artistic ability. However, despite our tendency to describe a person with advanced facility in drawing as "talented," "gifted," or even "genius," nearly everyone can develop a high proficiency in realistic drawing, regardless of one's inherited aptitude. As those with some experience in drawing know, those with an interest in drawing are driven to practice; as time progresses these budding artists seek out and begin to incorporate knowledge about perspective and drawing techniques into their practice. Interest translates to practice, and practice becomes proficiency as the artist matures. One who continues this training ultimately displays "talent" that amazes us, although it is actually often just the culmination of many hours of (enjoyable) work.

It is not particularly amazing that young children learn to read and write, yet if elementary school teachers spent the same amount of time teaching children to draw as they do reading and writing we would all be excellent draftsmen. Learning to draw is categorically no different from learning to write or learning a language. However, since this training is not an integral part of most elementary education, generally only those individuals with an early personal interest in the activity make it a part of their everyday lives, or receive specific instruction to improve their skills.

Creating a two-dimensional image that is a credible copy of the space relationships of natural objects as they appear to the eye is actually simple, if one employs a set of artistic conventions well known to humans for centuries. Success at this type of drawing depends on: (1) the ability to accurately depict the shape and texture of objects and the light that illuminates them, and (2) mastering the principles and techniques of perspective.

Unlike learning a new language (which children tend to learn more effortlessly than adults), learning to draw as an adult offers two major advantages. First, adults have advanced eye-hand coordination and fine motor control from years of practice at skills such as writing, typing, assorted sporting activities, and so on. Second, the principles of perspective and other drawing conventions tend to be conceptual, and therefore more readily assimilated by adults than children. In addition, it is easier for an adult to conquer the innate difficulties inherent to learning to draw.

The adult drawing student may encounter two major challenges. The first is a lack of confidence. Many with rudimentary drawing skills believe that the quality of their drawing corresponds directly with their innate ability and that this ability is a finite quantity. In other words, "This is the best I can do, given my limited talent." Adults are more likely to remember that if they just keep practicing, they *will* get better. Again, learning to draw, like learning a language or learning to read or write, is an ability that is intrinsically achievable by virtually all humans. Fortunately, a lack of confidence is usually a factor only at the beginning of this drawing course. As one's skills develop, self-assurance improves correspondingly.

The second challenge, ironically, arises from the reality that most adults *can* draw. Many adults are even exceptionally capable, but have developed deeply ingrained drawing practices and routines over the years that may be counterproductive to creating the most effective theatrical design renderings.

Take, for example, the costume designer who, while proficient at figure drawing, had the habit of drawing the left side of the body to a nearly complete state before he even began the right side. He noticed that this practice created problems with symmetry and balance in his figures, and was determined to make a change in his routine. He found that it was surprisingly difficult to change a custom that, over time, had become an unconscious muscle-memory action. Luckily, drawing habits are not addictive. By making a concerted effort, in a short time he was able to modify his routine by starting on the left side, then alternating back and forth between the right and left. This subtle behavioral shift in technique resulted in significantly better costume renderings.

Or, consider the scenic designer who had great difficulty creating a focus in her set renderings. An effective set rendering is not a detailed picture of the set, but rather, is descriptive of a particular moment in the play. Though beautifully drawn and painted, a typical rendering by this designer included as much attention to detail on less significant areas of the stage (for example, a masking flat) as to the area of the action of the play the rendering was supposed to portray. She was accustomed to beginning her rendering by creating an accurate line drawing of the set using measured perspective, as many designers do. She included every detail of the theater architecture, set, and major props in her perspective drawing.

As anyone who has employed the technique of measured perspective can attest, her layout drawing represented hours of work. Although labor-intensive, the detailed layout drawing had evolved to become an integral part of her design process. However, after spending so much time on the perspective drawing, when she began painting, she was reluctant to virtually eliminate major parts of her drawing to create an area of focus. The result was an attractive painting appropriate as an interior design rendering, but not very effective in visually communicating what an audience would see at a particular moment of a theatrical production. The solution for this designer was to change the way she approached her layout drawing. She continued to use the technique of measured perspective and drew the theater architecture and major lines of the set, but without including any detail. Then, after determining the scene in the play she would represent and the area of focus, she drew detail in only that area, creating a vignette of reduced detail around it. The result was an effective communication tool to describe the scenery, action, and mood of a particular dramatic moment.

Both of these designers faced and successfully met the challenge of overcoming their own ingrained habits. As you work through the exercises in this section, keep in mind that your ultimate goal is to produce effective design renderings and drawings. Any ingrained or unconscious habits that you might have that interfere with this goal will need to be identified and modified. Everyone can learn to draw or improve existing drawing skills; as an adult, you are particularly well situated to do so.

The exercises in this book are tailored to aid the theatrical designer in developing the drawing skills necessary to create renderings that are effective visual communication tools. Keep in mind that, regardless of one's area of specialization, versatility is an asset. Therefore, costume designers should not avoid architectural subjects or perspective drawing, nor should lighting designers balk at figure drawing.

Chapter 1

The Benchmark Drawing

This chapter begins with an exercise designed to measure one's existing drawing skills. Follow the instructions outlined in this chapter for setting up and completing the exercise, without reading ahead, so that your drawing is an accurate reflection of your current skills. The purpose of this exercise is to create a drawing that will be an assessment tool and a point of reference for later evaluation of your progress as you work through this book. After you have completed your benchmark drawing, this chapter will discuss typical behavior and results particular to the beginning, intermediate, and advanced student. As part of this discussion, procedures are outlined for analyzing one's own drawing for specific areas that need improvement.

SETTING UP THE STILL LIFE

Set up a simple still life on a table. Cover a small cardboard box with a piece of dark colored fabric large enough so the fabric drapes in folds over the box and onto the table in front of the box. Choose several (four or five) recognizable objects for your still life. One should be a small bust of a human head or torso. The other objects can be anything—a book, a teapot, a cup and saucer, or a wine glass are classics—but choose objects that are smooth in texture and light in value. Arrange the objects on the fabric

on top of and in front of the box. If possible, arrange the still life in front of a blank wall so that you can focus on the objects without background distractions. If you do not have a blank wall available, create a backdrop for your still life with a large piece of illustration board or similar material. Arrange the lighting so there is a strong top side light on the still life.

Figure 1.1 Sample still life setup for benchmark drawing.

DRAWING THE STILL LIFE

Find a position where you have an unobstructed view of the arrangement. Assume a drawing position that you feel comfortable with, either standing or sitting. Using a number two pencil and a piece of drawing paper at least as large as 11 × 14", sketch the still life. It may be helpful to tape the paper to the table. Your primary goal in this exercise is to faithfully record what you see. Draw continuously for one hour and then stop regardless of how complete the drawing is. Date and save this drawing. This is your starting point and a point of reference for measuring your future progress.

Analysis

After reading this section, you will be able to critically examine your own drawing for specific areas of improvement. This section is broken down into three categories: the beginning, intermediate, and advanced level student. Read all three of these sections first to determine which seems most appropriate for your own current level of skill. For each skill level, one or two sample student drawings of the previously depicted still life are discussed. Use these samples to determine your skill level. Keep in mind that these are not necessarily discrete categories; for example, even if you primarily identify yourself as an intermediate student, there may also be information in the beginning or advanced sections that will be of help.

BEGINNING LEVEL

For the person who draws infrequently or who otherwise has little experience with sketching, the benchmark still life exercise is particularly important, although it can be a frustrating experience. You may have a tendency toward viewing your work as unfavorable compared with the work of others. It is important to keep in mind that this exercise is not a competition. You will progress at your own pace from your own starting place. It is not helpful to compare either your benchmark sketch or rate of progress with other students (other than to assess your current skill level), since your starting place and progress rate will be unique to you. Some will improve dramatically at the onset and then hit a plateau at which it seems no progress is discernable for quite some time. Others will be thwarted by what

seems like no forward movement at first and then, suddenly, see a dramatic leap in drawing facility. Some may even think for a while that their skills have deteriorated. Consider that as long as you continue to practice drawing, your ability will develop, but that the rate of progress is not always incrementally constant.

General Description of the Beginning Student

If you are a typical beginning level student, it is likely that you rarely, if ever, draw as a part of your everyday life. Some of the possible markers of the novice might include one or more of the following: (1) you do not yet have, or have forgotten, in-depth knowledge of basic drawing techniques and conventions; (2) you may need practice in eye–hand coordination; (3) you may find every attempt at drawing to be challenging; (4) while doing your benchmark drawing, you were not sure how to begin the drawing, what size it should be, how to place it on the page, or how to finish in the time allotted; and/or (5) the most frustrating of all and yet most common, you could see with your *eyes* exactly what you wanted to commit to paper, but could not command your *hand* to create the correct shapes. Not surprisingly perhaps, almost all beginning students tend to have some or all of these same difficulties and frustrations. However, identifying behavior that leads to unsuccessful results is the first step in improving one's skills.

Assessing Your Experience with the Benchmark Exercise: Beginning Student Behavior

In the completion of the benchmark drawing, there tends to be a standard set of behaviors that typifies the beginning, intermediate, or advanced student. If you are a beginning student, the following list suggests several possible things you did while you were drawing the benchmark exercise. Some are contradictory. To begin the assessment of your skill level, recall your experience while you were completing the exercise to determine if you identify with any of the following behavioral traits.

- It took you a long time to get started with the drawing because you were not sure of what to draw first. As a result, you did not get to finish to the extent you had intended.

- You found yourself erasing and re-drawing nearly every line.
- You started over on a new sheet of paper several times.
- You stopped drawing before the hour was up either because you were frustrated with the results, or you did not know what else to add to the drawing.
- During the exercise, you mostly concentrated on your drawing and looked briefly at the still life only occasionally to keep yourself on track.
- While you were drawing you held your pencil the same way as when you write.

Take note of any of the previous descriptions and see if you identify with any of them. In the next chapter, you will learn techniques that assist you in overcoming some of these obstacles while developing good productive drawing habits.

Although it is helpful to look at your behaviors and routines in completing the benchmark drawing, ultimately the drawing will be used to designate your initial skill level. We will now examine some typical beginning-level benchmark drawings.

Examining the Benchmark Drawing: The Beginning Level

The following is a list of typical descriptions of beginning level drawings. They are grouped into categories, each of which is discussed at length in subsequent chapters. As you read the list, refer to your benchmark drawing to determine which descriptions pertain to your effort.

Drawing What You See

- The objects you drew are identifiable, but do not look like the actual objects in the still life; rather, they appear to be generic representations of the types of objects in the still life.
- The contours of objects are not accurately drawn. For example, perhaps the opposite sides of objects are not as symmetrical as they are in real life, or one part of an object appears too large or too small.

If either of these are descriptive of your drawing, you are, to some degree, relying on your memory of what everyday objects look like, and drawing a symbol provided by your brain rather than what you are actually seeing. It will be helpful for you to refer to the section Stored Visual Memories in Chapter 2.

Perspective

- The objects you drew are not in proportion to each other. For example, the wine glass appears to be greatly oversized compared with the teapot.
- The objects look flat, not three-dimensional as if they are receding in space.
- All of the objects appear to be on the same plane in the foreground of the drawing.
- Some objects that you drew appear to be falling over and/or the plane of the tabletop appears to be tilted upward.

There are certain perspective drawing techniques that fool the eye into believing that objects drawn on a flat piece of paper appear to be three-dimensional. For example, according to the rules of perspective, to make a true circle look as if it is receding in space it must be drawn as an ellipse, or oval. Also, all verticals are true verticals but horizontal lines recede to a vanishing point on the horizon. To learn more about the rules of perspective, refer to Chapter 4.

Three-Dimensional Modeling

- The objects you drew were each uniformly dark or light in value.
- It is difficult to determine from your drawing where the light source is located.
- All the objects in your drawing have a uniform outline, such as in a graphic illustration.

The ability to reproduce the naturalistic play of light and shadow on objects in your drawing is one of the crucial elements of realistic drawing.

Each object in your drawing should have an area that is shaded dark and a corresponding lighter area opposite. For more about this technique, refer to Chapter 5.

Composition

- The drawing appears to be too small in comparison with the size of the paper and is randomly placed on the paper.

- The drawing is too big for the paper and important parts of the still life are cut off at the edges of the paper.

You may not be aware that you always draw in the same scale. Every time you draw the same type of object—for example, a human head—it is always the same size, within a fraction of an inch. Become familiar with your default scale and place your drawing on the paper accordingly. Keep in mind, the way you place your drawing on the paper has an emotional effect on the viewer. This choice of placement should become a conscious decision every time you create a drawing. For more information on drawing placement and composition, refer to Chapter 3.

Figure 1.2 is a beginning student's benchmark drawing. The artist opted to draw only one of the objects in the still life, and the effort does not appear to represent an hour's worth of drawing. He was probably overwhelmed by the complexity of the arrangement and restarted on a new piece of paper several times, but each time was dissatisfied with the product. Perhaps he was intimidated by the features of the bust and foreshortened handle of the teapot, but felt more confident drawing the shape of the wineglass. The composition is awkward with the glass base nearly touching the top edge of the paper.

Still, this effort shows a high degree of potential. The student carefully observed how the lines of the object intersect. His first attempt at drawing the stem placed it too close to the far edge of the base, and this miscalculation was erased and corrected. He observed that the glass is shaped like a cylinder; one end of the stem must appear to connect at the center of the bottom of the cylinder and the other end to the center of the base. He also perceived that the mouth of the glass and the base appear in perspective to be similarly shaped ovals and parallel to each other. Many beginning students will draw the base and mouth of the glass as round shapes, since in reality they *are* circular. The sample 1 artist, however, is drawing what he is seeing, not what he knows to be the actual shape of the object.

Figure 1.3 shows another beginning student's drawing. This beginning drawing has many positive attributes: (1) the objects are relatively proportional to each other; (2) by including detail in the drape of the fabric, the teapot, and the spine of the book the student has clearly made some careful observations; (3) all the objects drawn have been worked to the same degree of completion; and (4) the drawing fits attractively on the page. However, the objects drawn are representational rather than realistic, they do not recede into space accurately, and the source of light is not clearly indicated. This artist will want to continue to work on seeing and observing, perspective drawing, and three-dimensional modeling.

Now that you have analyzed your benchmark drawing, you know where to concentrate your efforts at improvement. As you complete the exercises in this section, pay particular attention to these areas. For example, if you want to concentrate on composition, think about how you will position the drawing

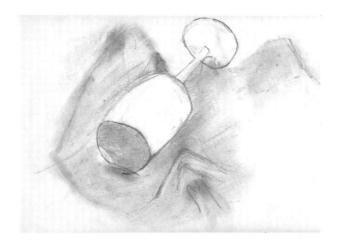

Figure 1.2 Sample 1 of a beginning student's benchmark drawing.

Figure 1.3 Sample 2 of a beginning student's benchmark drawing.

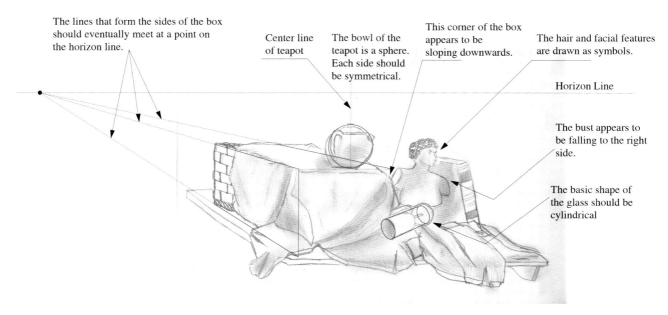

The lines that form the sides of the box should eventually meet at a point on the horizon line.

Center line of teapot

The bowl of the teapot is a sphere. Each side should be symmetrical.

This corner of the box appears to be sloping downwards.

The hair and facial features are drawn as symbols.

Horizon Line

The bust appears to be falling to the right side.

The basic shape of the glass should be cylindrical

Figure 1.4 Critique of beginning student's drawing.

on the page every time you begin a new exercise. If you find you have multiple areas that require development, work on one area at a time until you feel confident, then move on to the next area.

INTERMEDIATE LEVEL

General Description of the Intermediate Student

As an intermediate level drawing student, one or more of the following descriptions probably apply to you.

1. You have had at least some experience or instruction in drawing.
2. You draw for your own pleasure, at least occasionally.
3. There are some things you like to draw, and you draw those thing well. There are other things you do not enjoy drawing, and these you tend to avoid.
4. When drawing your design renderings, you often draw from your imagination rather than from a picture or from life.
5. You would like to improve the accuracy of your drawing, but are not sure how to begin.

Assessing Your Experience with the Benchmark Exercise: Intermediate Student Behavior

Some typical behavioral indicators of the intermediate student are listed below. You may recognize one or more of these as mirroring the experience you had while you were drawing the benchmark exercise.

- You may have found it challenging to draw some of the objects in the still life because they are things you usually never draw. (For example, perhaps you usually only draw the human figure.)
- You really enjoyed drawing one or two of the objects in the arrangement and spent most of your time working on them.
- You understand the rules of perspective, but perhaps you still had difficulty foreshortening objects that receded sharply into the background.
- After you had been drawing for a while, you realized that it would be impossible to fit the entire arrangement on the paper, even though that was your original intention.
- You may have had difficulty drawing all of the detail on some of the objects because the entire drawing was so small.

• When you finished the drawing, you were very satisfied with some parts, but not so much with others. For example, maybe you thought the texture and shadowing on the fabric was very successful, but you were not satisfied with how you drew the facial features on the bust.

Examining the Benchmark Drawing: The Intermediate Level

• There may be a wide range of drawing accuracy from object to object. For example, some objects may have excellent contours and shading, while another may exhibit inaccuracies in perspective.
• Most of the lines in your drawing are of uniform thickness and darkness, regardless of whether they describe areas of shadow or light. There is not much variation in the line weight of the pencil throughout your drawing.
• If you squint your eyes and look at your drawing you see mostly a shade of gray, with only a few areas that are clearly the white of the paper, and few that are deep blacks.
• Some areas of your drawing appear to be complete, but other areas look unfinished. The entire drawing may resemble a sketch rather than a finished drawing.
• The objects in your drawing look three-dimensional, but not necessarily realistic.
• The shaded areas of your drawing are very dark. The details of objects in these areas may have become obscured or perhaps you drew the detail darker than the shadows around them in attempt to make them stand out.

As an intermediate drawing student, you recognize that that you are more skilled in some areas than in others. Most likely, you will be familiar with the drawing conventions and techniques described in the next few chapters. You do not need to learn how to draw, but you do need to concentrate your efforts in specific areas to bring your drawing proficiency up to the next level. As you work through the exercises in this section, you will easily excel at some, but you will also find some exercises challenging.

Figure 1.5 Sample 1 of an intermediate student's benchmark drawing.

Figure 1.5 shows an intermediate student's benchmark drawing. This student drew all the objects using a good range of value, and used light and shade to make the objects look three-dimensional. The box and tabletop would appear more three-dimensional, however, if the different planes were given contrasting values. The wineglass gets lost among the folds of the fabric. The student realized this and attempted to create an area of contrast around the stem and base. But in reality the fabric on the tabletop is lighter in value than the edge of the glass that rests on the fabric. This student will benefit from more careful observation of the actual value of each area. A comparison of the drawing to the photograph of the still life in Figure 1.6 shows that the drawn objects are not proportional to each other.

Figure 1.7 shows another intermediate student's benchmark drawing. This student has good observational skills. Objects are relatively proportional to each other, there is a good sense of three-dimensionality, and the play of light and shadow on the objects in the drawing. However, the artist chose to leave out the tabletop and drapery leaving the wineglass floating impossibly in space. The oval that represents the base of the wineglass is inaccurately drawn, and the head stares straight out instead of tilting down as it does in the still life. This student needs to work on developing good composition instincts and on figure drawing.

The teapot is proportionately too large and tall.

The book is proportionately too short.

The top of the teapot aligns with the top of the bust.

The top of the book aligns just below the eye.

The top of the box is much lighter in value than the front.

Notice the value difference between the two planes.

Figure 1.6
Proportional comparison of drawing to still life.

Figure 1.7 Sample 2 of an intermediate student's benchmark drawing.

ADVANCED LEVEL

At this level, the improvements made in your drawing behavior and style will most likely be minute. Critically assess your drawing behavior and routines to identify and change those that are holding you back from reaching the next level of expertise. Ask yourself: "Is how I draw in some way negatively impacting my design rendering and drawings?" Perhaps you have mastered the proportions of the human figure but need more confidence when drawing faces or hands. Or, you easily draw realistic highlights and shadows but accurate proportion is sometimes difficult. The information in the following bulleted sections describes effective drawing habits and accurate, proficient drawing styles. From these lists, you may recognize certain areas for improvement.

General Description of the Advanced Student

If you are an advanced student (1) you most likely have had extensive experience, and probably training, in drawing; (2) your work is generally accepted to be of high quality and you recognize your own proficiency; (3) you may have a well-developed personal style of drawing; (4) you often draw for your own pleasure; and (5) you are adept at assessing the worthiness of your own efforts as well as others.

Assessing Your Experience with the Benchmark Exercise: Advanced Student Behavior

As an advanced student, you would describe the benchmark drawing exercise as an easy test. As you drew, you were relaxed and comfortable. You enjoy drawing, and the opportunity to draw undisturbed for a full hour was a pleasant experience. Some typical behavioral indicators of the advanced student include some or all of the following list.

- In the first minute you drew, you roughed the drawing in to determine if it would fit attractively on the paper.
- You were confident in your initial placement of the drawing; or, if not, recognized immediately what adjustments were needed and made them.
- As you worked on the drawing, you moved from one area to the next, so that at any given time the entire drawing was in a roughly equivalent state of completion.
- You looked at the negative space around objects and noticed where objects overlapped each other to ensure the accuracy of your drawing.
- If necessary, you extended your arm and used your pencil as a measuring tool to determine the relative size and proportion of objects.
- You drew light and shade accurately for each object and took note of the objects' cast shadows on each other.
- Each element in your drawing is in perspective and proportionate to the whole.

Examining the Benchmark Drawing: The Advanced Level

Figure 1.8 shows an advanced student's benchmark drawing. This student has realistically rendered the objects in the still life, and shows an understanding of the effects of light and shadow. The objects are accurately placed in the drawing and are proportional to each other. However, there is room for improvement. The book is not readily recognizable as a book, and the oval of the top of the wineglass is inaccurate. The drawing is a partial view of the still life in the photograph. The book is cut off by the edge of the paper on the right side of the drawing. The bust is crowded over to the right side of the drawing, while the less interesting, and unfinished, drapery below the teapot is given ample space. Lightly sketching in the entire drawing before working on detail would have given this artist more control over the composition of the drawing.

The more experienced and proficient you are at drawing, the more meticulously precise your self-critique. Examine every detail of your drawing with a critical eye, assessing your own work against each item in the following list.

- Your drawing has a definite focus. When looking at your drawing the eye moves naturally to this area, and the other elements in the drawing are in proportional balance to this focus.

Figure 1.8 An advanced student's benchmark drawing.

- You have used value contrast proficiently in your drawing to draw attention to certain areas and to create the illusion of three-dimensional space. There is a subtle range of value in the drawing from the white of the paper to very dark blacks.
- There is variation in the quality of the lines in the drawing and you have used line to accurately describe the contours of objects.
- The shadows in your drawing appear to be translucent and follow the contours of objects on which they fall.
- You have accurately described the different textures of each object.
- Your drawing has a satisfying feeling of completion; it appears neither unfinished nor overworked.

CONCLUSION

After completing the benchmark exercise and analysis of this drawing, you are ready to take your drawing skills to the next advanced level. Keep in mind that your individual progress will depend not only on your exerted effort, but also on how you process information. For example, if your goal is to modify an ingrained habit in your drawing behavior, you will learn new techniques that will replace the old behavior. However, you may find that although you have intellectually assimilated the new techniques, the muscle memory in your hand prevents you from easily integrating them into your drawing routine. Eventually your hand will re-learn what your brain already knows, but this will take a different amount of time for each individual.

The most important thing when learning to play a musical instrument or learning a new language is to practice as much as possible. The same is true for learning to draw. Regardless of your current skill level, the more you practice, the more skilled you become.

Chapter 2, The Sketchbook, will help you set up a schedule for drawing every week. It discusses appropriate subjects for costume, scenic, and lighting designers to draw. As in this chapter, you will continue to critique your own work.

Chapter 2

The Sketchbook

If you draw only when required to for your job as a designer, you will maintain, but probably not exceed, your present level of proficiency. It is a good idea to acquire the practice of drawing in a sketchbook on a regular basis. For the same reason a writer keeps a journal, a musician practices daily, and an athlete maintains a training schedule, a theatrical designer should keep a sketchbook and draw for at least an hour every week. Dedicating just an hour or two a week, every week, to drawing in the sketchbook will result in the ability to more quickly and confidently use your skills to illustrate your design ideas. You will find that as you become progressively better at drawing, you will use this skill more often as a tool in communicating your ideas to directors and other designers. You will also notice your design renderings getting progressively better.

THE SKETCHBOOK DRAWING SESSION

Ideally, your sketchbook drawing sessions should be at the same time each week. You should draw undisturbed for at least one hour and possibly up to three hours. Your goals are to (1) target certain areas for improvement, (2) experiment with new materials and techniques, and (3) complete a drawing during the session. The drawing session should be wholly dedicated to these goals. This precludes using the session as a time to work on your current design drawings or on any other assignments.

Selecting Subject Matter

The only rule concerning subject matter is you may not draw from your imagination. You must be looking at and copying your subject as you draw. As theatrical designers, drawing is a tool, and for our purposes, drawing proficiency is defined as the ability to accurately portray what is seen. The images in your mind have been processed from images seen in the past. This processed information has been stored more or less accurately based on your dexterity at seeing and drawing. If you draw from your imagination you will not become a better designer.

Often, scene designers choose to draw landscapes or architectural scenes or details; costume designers choose figures, portraits, draped fabrics, etc.; and lighting designers choose scenes with dynamic lighting and highlight/shadow contrast of any subject matter. However, it is an excellent idea to experiment with all types of subject matter. Everyone should be able to accurately portray the human figure and be proficient at architectural perspective and the effects of light and shadow on objects.

You may choose to draw from life, or from a photograph or other two-dimensional graphic image.

Beginning students may find life drawing to be very challenging, at first, because you must selectively choose, from your panoramic vision field, how much of what you see will be represented in your drawing. Because the subject is actually occupying three spatial dimensions, the transformation of the subject to the flat surface of the drawing paper requires more mental discrimination than copying a two-dimensional graphic image. In addition, the extended distance between the eye and the subject matter makes it difficult to simultaneously look at both the subject and at the drawing. Concerted effort is necessary to continually adjust the eyes from the subject to the paper. This action can be tiring and often results in excessively focusing the eyes on the drawing. However, drawing from life (for example, a human model, a landscape, or interior or exterior architecture and decoration) is the most efficient way to improve drawing skills, as it quickly develops eye/hand coordination.

Copying a two-dimensional image, of course, has distinct advantages. The forms are pre-flattened from three dimensions to two, a composition has already been established, and the two-dimensional image is portable. If the color saturation in the image distracts you from establishing value contrast in your drawing, photocopy it in black and white. Even better, if you have the available hardware and software, scan the image into an image-editing program such as Adobe Photoshop and de-saturate the image, leaving the true value contrasts intact.

Photographs, graphic images, and artist's paintings or drawings are all useful images to explore in your sketchbook. Do not draw anything downloaded and printed from the Internet. The image will likely be too pixilated unless it is thumbnail sized and hence too small. Copying the drawing techniques of the great masters is an excellent way to learn how to manipulate drawing mediums, exposing you to various notably superior techniques of line quality, tonal value, and use of perspective. You may choose to integrate some of these techniques into your own work, or use what you have learned as a starting point for your own original techniques. Concentrate on a particular artist for several sessions before moving on to something different. Artists such as Daumier, Van Gogh, Corot, etc., were masters at drawing and are well worth studying. Although good representational drawing is your ultimate goal, copying abstract images is also useful, as long as you draw what you see.

Targeting Areas for Improvement

After analyzing your benchmark drawing, you have identified elements of your drawing style and/or behavior that need improvement. The sketchbook is an excellent way to organize your efforts.

A beginning student may identify several areas that need improvement and it can seem an overwhelming task to fix everything at once. Focusing on one area at a time through sketchbook drawing is a way to manage improvement efforts. For example, a student who needs to work on proportion *and* three-dimensional modeling *and* composition may choose to concentrate on proportion for several weeks by working on accuracy in line drawings and ignore other considerations until advancement is made in this target area.

An advanced student might focus on a specific drawing element that directly affects that designer's renderings. For example, a costume designer who has always had difficulty depicting hands, yet only draws when renderings are due for a production, will often invent a shortcut method for representing hands, or try to avoid drawing them altogether. Of course, she is designing costumes not hands, but a poorly drawn hand will usually detract from the quality of the rendering, and a one-line vignette of the hand may be incongruous with the style of the rendering. Hiding the hands behind the back or using the same shortcut to indicate hands in every rendering, limits the creativity of the designer, which creates the risk of reducing a very expressive part of the body to an emotionless symbol. However, if this designer spends a few hours a week observing and drawing hands in her sketchbook, she will soon find herself enthusiastically using hands in her design renderings to enhance her depictions of the theatrical characters.

Experimentation: Venture Outside of Your Comfort Zone

Experimentation may be defined as any new subject choice, drawing technique, or use of media. Every time you draw, you should consciously choose the materials, subject matter, and paper (texture and size) used.

Most of us have a "comfort zone" with regard to our drawing styles. Instinctively and habitually, an individual will select the same types of images and draw them in the same scale using the same techniques. It is natural to prefer the materials and techniques already mastered. Experimenting with the unfamiliar is often an uncomfortable experience. Many people report that changing anything about their drawing routine feels awkward and that the results are unsatisfactory compared with their usual work. It is helpful to remember that when you experiment, it is normal to experience a learning curve at the beginning. As you become familiar with new materials and techniques, all of your inherent knowledge and expertise in the fundamentals of drawing will be evident.

DEVELOPING GOOD DRAWING HABITS

You may have developed drawing methods and routines that you feel comfortable with, and you may be understandably apprehensive about changing a routine that has produced satisfactory results. However, to achieve improved results be prepared to alter anything and everything about your drawing routine. You must be willing to embrace new subject matter, materials, and paper (texture, size, vertical/horizontal orientation). You must be enthusiastic about experimenting with alternative ways of holding the pencil, posturing yourself as you draw, and laying out and proceeding toward completion of your drawing.

Getting Started

Before you begin to draw, collect all the tools and materials you will need during your session and arrange them in a logical and comfortable manner. When choosing live subjects to draw in your sketchbook, keep the following guidelines in mind:

1. Avoid overly complex or busy compositions. Your goal is to complete a drawing during the session. Be realistic about how much you can complete in the time allotted.
2. Draw standing up with your drawing surface tilted at an angle to minimize the distance your eyes move from the subject to the paper. Hold the pencil or crayon between the thumb, index, and middle fingers. Keep the wrist stiff, letting the motion of the elbow direct the hand.
3. For the hour or more you will be drawing, confirm that the lighting conditions will

remain relatively consistent and that there is plenty of light illuminating your drawing paper.
4. Expect a person who is posing for you to require a break every twenty minutes. If the pose will continue after a break, use spike tape to mark the position.
5. Keep your drawing position constant. Unlike drawing from a two-dimensional image, your perception of the live subject will change with every eye movement or shift in your posture.
6. If possible, before you begin take a digital picture of your subject from the exact position you will be in when you draw. This will aid in re-orienting your position if you happen to move, and will also be useful if you need to continue your drawing session away from the subject.

A few times during your drawing session, step back and critically appraise your drawing. Set the drawing up vertically under plenty of light and back away a few yards. Ask yourself the following questions:

Is the drawing placed artistically on the page?
Is there a logical focus to the drawing?
Is there a variation in line weight?
Is there a variation in value?

Warming Up

At the beginning of your drawing session, take the time to warm up, as you would stretch before exercising. Execute a few twenty-second drawings of your subject. These drawings should be roughly the same size as your final drawing. Look exclusively at your subject the entire twenty seconds. This exercise will loosen up and activate muscle memory in your arm. During this exercise, you may identify parts of the subject that are particularly challenging for you to draw; parts that you will want to pay close attention to in the final drawing. It is useful to experiment with solutions to the challenges in the throw-away drawings.

Stored Visual Memories

As previously mentioned, people have stored visual memories of nearly everything they have seen, whether in reality or as a graphic representation. The more frequent the visual input the more detailed the memory of the object becomes. For example, very young children have no problem drawing a human figure from memory with all of the standard features including the requisite number of fingers and toes. Examining a characteristic drawing of a human figure done by a six-year-old child shows that the figure is frontally oriented to the viewer with the fingers splayed out and the feet drawn pointing down. The facial features are all represented, yet stylized. The eyelashes and hair are drawn as lines. The child has memorized the components of the figure and although the drawing probably resembles a person known to the child, it is not an accurate portrait of anyone.

Perhaps because most of us draw as children in grade school but fewer of us continue to draw as we age, we continue to extract information from these early memories when we draw as adults. One of the most common difficulties in figure drawing is avoiding a subconscious tendency to draw the figure, especially the head and face, in a position frontal to the viewer. Drawing the body or parts of the body in foreshortened positions is a difficult challenge. For many of us, our stored memory image of a body is standing straight up with the arms down at the sides. Perhaps the memory image gets a bit blurry at the feet (which will appear foreshortened in a standing pose), so the solution is to draw the feet pointing straight down or straight out to the sides. The same inaccuracies in stored memory images occur when drawing architectural objects or scenes. Horizontal planes present a particular challenge, because the natural tendency is to draw them in plan view. For instance, a standard side chair drawn in a frontal position from memory will no doubt include a back, a seat, and four legs. However, often the drawing shows too much of the seat (the horizontal plane).

The best way to circumvent the memory images hard-wired into your brain is to disassociate the object you are drawing with any stored visual memory you have. Avoid drawing for more than about ten seconds without referring back to your subject. Tell yourself the figure you are drawing is not a human figure or a chair or building—it is a collection of shapes and lines against a background. Instead of trying to translate what the plan view of a chair seat looks like in perspective, draw the lines and shapes that you actually see.

Chapter 3

Composition and Elements of Design

COMPOSITION

The term composition refers to the aesthetic wholeness of the drawing. Every element of a drawing contributes to its composition, including the placement of the media strokes on the page, the length, thickness, and texture of the strokes, the range of value, even the texture of the paper. In a successful drawing, all of these elements in combination subconsciously evoke emotional or conceptual meaning greater than the sum of its parts.

Composition in theatrical design renderings refers both to the aesthetics of the scenic or costume design itself, and of the visual representation of the design on paper. Theatrical designers use line, shape, size, and proportion of objects, texture, value, and color to enhance the meaning of the playscript. The drawing style of a design rendering should compliment the design concept.

Page Format and Drawing Placement

A scenic artist would be setting himself up for disaster if he failed to lay out a backdrop before painting it. Although the scale is different, the same type of careful planning is necessary when beginning a

drawing. Make an artistic decision at the onset about the size and shape of your final drawing. Will it be a square? Will it be a rectangle? If a rectangle, will it have a horizontal or vertical orientation?

Placement of the drawing on the page evokes similar emotional responses in the viewer as the compositional styles discussed above, and can be used to enhance the concept of the design. A costume design rendering placed squarely in the center of the page suggests something different than a figure placed to one side or the other. The amount of negative space, or blank paper, around the figure also impacts the final composition.

Whatever page format and drawing placement you may choose, it is absolutely imperative to lightly sketch out the entire drawing on the page before committing to final pencil strokes and details. It is extremely difficult to accurately complete a drawing by wholly finishing parts of it in succession. A classic example is trying to successfully draw a human figure by fully drawing the head, then the neck and shoulders, then the torso, etc. Drawing in this manner virtually eliminates control over the placement of the finished drawing. Even if you have accurately drawn all the parts in proportion, the figure may appear to be awkwardly placed, or the feet may be cut off at the bottom of the page. More common, this method of drawing results

Figure 3.1 Drop elevation for *Oklahoma!* by Bruce Brockman evokes loneliness.

Figure 3.2 Sketch for *Hamlet* evokes apprehension and danger.

Figure 3.3 The compositional layout of this rendering by Xuzheng He evokes vastness and serenity.

Figure 3.4 The actors are the focal point in this set rendering.

in serious proportion inaccuracies that could have been identified and easily corrected early on in the drawing session. For the same reasons that it is advantageous to initially lightly sketch in the drawing in its entirety, it is useful to continuously work all parts of the drawing to a roughly equal measure of completion.

Defining a Focal Point

A scenic design rendering often describes a particular moment in the time sequence of the play. Choosing this moment predetermines the focal point of the drawing. The focal point is nearly always an actor or group of actors. The other areas of the setting, which are not the focal point, will be darker and less color saturated. By contrast, the successful costume design rendering accurately illustrates the period style and drape of the costume on a human figure. Each element of the costume should be sufficiently detailed to thoroughly describe the designer's vision.

ELEMENTS OF DESIGN

Line

Given the nature of drawing media, a drawing inevitably consists of lines. They may be short, hair-thin crow quill ink pen lines or long broad strokes made with the edge of a charcoal stick, and every width and length between these extremes. As a general rule, variation in line width and length is necessary to produce realistic results. The effect of light on an object results in variation in the contour surface, and rarely in life does an object exhibit a line, uniform in width and value, around its edges. A lack of line variation tends to impart a graphic or cartoon-like appearance, which, although perhaps visually appealing, represents a stylistic affectation and not reality. Line quality also contributes to the emotional impact of the drawing. Short, jagged diagonal strokes may evoke energy or a feeling of anxiety. Dark thick lines may suggest danger, violence, or virility. Thin curving lines may imply humor, triviality, or sensuality.

Line width and length also convey a sense of scale in a drawing. For example, lines that depict the texture of tree bark in the foreground of a drawing will necessarily shrink proportionally as the trees recede into the background of the scene. Likewise, smaller objects may require rendering lines in shorter thinner strokes.

Texture

Texture refers to the patterns created by various drawing media and media on different types of paper, as well as the representation of the realistic tactile surface of an object. Every stroke of the pencil, pen, or charcoal stick creates a texture that is further complicated by the texture of the paper, and sometimes by the texture of the surface on which the

Figure 3.5 Examples of line variation.

Figure 3.6 Line variation used to depict texture and distance.

paper rests. This innate nature of the materials can be harnessed to enhance the textural effects required in the rendering. However, sometimes the texture quality of the materials or the manner in which the texture is applied can be a detriment. For example, in Figure 3.7 the long directional pencil strokes describing the sky create a visible texture that pulls toward the foreground of the picture and muddles the illusion of distance. For scenic and costume designers, it is crucial to be able to accurately depict realistic textures in their renderings. Wood, marble, fur, wool, silk, velvet, stone, brick, feathers, leather, steel, brocade, and a myriad of other textures must be faithfully depicted.

Value Contrast

For scenic and lighting designers the use of value contrast in design renderings has momentous importance. Consider the scenic design rendering as a specific moment in the action of a play. The rendering attempts to simulate as faithfully as possible what the audience will be seeing at that particular moment. In the actual production experience in the theater, everything and everyone is completely black with all the stage and house lights off. During any given minute of the play the action and setting the audience is permitted to see is controlled by the amount and the direction of light. The same is true in a scenic design rendering.

Figure 3.7 Pencil strokes create a texture that works against the depiction of distance in this image.

The value of an object is assigned relative to light and dark—white (#1) on one end of the scale, and black (#10) on the other—with descending gray tones in the middle. Value must be considered relative to the gray scale and not the color spectrum. Although spectrum yellow is obviously lighter in value than spectrum violet, a dark yellow ocher may be darker in value than a pale tint of violet.

Each object or element has an innate value that is modified by the amount and direction of light cast upon it; for example, a solid blue sphere may have a medium dark value, perhaps a #7 on the gray scale. Holding the sphere in your hand and turning it around, the value appears uniform over the entire object. However, set the sphere on a table and direct a beam of light at it from an angle, and an area on the side nearest the light source appears to have the lightest value on the sphere and an area opposite the light source the darkest value, with several different values between these extremes.

Value contrast is defined as the degree of lightness or darkness of an object or area of a drawing in relationship to the darkness or lightness of adjacent objects or areas. The sphere discussed above will appear dark against a white background, but quite light against a black background. Manipulating the value of adjacent areas of a drawing causes backgrounds to recede, emphasizes areas of focus, and clarifies or blurs the outlines of objects. It does the same thing the lighting designer does in the theater—it controls how the viewer looks at the drawing. In the illustration of the gray scale below, an interesting optical illusion is apparent. Each gray square contains a solid, even coat of pigment, yet the right-hand edge of each square appears lighter than the left-hand edge.

Value contrast is a relative phenomenon. In a pencil drawing done exclusively with an HB graphite pencil on white paper, the surface of the paper is the lightest value (#1) in the drawing, even though the paper may not be pure white. The darkest value (#10) is as dark as the HB pencil will mark the paper with maximum pressure without tearing through the paper, although this will certainly not be black. Progressively less pressure with the pencil will produce lighter and lighter values, but however lightly the pencil marks the paper, the mark will always be a darker value than the paper.

Figure 3.8 The gray scale.

Figure 3.9 An example of a rendering by Xuzheng He with high value contrast.

Chapter 4

Perspective

Although our eyes register perspective effortlessly, reproducing the effects of perspective (a sense of space and depth) in a drawing requires knowledge of how perspective works and a grasp of perspective drawing techniques. Mechanical perspective techniques use geometry to plot points on a drawing replicating more or less accurately what we see in three dimension on a two-dimensional surface. When drawing from life, accurate results are possible without using mechanical techniques if certain facts about how we see objects in perspective are considered.

THE HORIZON LINE

The horizon line is an imaginary horizontal line across the drawing paper that represents the eye level of the viewer. (*Horizon line* and *eye level* are equivalents and used interchangeably.) The viewer will observe the top faces of objects below the horizon line and the bottom faces of objects above the horizon line.

SINKING AND RISING TOWARD THE HORIZON LINE, DIMINISHING SIZE, OVERLAPPING FORMS, ATMOSPHERIC PERSPECTIVE

Four important rules about drawing in perspective are:

1. Objects in a perspective drawing get closer to the horizon line as they recede away from the viewer. For objects (or parts of objects) *above* the horizon line that are on the same horizontal plane, as objects get *farther away* from the viewer, they move progressively *down* toward the horizon line. For objects (or parts of objects) *below* the horizon line that are on the same horizontal plane, as objects get *farther away* from the viewer, they move progressively *up* toward the horizon line.
2. Objects are progressively smaller as they get farther away from the viewer.
3. Objects that are closer to the viewer overlap and partially obscure objects that are farther away. (The edges where objects overlap create handy reference points to help place objects in the drawing in the correct positions relative to each other.)
4. As objects recede into space, surface detail diminishes, value and color intensity diminish, and linear clarity becomes blurred. This phenomenon, called atmospheric perspective, is obvious when viewing an open landscape with mountains off in the distance.

All of the first three rules of perspective must be complied with to execute an effective perspective drawing. Let's see what happens if you do not obey the rules. Figure 4.1 illustrates six rectangles and a horizon line. Imagine the drawing is a front view

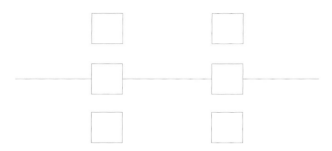

Figure 4.1 Cubes in front view with no perspective.

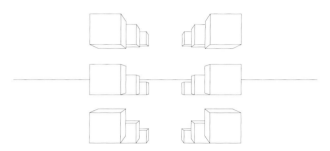

Figure 4.2 In this drawing, objects diminish in size and overlap as they get farther away, but they do not recede toward the horizon line.

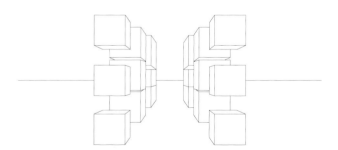

Figure 4.3 Here, rule #1 is obeyed and #3 is obeyed as much as possible, but rule #2 is not.

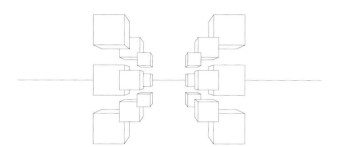

Figure 4.4 This drawing ignores rule #3 with disastrous results.

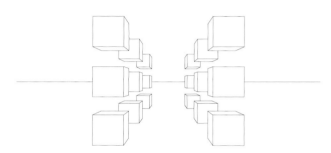

Figure 4.5 The first three rules of perspective are evident in this drawing.

with no perspective. The rectangles are solid objects with three dimensions, and two more rows and columns of identical objects sit behind them. Your objective is to draw the eighteen identical objects in perspective. Figure 4.2 shows what happens if rules #2 and #3 are adhered to, but rule #1 (objects recede toward the horizon line) is not. The illusion of perspective is not accomplished. Figures 4.3 and 4.4 show the ineffectiveness of not complying with rules #2 and #3, respectively.

In Figure 4.5, the rules of perspective are obeyed and an effective perspective drawing is the result. The middle and back rows of solid objects below the horizon line are successively higher on the page than the front row of objects, while the middle and back rows above the horizon line are successively lower. The middle and back rows are receding toward the horizon line. All of the solid objects would, in reality, be the same size. Because the middle row of solids are smaller than the front row, they appear to be farther away than the front row. The back row, drawn even smaller, appears to be farther away than the middle row. Finally, the fact that "closer" objects overlap those that are "farther away" completes the illusion that objects are receding into space.

Another way of illustrating the four rules of perspective is to imagine a football game with the quarterback on his own forty-yard line looking down the field for a receiver. He has a few seconds, so he whips out a drawing pad and quickly sketches all the players on the field. He is 6'7", the tallest on the team, so all the other players are below his eye level or the horizon line. His offensive line is closest to him, so the feet of those players are near the

Figure 4.6 Atmospheric perspective in paint elevation of landscape drop.

bottom of the paper. They are larger than any other players on the field and overlap the defensive line trying to sack him. The drawings of the offensive and defensive line players have crisp outlines and include minute detail including grimacing facial features and grass stains on the uniforms. Scattered out down the field are receivers and defensive backs. The players are progressively smaller and less distinct and their feet are higher on the drawing (closer to the horizon line) as they move farther away from the quarterback. The player closest to the goal line is the smallest and most indistinct, and is based higher on the page than any of the other players.

To summarize, the way we see objects in a perspective drawing is determined by the horizon line. Objects get progressively closer to the horizon line, and smaller, and less distinct as they recede from the viewer. Closer objects overlap objects that are farther away.

VANISHING POINTS

One-Point Perspective

To see all sides of a solid three-dimensional object, one would have to move 360 degrees around the object. Because this is impossible in a two-dimensional drawing, we see only one view of the object. We see some but not all sides of the object. For example, only three sides, at most, of a rectangular solid are visible at once. If we place a solid cube on a table and we observe the cube straight on so that the front face is not at an angle, we see one or two sides of the cube, depending on the eye level of the viewer. If the center of the viewer's eye level and the cube center point are aligned, we see only the front face of the cube as a true square. Move the cube slightly to the right or left and we see the front face as a true square and a sliver of the right or left face, respectively. As the cube continues moving laterally, we see the side face as a progressively wider rhomboid. If the cube is centered on and slightly below the horizon line, we see the front face as a true square and a sliver of the top face. As the horizon line rises we see the top face as a progressively wider shape. If the cube also moves to the right or left, we see the front, top, and one side of the cube. We see the true shape of the front face (a square) because it is fully facing the viewer. The shapes of the top, and left or right faces appear distorted because they are receding in space. The shape of the distorted face is similar to a rhomboid. The vertical edges of the side faces remain vertical, but the horizontal edges we see are not parallel. They appear to converge in space at a point in the center of the horizon line. The point at which real parallel lines appear to converge in perspective is called a *vanishing point*.

In a perspective drawing where all the objects are oriented frontally to the viewer, the side edges will converge to one vanishing point (referred to as the *center vanishing point*) located in the center of the drawing on the horizon line. Because the sides of each frontally oriented object recede to only one point on the horizon, this device is known as *one-point perspective*.

NOTE: All true vertical lines remain true verticals in one-point perspective and are never distorted from true vertical.

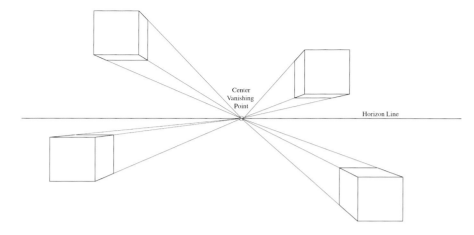

Figure 4.7
Cubes facing the picture plane above and below the horizon line, drawn in perspective.

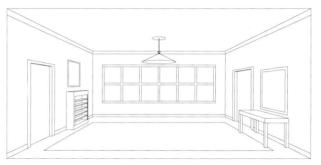

Figure 4.8 Perspective drawing of a room in one-point perspective.

A classic example of one-point perspective is a drawing of a room where one wall is removed and we see the two side walls, ceiling, floor, and back wall, which is frontally oriented to the audience, as in Figure 4.7. The back wall is a rectangle, but all the other walls are rhomboids. All vertical lines in the drawing are vertical, and all horizontal lines that are parallel to the back wall are horizontal. All lines that are perpendicular to the back wall recede to a center vanishing point in the middle of the back wall. In addition, the horizontal lines comprising all trims, moldings, shelves, picture frames, etc., that are perpendicular to the back wall also recede to the center vanishing point.

Two-Point Perspective

When a three-dimensional object is situated at an angle to the viewer, two vanishing points on the horizon line are required to accurately illustrate its shape in perspective. All the visible faces of the angled object appear distorted from its true shape. Place a solid cube on a table as in the previous discussion of one-point perspective, but orient the cube so a corner faces the viewer with the diagonal axis of the top face perpendicular to the center vanishing point and somewhere below eye level. In this position we see two distorted side faces and the distorted top face of the cube. Because the cube's diagonal axis is aligned with the center vanishing point, the side faces are identical mirrored shapes. The top and bottom horizontal edges of the right face converge at a point on the horizon line to the right of center, the top and bottom horizontal edges of the left face converge at a point on the horizon line to the left of center, and these two vanishing points are equidistant from the center vanishing point. These two points are referred to as the object's *left* and *right vanishing points*. The vertical edges of the side faces remain vertical. Because the top face of the angled cube consists of no vertical lines, all four edges of the shape are seen in perspective. The edges of the top face that abut the left side face, and its opposite parallel face, converge to the left vanishing point. The edges of the top face that abut the right side face, and its opposite parallel face, converge to the right vanishing point. If we angle the cube so the top face's diagonal axis is no longer perpendicular to the center vanishing point, the two side faces will no longer be identical mirror images. One side face will appear wider than the other. The vanishing point for the narrower side will be closer to the center vanishing point and the wider side will have a vanishing point farther away from the center.

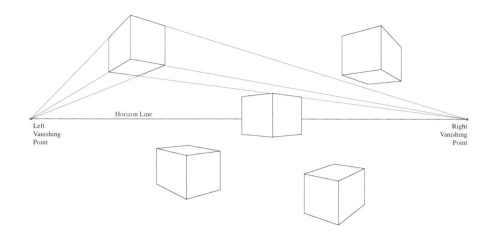

Figure 4.9
Cubes drawn in two-point perspective.

Figure 4.10 Paint elevation of cityscape utilizing one- and two-point perspective.

In a perspective drawing, all parallel lines converge at the same vanishing point. This means that all objects or lines in the drawing oriented at the exact same angle to the viewer will share a vanishing point.

Round Objects in Perspective

Objects with rounded sides, lacking edges and clearly delineated faces, can be confusing to draw in perspective. A true sphere will always appear as a perfect circle in a perspective drawing. For example, the round globes of a row of streetlights will get smaller as they recede from view, but they will always appear round. By contrast, the only time a perfect circle will appear in perspective is when it is frontally oriented and aligned with the center vanishing point; otherwise it will appear as an oval, with the width of its short axis dependent on its angle to the viewer. Ovals are difficult figures to draw, and unless rendered correctly, will not read to the viewer as a circle in perspective.

WORKING WITH TWO-POINT PERSPECTIVE

Drawing a cube in two-point perspective is a straight-forward task, but most objects are more complex. Drawing accurately in perspective requires knowledge of more sophisticated techniques. Exercise 8 in Chapter 7 explains how to find the center of a plane in perspective, divide a plane in perspective into equal parts, accurately draw inclined planes, and draw circles, cylinders, and cones in perspective.

Three-Point Perspective

Most perspective drawings utilize two-point perspective. A drawing with objects rendered at various angles with respect to the viewer is generally more visually interesting than one in which all the objects are frontally oriented. Recall that when employing one- and two-point perspective, true verticals remain vertical. *Three-point perspective* is utilized to illustrate vertical distance. Objects that are both at an angle to and high above or below the viewer (in a drawing of a skyscraper, or a view down a mine shaft, for example) require that the vertical as well as the horizontal lines comprising the object converge. This is the same principle outlined in rule #2 listed previously. Objects get smaller as they recede from the viewer. The horizontal lines of the object converge at their left and right vanishing points in the same manner as two-point perspective. In addition, the vertical lines describing the object also recede toward each other to a point either above or below the horizon line. In the drawing of a skyscraper in Figure 4.11, the bottom of the building is noticeably smaller than the top, and hence appears to be very far away.

Foreshortening

Foreshortening describes the truncating of an object's length in perspective. The true length of an object is perceivable only in plan and elevation views. As the object is rotated out of one of these views, it will always appear to be proportionately shorter than its true length. To observe this phenomenon, hold a pencil at arm's length at your eye level with the point directed at the ceiling. Slowly rotate the point toward your face. Observe how the pencil appears to become shorter as it rotates toward you until, with the point directed at your forehead, you see the wood part of the pencil as a circle and the lead as a black dot in the middle of the wood. Any plane of a three-dimensional thing that is rotated away from the viewer is foreshortened.

We know that geometric shapes become distorted from their true forms when viewed in perspective. However, translating the technique of drawing a cube face in perspective to a human face can present quite a challenge. In Chapter 2 we discussed the common tendency of drawing the human figure by default in a position frontal to the viewer. Consider that every three-dimensional object, including one as complicated as the human figure, can be reduced to a series of parts that are variations on four simple geometric shapes—sphere, cube, pyramid or cone, and cylinder. The ability to accurately draw these shapes in perspective, turned at every possible angle, will facilitate developing the proficiency to render more intricate objects.

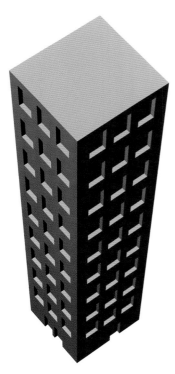

Figure 4.11 A tall building drawn in three-point perspective.

Chapter 5

Three-Dimensional Modeling

In drawing the three-dimensional modeling technique uses value differences to replicate reflected light and shadow on objects in the drawing. A drawing without the effects of light and shadow is essentially a line drawing, similar to a black line cartoon used in scene painting layout. Including three-dimensional modeling in a costume rendering provides additional information about the design that is lacking in a simple line drawing, and is a virtual necessity in set and lighting renderings.

This chapter breaks the intricate process of making a line drawing look three-dimensional into definable steps that mirror the steps of trompe l'oeil painting. Exercise 2 in Chapter 9 details the steps in drawing three-dimensionally modeled geometric shapes.

THE FUNDAMENTALS OF TROMPE L'OEIL

The French term *trompe l'oeil* means "deceives the eye." It refers to a style of painting, perfected during the Renaissance (and used extensively in theatrical backdrop painting), that creates the illusion that the objects in the painting are three-dimensional. The three fundamental elements in a successful trompe l'oeil painting are an accurate drawing of the objects in perspective, convincingly rendered textures on the surfaces of the objects, and an accurate depiction of the play of light and shadow on the objects from a predetermined light source or sources. These fundamentals can easily be applied to drawing, and once mastered, smooth the transition from drawing to the use of color media.

The Cartoon

To successfully render an object in the style of trompe l'oeil, the object must be accurately drawn in perspective. This drawing is referred to as a cartoon. It is a line drawing of all of the objects to be depicted. Within a single drawing, all of the objects are drawn in relation to one horizon line and point of observation. From this point of observation, objects in the drawing recede in space according to the rules of perspective. In addition, each of the objects in the drawing is depicted as an accurate representation of itself and is accurately drawn in relation to all other objects in the drawing.

For example, in a set rendering of a realistic box set, all objects (including walls, furniture, props, actors, and any depicted theater architecture) are drawn as if seen from a single vantage point with accurate outlines appropriate to each object, and each of the objects is in logical proportion to each other. Three-dimensional modeling of the rendering should not take place until it is determined that the cartoon is as accurate as possible.

Figure 5.1 Cartoon of a drop paint elevation.

Base Value and Surface Texture

The next step in successful trompe l'oeil painting is an accurate depiction of the base value and surface texture of each object in the rendering. Any object to be rendered has a hue or hues that is quantifiable under neutral light. In a drawing, the base color of an object is reduced to a value on the gray scale. The base value is the "color" of the object translated to a gray scale value that will be roughly midway between the lightest and darkest parts of the object when affected by a light source. Referring to the gray scale, choose a base value for each object or area that is between #3 and #8, inclusively. This will ensure that there are at least two value steps that are lighter and darker to represent highlight, zinger, shade, and lowlight (defined below). For objects that are intrinsically white, the base value should be rendered as #3; for black objects, the base value is #8. Every object has basic value and texture properties that will be altered by how the object is illuminated. Drawing the object realistically as to base value and texture first, and then adding the effects of light and shadow later simplifies the process by breaking it down into logical steps. For example, in a trompe l'oeil rendering of a marble column, it simplifies the process to draw the marble texture (including accurate value and realistic veins and other details particular to a certain type of marble) before modeling the column with light, shade, and cast shadow. Similarly, it can be helpful in a costume rendering to draw the texture and pattern of a piece of clothing before adding the affects of a light source.

Figure 5.2 Marble texture on a column.

Figure 5.3 Fabric textures in a costume rendering of Sir Anthony Absolute for *The Rivals* by Patrick Holt.

Figure 5.4 The affect of sunlight at noon.

Figure 5.5 The affect of sunlight in late afternoon.

Figure 5.6 The affect of moonlight.

Figure 5.7 The affect of incandescent light.

The Light Source

After all objects in a drawing are based in, the next step is to determine a light source and accurately describe its influence on the objects in the drawing. The type of light source and the strength of the illumination determine how the objects in a trompe l'oeil drawing will be rendered. Midday sunlight illuminates differently than candlelight or moonlight. At midday on a clear day, the sun is as strong and high overhead as it will be on that particular day.

Objects affected by midday sunlight on a clear day have high contrast of light and dark, and cast clearly defined short dark shadows. The weather affects how sharp or soft shadows will appear. The time of year and latitude also affect the strength and length of shadows. Moonlight creates shadows that are dark and soft. The affect of artificial light on objects varies with the light source, but is never as bright as sunlight. Firelight, candlelight, incandescent light, florescent light, neon light, and flashlight all illuminate differently and can be accurately described in a rendering.

The light source or sources may be placed anywhere around the objects that will be drawn

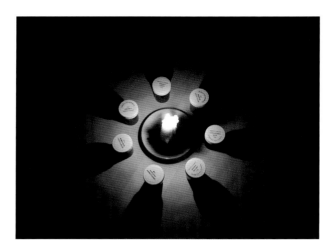

Figure 5.8 The affect of candlelight.

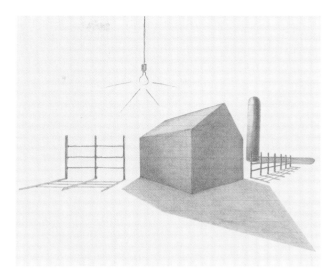

Figure 5.10 Radiating light rays affecting objects in a drawing.

Figure 5.9 Light source above and to the right.

and three-dimensionally modeled. The placement of the light source determines what areas of three-dimensional objects are light and dark and where shadows fall. For example, a light source placed above and to the right of the objects will result in lighter areas toward the top and right sides of objects, and darker areas toward the bottom and left sides.

Whatever the light source, it directs what may be described illustratively as lines of light (rays) at the objects in the drawing. If the light source is the sun, these lines are considered to be parallel due to the great distance of the sun from the earth. If the

light source is artificial, it is a point source from which the lines of light radiate.

To illustrate how the light rays will connect with an object in the drawing, it is helpful to place the light source (represented as a circle) in the drawing, and draw a straight line from the source through the center of an object and out the other side. If the light source is the sun, draw a line from the circle representing the sun to the center of your paper (or central vanishing point, if a perspective drawing). Then draw a line parallel to that line through the center of an object. If the light source is artificial, simply draw a line from the light source through any object. Along this linear axis, parts of the object that are closest to the light source will appear light in value in the drawing. Parts of the object at the other end of the linear axis (farther away from the light source) will be darker in value.

The line of light discussed above that penetrates an object is a two-dimensional representation of the light source's position relative to the objects in the drawing. It describes only the left or right and up or down position of the light source, but not front or back in relation to the objects. To understand exactly how light will affect objects in the drawing, it is necessary to determine the depth of the light source. Is the light source behind, directly above, or in front of the objects in the drawing? To illustrate this, Figure 5.11 depicts the same drawing in Figure 5.10 from a top (or plan) view. The light source in this

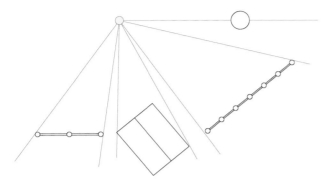

Figure 5.11 Top view of drawing in Figure 5.10.

view is clearly in front of the objects in the drawing. Therefore, areas of the objects that are closer to the viewer will be lighter in value, and the objects will cast shadows away from the viewer.

Shade and Lowlight

The area of a three-dimensional object that is opposite the directional light source will be darker than its intrinsic base value. The term *shade* describes this darker area. The shaded side of an object that has a very light base value will usually be lighter in value than the shaded side of an object with a dark base value. (This is true unless the light source is intensely bright in an otherwise dark environment and in close proximity to the objects creating very high contrast where objects appear white on the lighted side and black on the side away from the light source.) The shaded area is at least one value step on the gray scale darker than the base.

The position of the light source determines the placement of shade and what percentage of the object is shaded. The object's physical contour determines the shape of the shaded area. For example, a cube, or any similar object, has sharply defined planes. For any object with sharply defined planes, each plane will have a different value according to its position relative to the light source. The entire plane opposite the light source will be shaded. The difference in value is most defined at the lines where planes meet. Conversely, a sphere has no sharply defined planes. The shaded area of a sphere resembles a crescent that is perpendicular to the line-of-light axis discussed previously. The shift from light to dark on a spherical object is typically not a hard line, but rather a soft, blurred transitional area.

Figure 5.12 The shaded areas of objects in this drawing are highlighted.

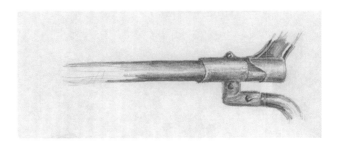

Figure 5.13 An example of lowlight.

The term *lowlight* refers to the area—proportionately very small—of the shaded side of an object farthest away from the light source that is even darker than the shade value. An object's lowlight value is at least one step darker on the gray scale than its shade value. The use of lowlight adds additional depth and contributes to the realistic effect of the three-dimensionally modeled drawing.

Figure 5.14 The use of cut line in a drawing.

Figure 5.15 Objects with various surface textures and their highlights.

Cut Line

The *cut line* is a very dark thin line—used very sparingly—that describes the distinction between objects, and between an object and the shadow it casts. In a black and white drawing, the cut line is black or the darkest value in the drawing. Typically, cut lines are placed at the point or edge where an object touches the surface of another object, and along the edge that adjoins the cast shadow. They may also be placed at the corners of the shade side to create a crisp definition of the object. As a general rule, cut lines should not be placed on plane edges that face the light source. The judicious use of cut lines is necessary to avoid the appearance of outlining.

Highlight, Zinger, and Reflected Light

After adding base value, shade, lowlight, and cut line to the original cartoon, the effect of three-dimensionality will be profound. However, since all the objects in the drawing were assigned a base value of at least #3 on the gray scale, there is no white (or light) on any of the objects. Creating the appearance of light on the objects can be accomplished in one of two ways: adding it with a white drawing medium (white colored pencil, pastel, conté crayon), or subtracting darker values with an eraser to reveal the white of the paper. If the paper is not white, it will be necessary to add white pigment of some variety. The subtractive technique works well with graphite or charcoal on white paper. On light-colored (but not white) paper, using both the additive and subtractive method may be advantageous.

Three terms are used in defining and describing light. *Highlight* is the most prevalent light in the drawing. It is essentially the opposite of shade, and is placed at the opposite end of the line-of-light axis. All objects will appear lighter on the side closest to the light source, but the material composition of the object can greatly affect how the light appears to the viewer. Objects with coarse textures and/or matte surfaces have dull highlights with very soft edges relative to objects with smooth textures and/or shiny surfaces, which have bright highlights with sharper edges. Accurately depicting the highlight of an object is essential in describing its surface texture.

The term *zinger* refers to parts of the highlight that are even more intensely bright than the highlight. In a black and white drawing, the zingers will be the only areas that are truly white. Within a highlight, a zinger function is the opposite of that of the lowlight. As with highlight, objects with coarse texture and/or matte surfaces have very low contrast, zingers, if any. Shiny, smooth objects have bright, clear zingers. A sphere will have a zinger at the exact point that the line-of-light axis penetrates the surface of the object. Zingers, like cut lines, should be utilized sparingly. Like cut lines, they can also be used to accentuate edges and make object contours appear more defined. Typically they are placed within highlights and on edges on the light source side of objects.

Cast Shadow

Cast shadows are added after all other aspects of the three-dimensionally modeled drawing have been completed. Because light rays cannot penetrate a solid, non-translucent object, the area behind an object and opposite the light source appears as a dark shape mimicking in two dimensions the shape of the object. This dark shape is the *cast shadow*. A cast shadow has three basic properties.

One may recall, in the book *Peter Pan* by J. M. Barrie that Peter's shadow became detached and he stoically endured as Wendy sewed it back on to the soles of his feet. This literary reference points out the first basic property of cast shadows: a cast shadow of an object resting on a surface (like a person standing on the floor) always connects at the point of contact between the object and the surface. Conversely, a floating or flying object (such as a cloud or an airplane) will have a cast shadow that is not connected to itself.

The second property of a cast shadow is translucency. Unlike Peter's shadow, a cast shadow is not a tangible object that can be misplaced or held in the hand. In some very high contrast lighting situations, shadows may appear to be opaque, but in the tricky business of making two-dimensional lines and shapes on paper appear to be three-dimensional, it is best to emphasize the translucent character of cast shadows to differentiate them from solid objects. For this reason they are added in at the end of the drawing process. All of the textures, shades, high-lights, cut lines, etc., that have already been drawn in will be subtly visible beneath the cast shadow. This device greatly contributes to the realism of the drawing.

The third basic property of a cast shadow is that it follows the contours of any other objects that it crosses. For example, the cast shadow of a person standing near a wall in a room may have a cast shadow that begins at the feet, travels horizontally along the floor, and then angles up vertically as it intersects with the wall. If a cast shadow crosses multiple objects of different dimensional sizes, an interesting phenomenon occurs: the cast shadow appears to be closer to the object casting the shadow and proportionately smaller, or narrower, the closer it gets to the object on which the shadow is cast is to the light source (for example, a streetlight casting a shadow on a sidewalk and street where the sidewalk is half a foot or so elevated from the street). Assuming an overhead light source, the cast shadow on the sidewalk will be slightly narrower than the shadow on the street. In reality, with only a six inch difference between sidewalk and curb, this phenomenon would be barely discernable in sunlight given the great distance of the sun from the earth, but would be quite noticeable under artificial light. It is advantageous in trompe l'oeil drawing to emphasize this phenomenon for realistic effect.

Although a cast shadow roughly mimics the object to which it is attached, the placement of the light source causes various distortions of this shape. To illustrate this concept, Figures 5.17 through 5.22

Figure 5.16 Highlight, zinger, and reflected light in a drawing.

Figure 5.17 Cast shadow at noon.

Figure 5.18 Cast shadow at 1 p.m.

Figure 5.21 Cast shadow at 4 p.m.

Figure 5.19 Cast shadow at 2 p.m.

Figure 5.22 Cast shadow at 5 p.m.

Figure 5.20 Cast shadow at 3 p.m.

track the changes in an object's cast shadow as day approaches night.

Under an artificial light source, from which light lines radiate, a center overhead light source in a room will produce a myriad of different shadow angles on objects placed throughout the room. It is possible to plot the exact shape and size of cast shadows using perspective drawing techniques. However, in most costume renderings, drawing a precisely accurate cast shadow is not necessary.

Figure 5.23 Examples of interesting cast shadows.

Figure 5.23 cont'd

A dark, translucent shape that approximates the pose of the figure casting the shadow and angling away from the point source of light is sufficient to complete the sense of realism. Carefully observing shadows in real life, photographing various examples, and drawing them in a weekly sketch is an excellent way to learn about the properties of cast shadows. The following images catalog some interesting cast shadows to begin your collection.

Chapter 6

Figure Drawing

It is obviously necessary for costume designers to study and draw the human figure, but truly anyone whose job description includes the ability to draw will benefit from making the effort to become adept at drawing the body. With its myriad moving parts, expressions, and variations among individuals, the human body is a rich trove of readily accessible source material for the artist. Depending on model, pose, and lighting, a figure drawing can look clinically realistic, emotional and expressive, like a landscape, or even completely abstract. If you can proficiently draw the human figure, you can draw anything.

For costume designers, it is absolutely imperative that you become proficient at drawing the human body. It is as important as studying anatomy is for a doctor. If you are unwilling or unable to do so, you should choose another career. Your profession is designing ornamentation for an object (the body). If you are not completely familiar with all aspects of this object, you will not be successful at clothing it. It is a normal human reflex to subconsciously react negatively to a badly drawn rendering. Although many people are incapable of drawing a figure, almost all of us can tell if a figure is drawn inaccurately. Having good drawing skills will inspire confidence in you from the director and other designers that you work with. Good renderings also minimize confusion in the costume shop about your designs. Because this skill is so

important, the costume designer must be prepared to spend a great deal of time practicing to draw the body.

Of all the images in the universe, the human body is the single most recognizable to us. Although we probably do not remember, no doubt the first image most people see and register is human. Because we are intimately familiar with our own bodies, this intuitive knowledge of what each of us looks like acts as a detriment when attempting to draw a specific individual human form. Lacking formal art training as children, by adulthood the imagery in our minds of the human form is so iconic that, when attempting to draw accurately from life, it requires concentrated effort to ignore our stored symbolic image memories of the human form. If your symbolic image memories of human figures resemble the male and female icons on restroom doors, you are not alone, but it will require some effort to ignore the impulse to draw humans as forward facing, standing stick people.

Practice is the only way to improve drawing skills. Make a commitment to drawing a live, nude human for an hour every week. Art schools and local arts councils often offer weekly open life drawing sessions for a fee. It is crucial that the model be nude, because if you are not familiar with the muscles and bones of the body and how they move, you will not successfully be able to clothe the body. If a live model is not available, you can copy drawings or photographs of nude figures. In either case, follow the process described in Exercise 1, Chapter Seven by warming up with twenty-second poses before gradually increasing the amount of time spent on each drawing. You will see improvement after a few weeks if you make a concentrated effort to draw what you see rather than what you think you see.

MOVEMENT AND BALANCE

Depicting a sense of movement in theatrical renderings of human figures, although not necessary to convey the information required of a designer, animates the renderings, makes them more appealing to viewers (i.e., the director), and helps make clear the characters' personalities. The primary purpose of a costume rendering is to clearly show the style, color, texture, and fit of the clothing the actor will wear on stage. A sense of movement in the figure should not detract from the primary purpose, but it does help "sell" the design to the director in the design phase. Wooden, poorly drawn figures are difficult to get excited about, regardless of how brilliant the design.

Even movement in a figure drawing that is as subtle as a tilt of the head or a slight curving of the spine is appealing compared with a full frontal "attention" pose with arms hanging straight down, weight equally distributed on both feet, and the face staring straight ahead. Michelangelo's sculpture of David, as photographed in Figure 6.1, is an excellent example of the use of subtle movement in a figure who is otherwise inactively standing. Called a contrapposto pose, the weight of the body is concentrated on one leg. This creates tension in the muscles of the weight-bearing leg, and makes the left hip jut out to the side slightly with the left side of the pelvis higher than the right. The right leg is slightly bent at the knee and angles out to the right, and bearing little of the body's weight, it is more relaxed. To counteract the raised left hip, the waist is slightly bent and the spine curves toward the left, which causes the right shoulder to rise higher than the left. The right arm is bent at the elbow and angles to the right. To complete the sense of balance, the figure's head is tilted slightly to the right, and we see his face in three-quarter profile. These minor variations from the "attention" pose create interesting angles

Figure 6.1 Michelangelo's David.

and shapes created by the negative space of the background.

To make sure that you are creating a sense of movement in your figure drawings, always start the drawing with lines that indicate the movement: the curvature of the spine, the angles of shoulders and hips, the tilt of the head, and the angle and position of the limbs. Build detail on top of these lines of movement to maintain the vitality of the pose through to the end of the drawing. It is also crucial to establish a vertical balance line between the head and feet. To remain balanced, the head must be directly above the point of balance created by the position of the feet. For a standing figure with weight equally distributed on each foot and the feet shoulder width apart, the head will be centered above the feet. The vertical balance line will extend from the point of the chin to a point on the floor midway between the feet. As weight shifts onto one foot, the head moves proportionately closer to the weight-bearing foot to keep the body upright. Look again at Figure 6.1 and notice that David's chin is almost directly over his left (weight-bearing) foot.

PROPORTION

Each human is unique, and differences in height, weight, gender, race, and age from person to person are obvious to us. But the basic proportions of the typical adult human figure are generally the same for all. (Children have different body proportions than adults that change as they grow, but the proportions are generally the same for all children in similar developmental stages.) The size of the head in relation to height, the relative lengths of the torso and limbs, and especially the placement of the facial features for most humans fall within a very narrow range. This is convenient for architects, manufacturers of furniture, and theatrical scene designers who design according to the proportions of the average human.

The Head as a Unit of Measurement

Artists have long used the human head as a point of reference when drawing the figure. The length of the head can be used as a unit of measurement for determining height and the proportions of the body. For a figure standing erect and facing front, you can determine how many head lengths tall the body is, and where the features of the body line up with various head lengths. When drawing from life, you can use your pencil as a measuring tool to determine the length of the model's head. This procedure is detailed in Exercise 1, Chapter 7. When copying a photograph or drawing, simply use the actual length of the head as a unit of measurement, as shown in Figure 6.2.

Many artists consider the ideal figure to be a total of eight head lengths in height when standing erect. Michelangelo's David, pictured in Figure 6.1, is eight heads tall. Comic book superheroes are typically drawn as eight-and-one-half heads in height. Fashion illustrations often depict figures as tall as ten heads. In these idealized figures, extra length is added to the lower half of the body, and proportionately to the arms. Most people are not eight-and-one-half, or even eight heads tall, and no real body

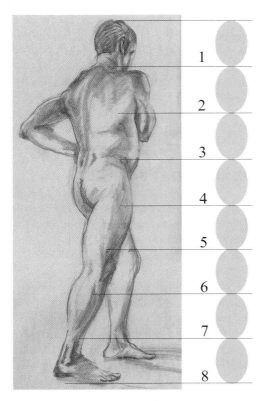

Figure 6.2 Using the length of the head as a unit of measurement.

is ten heads tall. Most adults are somewhere between six-and-one-half and eight head lengths tall. Seven to seven-and-one-half heads tall is most common. To find your own head height, measure the vertical length of your head from the crown to the chin, and divide this number by your total height in inches.

The number of heads tall a figure is has nothing to do with the actual height of the individual, but rather it is the proportion of the size of the head to the height. A figure drawing six heads tall will appear to have an abnormally big head and short limbs; while one eight heads high will appear to have very pleasing, beautiful proportions. (This is why artists typically draw their models at eight heads regardless of their actual proportions.) Costume designers can use this convention in their renderings to help visually describe the personalities of the characters in a play.

When drawing from life for the purpose of improving your drawing skills as a designer, never use an ideal or stylized formula to determine the height of the model. Always draw exactly what you see. After mastering life drawing you can always adjust height proportions in your renderings for artistic effect. Although each costume designer has his or her own rendering style, a costume rendering does not depict a clothing design for an idealized person or a fashion design for the masses, but a specific outfit for a specific character who inhabits the world of a specific play. Experience in drawing different body types is important because generic body types are not appropriate for all characters.

Standard Proportions of the Body

Although you should always draw what you see and not draw according to memorized formulas, it is helpful to learn some of the standard proportions of the body. The next part of this chapter details common standards of human proportion, and common mistakes made by inexperienced figure drawers. If you know what the standards are as well as the common pitfalls, perhaps you can avoid them in your own drawings. However, keep in mind that the standards are only guidelines. Memorizing only the standard measurements of the body, but never drawing from life, is analogous to only conjugating the verbs of a language you are attempting to learn, but never actually speaking the language. Instead of just memorizing the formulas for the ideal placements of the facial and body features, take measurements of your own body. If your measurements approximate (they certainly do not have to be exact) the "ideal" measurements, then you are living inside a very handy reference tool.

Heads and Faces

In a full frontal pose, the head is an ovoid wider at the top than at the chin. This shape should be fairly symmetrical. It is helpful to draw a centered vertical line through the head shape so the features of the face remain approximately symmetrical. If we then bisect the head horizontally and then horizontally divide the lower half of the head into three equal parts, we can roughly place the features of the face in their customary locations.

One of the most common proportional errors made by beginning students is placing the eyes too high on the head. It is easy to see on a model who is completely bald that there is nearly as much head above the eyes as there is below. The eyes are placed centered on or slightly above the horizontal line bisecting the head. This will vary with the individual model. Placing the eyes lower rather than higher may tend to make the model look more juvenile. (The features of babies' faces are quite close together and situated in the bottom third of the head.) Although this will need to be adjusted slightly for each individual, the eyes are spaced about one eye width apart (one-half an eye width on either side of the center vertical). The bottom of the nose hits roughly at the line one-third down from the horizontal line bisecting the head. You can begin by making the nostrils about as wide as the space between the eyes, and then adjust according to the individual. The mouth is placed either centered on or slightly above the line marking the bottom third of the lower half of the head. The width of the mouth is approximately the same as the distance between the pupils of the eyes. The eyebrows sit slightly above the tops of the eyes and typically curve down slightly to the sides to indicate the curvature of the head. In a frontal view of the head, the ears will be seen in foreshortened view. The top of the ear will typically line up with the eyebrow and the bottom of the ear with the bottom of the nose. The neck may appear narrower than the face, especially in female models, depending of the width of the jaw.

These proportion standards should be used only for reference, and should not be adhered to when drawing from life. Practicing until you memorize what generic features look like in frontal view can actually impede your ability to draw accurately. Typically the model's head will not be in a true frontal view, and you will create a successful drawing only by drawing what you see. Knowing the formulas for placing generic facial features on a frontal facing head will not help when the features are even slightly foreshortened. Another of the most common errors in drawing is making the features appear frontally oriented even though the head is tilted or in partial profile. The most important thing to remember about drawing the head and face is that the head is an ellipsoid, a three-dimensional rounded shape. The facial features change in appearance with each degree of tilt up or down, right or left.

In profile view it is clear that the head is a rounded shape and the features are three-dimensional. It is obvious that the face is not flat; it

Figure 6-3 The head in front view; self-portrait by Micha Rudack.

Figure 6-4 Detail of costume rendering of Tom Morgan by Patrick Holt for *Treasure Island*.

Figure 6.5 The head tilted down.

curves back at the upper part of the forehead and under the chin. The eyeballs are spheres that are covered by the skin of the eyelids. The pupil, that in frontal view is round, is rotated into a foreshortened oval. The nose juts out from the face, and the lips are distinct from each other. The best way to approach drawing the head and face is to draw an oval with the axis tilted in the proper direction according to the pose of the model, and then draw curved horizontal lines in the proper positions for eyes, nose, and mouth. These curved lines must be perpendicular to the axis of the oval.

The head and face are typically not the focus of a costume rendering, yet the expression of the face can greatly enhance its impact. Use the tilt and angle of the head to your advantage in describing the character's personality. Partial profile poses that emphasize the outline of the eyelids, nose, lips, and chin are very appealing. Emphasize the hair and,

Figure 6.6 Detail of costume rendering by Al Tucci.

Figure 6.7 Detail of costume rendering by Adam Dill.

obviously, any head adornments that are part of the design, but keep the facial features simple. Emphasize with lines the outlines of the features, but not surface detail such as wrinkles or plane changes. Do not be afraid to use dark shading to emphasize the three-dimensionality of the head and face, but keep plane transitions soft. Shading should be done with soft value changes rather than lines. The eye details should be the darkest value in the face. Emphasize the shape of the lids with dark lines. Draw eyelashes as a single mass rather than individual hairs. Emphasize the line between the lips with a dark value. The upper lip is typically darker than the lower because it slopes down away from an overhead light source. If the lips are parted and teeth are visible, do not emphasize individual teeth. Draw the teeth as a mass or simply a lighter area between the darker lips. Do not make the teeth too white, especially just under the upper lip because the upper lip naturally casts a shadow onto the teeth. Figures 6.6 through 6.9 show some examples of interesting costume rendering heads.

The Torso and Arms

In the ideal figure-of-eight head lengths, standing erect in frontal pose with the arms held down at the sides, the bottom of the second head length falls at the line of the nipples, and the bottom of the third head length falls at the groin. The shoulders are

Figure 6.8 Detail of costume rendering of Marcellus by Al Tucci for *Hamlet*.

Figure 6.9 Detail of costume rendering of Bumbo-Mumbo by Patrick Holt for *Faust*.

Figure 6.10 Costume rendering of Mrs. Malaprop by Patrick Holt for *The Rivals*.

typically between one-and-one-half and two-and-one-half head lengths wide, depending on the gender of the model. The lower end of this scale mainly pertains to female models, while the upper end describes the male. The line of the top of the shoulders is about one-third of a head length down from the bottom of the chin. The elbows line up with the waistline, the wrists with the groin, and the tips of the fingers fall about mid-thigh. Inexperienced students often make the torso too long and the arms too short. Use the guideline of the elbows at waist level and the wrists at groin level to regulate this proportion.

Many exciting clothing features happen at the waist: jackets are buttoned and waistbands, belts, and sashes are at, above, or below this line. Some styles, such as the 1920s' flapper style, de-emphasize any curvature in the torso, but many styles are more appealing when the natural variations of the torso are emphasized. For a normal weight person, the waist is narrower than the rib cage or hips. Overweight people typically carry extra pounds around the waist and torso than in the limbs. Practice drawing people of various sizes and weights, because not all play characters are slim and beautiful. Your costume rendering figures should reflect the body

type most appropriate for the character in the play, and not the generic male or female you are accustomed to drawing.

A costume rendering is essentially a drawing of a standing figure doing nothing but being a clotheshorse. To alleviate monotony in your renderings, position the arms, appropriately to the character, in interesting ways. Arms hanging straight down are not interesting. Bend the arms (held away from the torso so the costume is not obstructed). Put a hand on the hip, or have the figure holding an item appropriate to the character (cane, handkerchief, hand mirror, tankard, skull).

Hands

Hands are one of the body parts most feared by figure drawing students. A high percentage of students fear the hands so much that they simply do not draw them at all. In their drawings where the hands should be, there are ovals, amorphous blobs, or nothing at all. This is understandable considering the hand is such a complicated piece of equipment. The palm is a trapezoid-like shape with the wrist base slightly narrower than the finger base. The palm is covered with those wrinkles so beloved by palm readers, but so hard to draw. More wrinkles adorn the back of the hand where the outlines of bones and veins are visible beneath the skin. The fingers all have three joints, including the thumb, which is jointed where it attaches to the palm at the side of the base of the trapezoid. The fingers can bend forward at each joint, have some side-to-side movement capabilities, and each also includes a fingernail. The wrist, in conjunction with the elbow, swivels 180 degrees or more, and is capable of bending and swiveling at the same time. All this movement, though perhaps difficult to draw, makes the hand very expressive, a quality you will want to exploit in your renderings.

The only remedy for hand phobia is to tackle it straight on and practice drawing nothing but hands for a few weeks. You can draw your own non-dominant hand in thousands of positions. Simplify the hand into geometric shapes: the trapezoidal palm, small spheres for the knuckle joints, and cylinders for the finger parts between the knuckles. Keep your hand drawings as simple as possible and do not emphasize the wrinkles, veins, or fingernails. Since hands are unlikely to be the focus of any theatrical design rendering, the best approach to drawing hands is to become accomplished at drawing a few positions that work well in your renderings.

The Pelvis, Leg, and Foot

For the ideal eight head length figure, the fourth head length extends from the navel to the groin, comprising the pelvis area. The lower part of the body from the groin down to the feet equals half the height of the entire body. The top of the fifth head length begins at the groin and ends at the thigh above the knee. The sixth head length ends below the knee above the calf muscle. The seventh head length ends below the calf muscle, and the eighth at the bottom of the feet, which are foreshortened in a standing frontal pose.

This idealized figure has relatively long legs, which is generally considered to be an attractive feature. Interestingly, one of the more common blunders in figure drawing is to make the legs too short in relation to the torso. This usually occurs because the designer does not lay out the whole figure on the

page first, but begins by making the head too big for the size of the drawing paper. He then proceeds to draw the neck, torso, and so on down the length of the body. Because the legs get squeezed in to fit at the bottom of the paper, they end up too short.

Whether your model is seven or eight head lengths, or somewhere in between, put some movement into the lower half of the body. Unlike the arms, which may be bent at interesting angles or holding objects, the legs in most costume renderings are simply holding the body erect so as to plainly display the costume design. However, you can tilt the pelvis and distribute the weight of the figure on one foot, as in the contrapposto pose discussed at the beginning of this chapter. This will allow limited positioning of the non-weight-bearing leg in more interesting configurations. A slight bend of one knee and an angle to the lower part of one leg is much

Figure 6.11 The bend of the knees adds interest to this costume rendering of Bumbo-Mumbo by Patrick Holt for *Faust*.

more appealing than two legs that are mirror images of each other.

One thing that makes a figure drawing look particularly amateurish is the inaccurate placement of the muscles and bones of the legs, especially the calf muscle, the kneecap, and the bones of the ankle. Many costume designs expose the legs, so it is worthwhile to spend some extra time studying these muscles and bones.

Feet are rarely bare in costume renderings. Although it is necessary to be able to accurately draw the bare foot, it is a good idea to practice drawing feet wearing various styles of shoes with different heel heights. The toes of unshod, weight-bearing feet tend to spread out and look quite different than shod feet. Heel height also affects the appearance of the foot, ankle, and calf. Have your model occasionally pose nude but wearing different shoe styles. You will notice that a high heel tightens the muscles of the ankle and makes the calf muscle appear more prominent.

Exercise 1 in Chapter 7 describes a detailed format for drawing a nude model for a one-hour session. For costume designers, this area of study is mandatory. Use this format for your own drawing sessions at least once a week. Remember that good figure drawing skills, although they may not make you a great designer, will certainly make you a better designer.

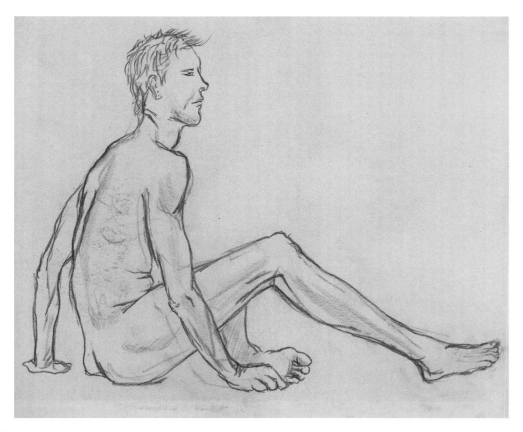

Figure 6.12 Figure drawing by Aimée Dombo.

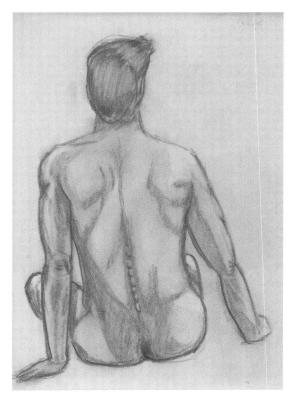

Figure 6.13 Figure drawing by Pam McGowan.

Figure 6.15 Costume rendering of Tom Morgan by Patrick Holt for *Treasure Island*.

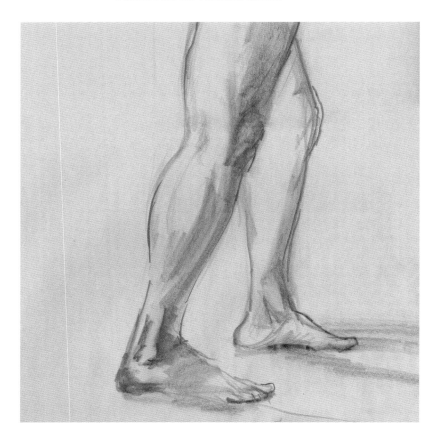

Figure 6.14 Figure drawing of lower legs.

Figure 6.16 Costume rendering by Al Tucci.

Chapter 7

Drawing Exercises

There are fifteen drawing exercises in this chapter, most designed to take approximately one hour to complete. To maximize drawing improvement, complete one exercise per week in addition to a weekly sketchbook drawing. Because each exercise builds progressively on skills developed in the previous exercises, it is best to start with Exercise 1 and continue in the order that they appear in this chapter. If you are just beginning to learn how to draw, or if it has been awhile since you did, read the first six chapters of this book before starting any of the exercises. Many terms and techniques you will need to know are defined and explained in these chapters.

For several of the exercises, including the first three, it is suggested that you work in charcoal on newsprint paper. Newsprint and soft vine charcoal, as drawing materials go, are inexpensive, and for beginners, you will avoid spending a great deal of money on drawings that are not quite frame-worthy. Soft vine charcoal is easy to erase from newsprint with a soft rag and a kneaded eraser, and you create value differences by simply varying the pressure of the charcoal on the paper. If you choose to use different drawing mediums and paper, it is still recommended that you use affordable charcoal and newsprint for the short warm-up drawings that begin each exercise. To avoid smudging your charcoal drawings, seal them with spray fixative after each drawing session, before you store or stack the drawings. Spray fixative must be applied in a well-ventilated area. If you spray directly on the drawing the charcoal will literally blow away from the pressure of the aerosol. Instead, direct the spray up away from the surface of the paper, and the fixative droplets will settle on the paper without disturbing the charcoal. Alternately, you can turn the drawing face down and heavily spray the back of the paper. The fixative will soak through the paper and seal the charcoal.

Save all the drawings you do, even if you are not satisfied with them. Tracking your progress is an important part of the process of learning to draw. In addition to regular practice, you also need constructive criticism to improve. Feedback from a friend or relative who believes everything you draw is museum quality is not constructive. Show your drawings to someone who is trained to evaluate artistic merit, will use the correct terminology when evaluating your work, and will provide useful suggestions for improvement. A critique should follow each of your weekly drawing sessions.

TOOLS AND MATERIALS

This is a list of the tools and materials you will need to complete all of the exercises in this chapter. Specific tools and materials that are necessary are listed at the beginning of each exercise. Most of these items are readily available at art or craft and hobby stores.

You will also need a carrying case for your supplies. Art stores carry hard plastic cases in a variety of sizes designed to hold art and craft supplies. Hard- or soft-sided fishing tackle boxes are typically much less expensive, but just as useful.

Artists' supplies tend to be expensive, and for those on a budget, there is, naturally, a compunction to spend as little as possible. Unfortunately, inexpensive art supplies are usually of poor quality and can impede your progress by producing disappointing results. Never buy art supplies at a grocery store or supplies designed for elementary school art classes. Buy the best supplies designed for professional artists and designers that you can afford, but shop around for sales and bargains. The best place to buy art supplies, unless you happen to live near a large discount art store, is the Internet.

One large pad of newsprint approximately 18 × 24"

One pad of white drawing paper approximately 11 × 14"

One large or several small sheets of white 4-ply Bristol, smooth illustration board, or hot-pressed watercolor paper

One book or several sheets of black drawing paper, Bristol, or illustration board

The black paper should be smooth textured with a matte finish. Do not use black construction paper, pastel, or charcoal paper

Two sheets of heavyweight vellum or marker paper approximately 9 × 12"

One sheet heavyweight poster or mat board

Set of graphite drawing pencils 4H, 2H, H, HB, 2B, 4B, 6B, 8B, for example

Very soft (8B or 9B) graphite stick

Soft vine charcoal sticks

Portable electric or manual pencil sharpener

Stomps of various sizes

Kneaded eraser

Standard (pink or white) pencil eraser

Eraser shaped like a pencil

Gum eraser

.05 mm mechanical pencil and lead

Waterproof black drawing ink

Water-soluble black drawing ink

Three different sized drawing nibs with holder

Fine crow quill drawing nib and holder

Sable or imitation sable watercolor brush size #4 or #6

Figures 7.1 through 7.3
Tools and materials.

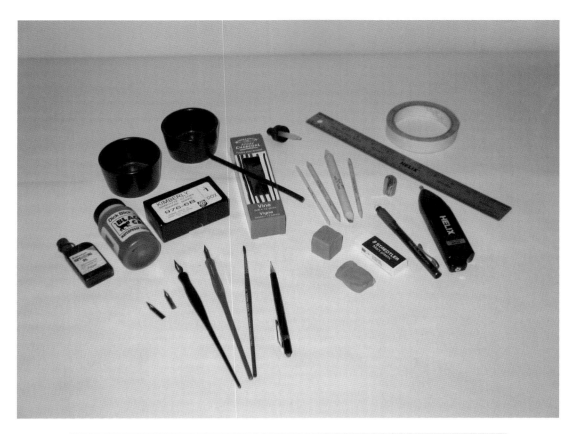

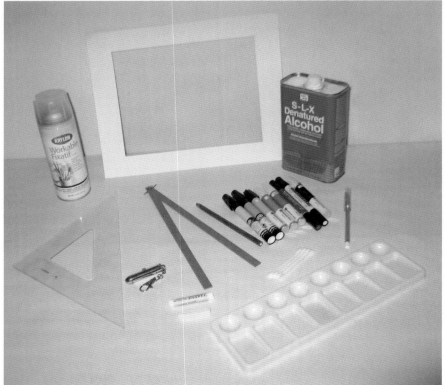

Figures 7.1 through 7.3 cont'd

Small watercolor palette
Two small water containers
Eyedropper
Cork-backed metal ruler or ruler with a metal edge
Large 45-degree plastic triangle
Masking tape
Art colored pencil, such as Prismacolor, in black, white, and shades of gray
Art marking pens such as Prismacolor, Pantone, etc., in black and shades of gray
Blending marker
White charcoal pencil
White soft pastel stick
White conté crayon stick
Spray fixative
Q-tips or cotton balls
Soft, absorbent, lint-free rags
Paper towels
Adjustable angle guide (This tool is comprised of two thin straight sticks of heavy cardboard or wood approximately nine inches in length, and attached together at one end with a round-head brass-plated paper fastener or bolt and wing nut.)
Picture plane tool (This tool is exactly like the mat for a framed picture. The opening of the mat will be the same size as the desired size of your finished drawing. See Exercise 11 for a detailed description. To construct this tool, you will need a piece of heavy mat or illustration board 11 × 17″, and an Xacto or utility knife.)
Digital camera (optional)
Denatured alcohol (optional)
Laser pointer (optional)

EXERCISE 1: FIGURE DRAWING FROM LIFE—SHORT POSES

The life drawing exercise is mandatory for costume designers, but is beneficial to anyone who wants to improve his drawing skills. Repeat this exercise once a week for three to four months and you will be astonished at the development in your drawing skills.

Soft vine charcoal is the preferred drawing medium for this exercise. Soft charcoal pencil, or very soft (9B) graphite pencil can be substituted for the vine charcoal, if desired. Draw on 18 × 24″ newsprint, using a full page for every pose. You will need 18 pieces of newsprint. Other materials needed

for this exercise are a soft cotton rag (useful for erasing large areas of charcoal), a kneaded eraser, an angle guide, and a pencil or straight thin dowel six or seven inches long to use as a measuring tool. A digital camera (optional) is useful for recording the model's poses so you can critique your work after the drawing session is completed.

For this exercise you are drawing a live, nude model. The purpose of the exercise is to practice drawing as accurately as possible the movement of the model's pose and the light and shade observed on the different planes of the body. The movement of a still figure refers to the curve of the spine, the tilt of the head, and the angles of all jointed body parts. You will be recording the angles of the shoulders and hips, the positioning of the limbs, and the tilt of the waist. An accurate portrait of the model's face is not a priority.

This session will last approximately one hour to one hour and twenty minutes, with rest time allowed for the model. Start by measuring the proportions of the model; give the model a short break, and then warm up with ten twenty-second drawings. Continue the session with four one-minute, and two five-minute drawings. Give the model another short break, and then do one twenty-minute drawing. If time permits, give the model a short break and then do an additional twenty-minute drawing (optional).

Draw in a quiet place where you and the model will be undisturbed for the entire session. Provide a private dressing area for the model and an elevated platform draped with fabric for the poses. Make sure

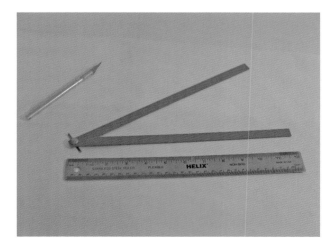

Figure 7.4 Angle guide.

Figure 7.5 The model as seen from the drawing station.

the model and your paper are well illuminated and that the model is posing against a neutral background. The lighting should be directional from one side or the other, so that one side of the body is clearly in shadow. Always draw standing up. Using an easel or other support, prop the newsprint pad up so it is nearly vertical and the top of the pad is at the level of the top of your head. If you are left-handed, position the easel and pad to the left of the model (the opposite if you are right-handed) and back far enough so that you can see the entire figure. Optimally, you should stand at such a distance that the model appears to fit on the newsprint page.

Measuring the Model

Before you begin the drawing session, it is recommended that you measure the proportions of the model. You will be measuring the length of the head, how many heads tall the models is, and where the head lengths line up on the body.

Ask the model to stand feet together in an attention pose facing you. The model's head should be as level as possible (as if balancing a book on the head), and the posture erect. Arms should hang to the sides with fingers extended. Standing at your drawing station, hold a pencil or thin dowel with your arm fully extended at shoulder height. With one eye closed, use the pencil to measure the length of the model's head from the crown to the chin, measuring down from the top of the pencil. Mark the head

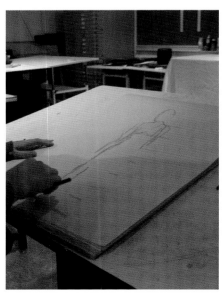

Figure 7.6
Measuring the length of the model's head.

length on the pencil. This is the unit of measurement that will be used to determine the model's proportions. Transfer this measurement to your newsprint, near the center top of the paper. Draw an oval representing the length of the head on your paper.

Fully extend your arm and pencil again, and line up the top of the pencil with the bottom of the chin. Note where on the body the next head length unit falls. It will likely be somewhere near the line of the nipples. Transfer the measurement to your paper. The next head length will be somewhere around the navel; the next somewhere around the groin, and so on. Make sure you accurately determine where the head lengths line up for your model, rather than using a proportion formula. Transfer head lengths to your paper until you get to the bottom of the feet. It is likely that your model will not be an even number of heads, and the last measurement will be a fraction of a head.

Use the head-length unit of measurement to find the width of the head, the width and length of the neck, and the width of the shoulders, waist, and hips. Sketch the model using these proportion guidelines, concentrating on the broad proportions of the body rather than details, such as facial features, hair, fingers or toes. Note where the elbows line up in relation to the torso, and the wrist and fingertips line up in relation to the lower body. Take your time with the drawing. After completing your proportional sketch, which may take up to twenty minutes, give the model a short break.

Keep this proportion drawing of your model close at hand during your drawing session, and refer back to it often. Although, as the model moves into different poses, the proportions will be distorted and foreshortened, the original proportion drawing will be a useful tool throughout the session.

Twenty-Second Poses

The purpose of the twenty-second poses is to warm up the muscles in the hand and arm as well as the brain synapses that control eye–hand coordination. The object is to record the entire pose in the time allotted. The result should be a quickly drawn sketch that describes the movement of the pose, without any detail. Do not erase unwanted lines or restart an unsuccessful attempt once the pose has begun. Do not concern yourself with detail, or the likeness of the model, but only with getting the pose on the paper. With each successive pose, correct the size of the drawing, if necessary, so that the figure fits on the paper.

Have the model count slowly to twenty-five and then take another pose after verbally announcing the change. The extra five seconds will give you time to flip to the next blank page and turn your paper vertically or horizontally, depending on the pose. These poses should be very expressive, conveying a sense of movement. A model can easily hold almost any pose for twenty-five seconds. Try not to look at the paper during these short poses; look only at the model. Take a second to look at the pose and decide if the rectangular newsprint pad should be oriented horizontally or vertically. That is, if the pose is taller than it is wide with the model in a standing position, use a vertical orientation. If the model is bending over or lying down, use a horizontal composition. Using sweeping strokes, draw from the elbow without bending the wrist. Because you will not be looking at the paper, it is helpful to continuously keep the charcoal in contact with the paper.

Use the following technique to draw the twenty-second poses. It is very effective at representing the movement of a pose. Near the top of the page, draw an oval or a line describing the tilt of the head, and then a sweeping line expressing the arc of the neck and spine. A line or scribble perpendicular to the base of the spine describes the hips, from which the legs are drawn consecutively, also as sweeping lines, jointed at the knees and ankles. Then retrace the second leg and continue back up the spine, keeping the charcoal in contact with the paper, and draw a line perpendicular to the base of the neck to represent the shoulders. Finally, draw each arm as a sweeping line, jointed at the elbow and wrist. With some practice, you will be able to accurately describe the motion of the entire pose in twenty seconds. You will eventually find that you have plenty of time to add some volume to the figure, for example, the rib cage, or the outline of the shoulders or thighs.

After warming up, you should have accomplished two important steps: first, you are comfortable with fitting the entire pose on the paper; second, you have captured the motion, in proportion, of each pose. If, at this point, you feel that these goals are not accomplished, continue the twenty-second poses until you feel fully warmed up.

One-Minute Poses

At this point, switch to one-minute poses. You now have three times as much time to draw as you did in

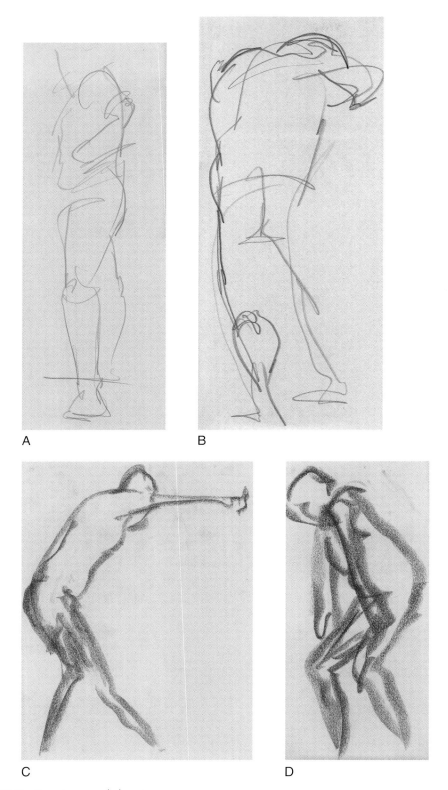

A

B

C

D

Figures 7.7A,B,C,D Twenty-second drawings.

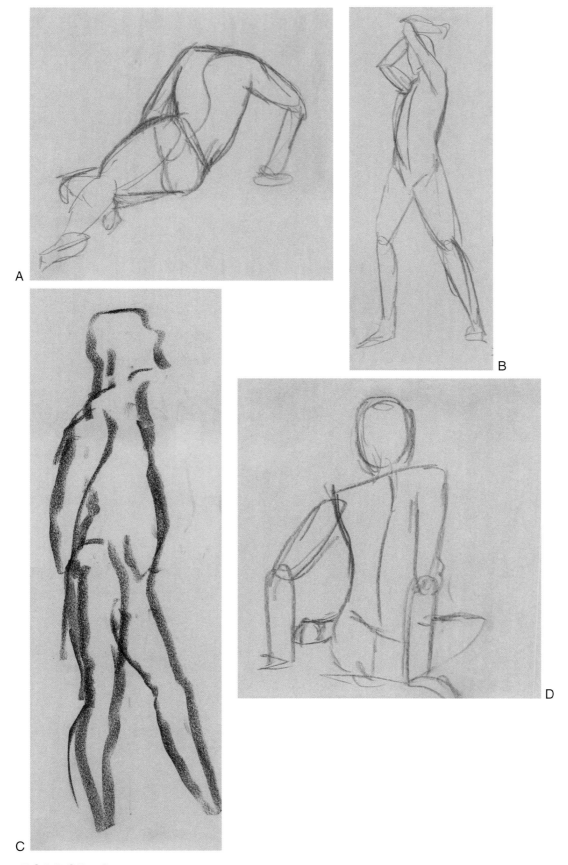

A

B

C

D

Figures 7.8A,B,C,D One-minute poses.

the first section, but not enough time yet to record fine detail. If you begin drawing eyes, fingers, or hairstyles in a one-minute pose, it will be at the expense of the rest of the figure. Unlike with the twenty-second poses, there will be at least a minimal opportunity to look back at your drawing, but the majority of the time, your eyes still remain on the model.

For the first twenty seconds, begin exactly as you did with the previous drawings to get the movement of the pose onto the paper, after which you still have twice as much time as you have already spent drawing. There are several ways to proceed with your remaining forty seconds: refine your sketch, add detail, or assess your sketch for the purpose of improving your next one-minute sketch.

Refining Your Drawing

At this juncture, you may decide to use the remaining time to make refinements to your sketch without adding any additional detail. Look briefly at your drawing and back at the model. Determine whether or not the rough sketch is proportional and if the lines angle in the proper directions according to the pose. Perhaps the head is too large, or an arm or leg proportionately too short, or crooked at a different angle than is represented in the pose. Using the cotton rag or kneaded eraser, make the necessary corrections.

Adding Detail

After drawing for twenty seconds you may have a satisfactory skeletal outline of the pose that does not require major correction. With forty seconds left of the pose, begin to add detail to your drawing. Block in the forms of the body as geometric shapes. Work for the same level of detail over the whole figure rather than attempting to completely flesh out one part. Begin to look at the contours of the body and how they combine with the background to form negative shapes. Time permitting, observe and emulate any obvious shadows.

Assessing Rather Than Refining

Use the additional time to assess your drawing, not with the intention of making changes to it, but with an eye to making adjustments in your next one-minute drawing. For instance, you can analyze scale

and placement of your drawing. Is the placement of the drawing on the page aesthetically pleasing? Perhaps your drawings regularly tend to end up awkwardly placed toward the top, bottom, or one side of the paper. As you begin your next drawing, deliberately begin the head at a point on the paper that will correct this placement.

In addition, you might wish to evaluate the size of the drawing on the paper. Is the figure either too big or too small for the paper? If your drawing is too small for the paper, start your next drawing with a larger head. This will unconsciously prompt you to draw the rest of the figure proportionately larger. Do the opposite if your drawing is too large for the paper: Start your next drawing with a smaller head.

Five-Minute Poses

Next, proceed with five-minute poses. It is most useful for costume designers if the model assumes a standing pose. For scenic and lighting designers, the pose is useful regardless of whether the model poses sitting or standing.

Again, start the five-minute pose exactly as if it were a twenty-second pose. Take the rest of the next minute to make sure that your initial rough sketch is accurate and well placed on the paper before adding additional detail. During this process, it is permissible to erase any incorrect or unwanted lines.

Checking for Accuracy

During the five-minute poses, you will have more time to refine the accuracy of your drawing. After completing the requirements of the one-minute pose, you still have four more minutes. Use at least one of these minutes to check that your drawing is accurate to the model's pose. Use your angle guide to determine the angle of a body part on the model (for example, the tilt of the head or a crooked arm or bent leg) by holding your loosened angle guide out at arm's length toward the model. Align one arm of the angle guide with one line of the body (for example, one side of the torso) and the other with another connected angled line (for example, the upper arm or the upper leg). Tighten the connection of the angle guide, carefully moving it to your drawing, keeping it in the same position. It is helpful if you think of the face and arms of a clock with the pivot point of the angle guide at the center of the clock. If you hold the arms of the angle guide up to the model,

A

B

Figures 7.9A,B Five-minute drawings.

and the arms of the guide point, respectively, to the two and the four on the face of the clock—indicating 2:20—ensure that when you transpose the angle to your drawing, the arms remain pointed at 2:20. Check all major angles in the pose in this manner.

You should also compare the proportions of the figure in your drawing with the head length measurements calculated at the beginning of this exercise. Is your drawing the correct number of heads in height? If not, it may appear that the head is too big or small, the torso too long, or the limbs too short. Make any necessary corrections before continuing with your drawing. If you find that major corrections are necessary, just start over. Newsprint is cheap, and there is no point in investing time in putting detail over an inaccurate skeleton.

Negative Space

Carefully observe light and shadow around and on the object and the negative space surrounding it. Often edges of objects are defined by the contrasting value of background space or the surface of another object that abuts it. If outlining is a regular routine for you, practice drawing your subject by drawing

only the negative spaces between objects. Alternatively, practice drawing the value contrasts you see as if they were solid objects. This will diminish a tendency to draw a representation of an object instead of how the object actually appears in your subject. For example, instead of drawing an arm, draw the shape of a value "object" that abuts the arm. Notice that the model's arms, legs, and torso, as they bend at angles to each other, create spaces against the neutral background. Focus on these shapes and emulate the exact shape of the negative space on your paper. If you can successfully draw the negative shape, you will have described accurately at least two contour lines of the body. For many people, an abstract shape is less intimidating than drawing a specific part of the body.

Alignment

Check to make sure the elements of your drawing are aligned accurately both vertically and horizontally. To do this, hold the angle guide (fixed in a straight line position) vertically at arm's length toward the model. Notice that certain points on the body line up with other points. Position the angle

Figure 7.10 Using the angle guide.

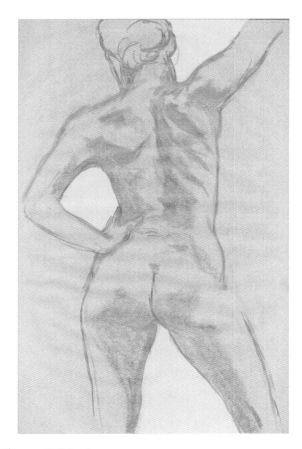

Figure 7.11 Drawing negative space.

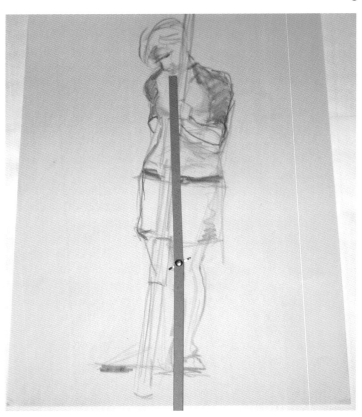

Figure 7.12 Using the angle guide to check vertical alignment.

Figure 7.13 Shading in the five-minute drawing.

guide so a vertical line runs through the top of the model's head. Observe where other parts of the body intersect with the vertical line. Remember that for a stationary figure to remain balanced, the chin must be centered over the weight-bearing center of the feet. Turn the angle guide horizontally and continue to check alignment of other points on the body. Make any adjustments that are necessary.

Adding Detail: Shading

With the rest of the time remaining, concentrate on creating volume, or a sense of three-dimensionality, by shading your drawing with the vine charcoal. Charcoal is a medium that lends itself to broad shading rather than fine detail. Add shaded areas as shapes. That is, look at the model and notice how darker areas assume specific shapes unto themselves. You will notice many gradations of light and dark over the whole of the model; these gradations are referred to as value—a measure of the degree of darkness ranging from black to white. Notice how

value differs on adjacent planes. The back of the hand, for example, is jointed at the wrist, base of the fingers, and at two knuckle joints. A relaxed hand has four different planes that will likely have different values. The facial features, similarly, can be broken down to planes of light and shade. Create detail in the face by drawing shaded smudges with the side of the charcoal rather than attempting to draw individual features as lines.

Put the darkest values in first. To make a plane look darker in value than an adjacent plane, concentrate on the area where the two planes meet. If you establish a deeper value on one plane at this location, the eye will read the entire plane as darker than the adjacent plane even if you fade the shaded area so the opposite side of the darker plane is in fact the same value as the lighter plane. Then, soften and lighten the shaded areas as necessary with the kneaded eraser (twisted into a point for small areas). The kneaded eraser will pick up charcoal like a sponge, if you just press over a shaded area rather than scrub in a traditional erasing manner.

After completing the five-minute poses, give the model and yourself a short break. Shake and stretch your drawing arm to loosen it up. During this break, if you go back over your twenty-second and one-minute poses and assess your progress, you will find that you have become more familiar with the forms and shapes of the model's body even as the poses change. Progressively your sketches are beginning to look more like one particular person than a generic human form.

The Twenty-Minute Pose

Twenty minutes is a long time to remain motionless. Choose a non-strenuous pose such as a simple standing or sitting position. If you choose a pose with an arm extended, provide a staff or pole for support. A half-sitting position on a tall stool is another option.

The twenty-minute pose is merely an extended version of the five-minute poses, just with more time to concentrate on accuracy and detail. As with

Figure 7.14 A completed twenty-minute pose.

the five-minute poses, begin by sketching in a skeleton. Take as much time as you need to make the skeleton as accurate as possible. Rub out any unwanted lines with the cotton rag and kneaded eraser. Following the same steps as in the five-minute drawing, check for alignment, use the negative space of the pose to help draw an accurate contour, and add shaded detail as volumetric shapes. Do not add detail or shading until the proportions of the drawing are correct; just start over if you feel your initial attempt is hopeless. Work on the whole drawing in stages so the completed drawing has no unfinished parts. Think of the twenty-minute pose as a five-minute pose with extended time to scrutinize every line and shape in your drawing for accuracy.

The amount of detail you will have recorded in twenty minutes will depend on the speed at which you draw, but typically the entire figure as a rough sketch, including facial features, hair, fingers, and toes, can be rendered with a sense of light and shade in twenty minutes. If you have a digital camera, take a snapshot of each pose that you draw and compare it to your finished drawings.

EXERCISE 2: THREE-DIMENSIONAL MODELING—DRAPERY

Soft vine charcoal is the preferred drawing medium for this exercise. Soft charcoal pencil, or very soft (9B) graphite pencil can be substituted for the vine charcoal, if desired. Draw on 18 × 24″ newsprint, using a full page for every drawing. You will need seven pieces of newsprint. Other materials needed for this exercise are a soft cotton rag, a kneaded eraser, stomps in various sizes, and an angle guide. Take pictures of the drapery set-up with a digital camera (optional) so you can critique your work after the drawing session is completed.

The purpose of this exercise is to accurately describe both the drape and affect of light on fabric. You will record the way the fabric falls in folds, the weight of the fabric, and the shading and highlights from a strong directional light source.

This session will last approximately one hour. Start by warming up the hand and arm with four two-minute drawings, continuing with two ten-minute drawings. Then take a short break to stretch and relax your drawing arm and hand. Finish with one twenty-five minute drawing.

Setting Up the Drapery Model

Choose two pieces of fabric approximately 4 × 4″, or larger, for this still life set-up. Choose solid colored fabrics with minimal texture and no pattern. One of the pieces should be of heavy weight such as canvas, upholstery fabric, sailcloth, suede cloth, velvet, or velour. The other piece should be lightweight fabric like satin, silk, chintz, or percale sheeting. Each fabric piece should be clearly different from the other in value; one should be noticeable darker than the other.

Set the still life up on an elevated platform, such as a large table set in front of a neutral background. Set various size boxes or other bulky items on the table as a support for the fabric, and arrange the fabric attractively, completely covering the support items. Include a tall narrow item such as a sturdy candlestick to create a peak in the draped fabric. Step back and look at the arrangement, critiquing it for aesthetic merit, and adjust as necessary. The idea is to design an arrangement that will be challenging to draw for an extended period, but not so complicated as to be frustrating to draw. You will be drawing the entire arrangement in each step of this exercise, so make it interesting, but keep it simple.

For this still life set-up, you will need a strong directional light source. The light source should originate from above the set-up and from one side only, so that the drapery is clearly highlighted on one side and in shadow on the other. An optimal situation is to set up the drapery arrangement in a lighting lab where you have total control over the placement and intensity of the instruments. If not, a photography studio floodlight on an adjustable tripod works well, but you could also implement overhead track lighting, as long as the light comes only from one direction and is powerful enough to permeate any other ambient light in the room.

The Two-Minute Drawing

Now you are ready to draw. As in the figure drawing exercise, draw standing up with the newsprint pad nearly vertical, and at enough of a distance from the still life that it appears to fit on the paper. Observe whether the still life is taller than it is wide, or wider than it is tall, and orient your paper accordingly, either vertically or horizontally.

Figure 7.15 The drapery still life.

Figure 7.16 A two-minute drapery drawing.

Begin with four two-minute drawings. These drawings have the same purpose as the twenty-second drawings in Exercise 1—warming up the arm, hand, and the brain synapses that involve eye—hand coordination. Use these drawings to familiarize yourself with the proportions of the drapery set-up, and to get proficient at fitting the whole arrangement attractively on your paper. You may want to move your drawing station to a different position after completing each two-minute drawing, and choose your favorite position from these for the longer drawings later in this exercise.

During the first twenty seconds of the two-minute drawing, rough in the perimeter of the still life and the major fold lines in the fabric. Draw these first lines in very lightly, in case you need to erase them. Use as much of the paper as you can, and fit the entire arrangement on the page. (Whatever parts of the arrangement are on the tabletop is sufficient; it is not necessary to include excessive amounts of fabric hanging down from the horizontal surface.) Because

costume and set renderings are nearly always drawings of the entire set or the whole character, it is good practice to draw the entire set-up, whether a figure or still life. If your initial attempt is too small or too large for the paper, take note of what corrections you should make, then rub out the first drawing and begin again. Use your angle guide to make sure all the fabric folds are properly positioned in your drawing.

Notice that the heavier fabric in the still life drapes differently than the lighter fabric. Draped heavy fabrics have bigger, softer folds, while lightweight fabric drapes with thinner, crisper folds. For either fabric, draw the folds as areas of light and shade, rather than as lines. With the strong directional light source, each fold will have a dark side and a light side. The geometric solid that the majority of the folds will most represent is a cylinder. Because the folds are curved shapes, the transition between the shaded and lighted sides of the curve will be soft, and the light will hit the curve at spot away from the edge of the fold.

Figure 7.17 A ten-minute drapery drawing.

An easy way to describe the light on these curves is to use the side of the charcoal stick to shade the whole fold, and then use the kneaded eraser to remove the charcoal only in the area where the light should be. Use your stomp to soften and blend the transition between the shade and light. Begin this process during the two-minute drawings, even though you will not be able to finish in two minutes. This process will get you familiar with the technique of shading, and you will not have to change techniques as you move into the longer drawings.

The Ten-Minute Drawing

Start the ten-minute drawings in exactly the same way as you did the two-minute drawings. Make sure you have a light, accurate sketch of the whole arrangement that fits on the paper before you add detail. Complete two ten-minute drawings, changing

Figure 7.18 A twenty-five-minute drapery drawing.

the position of your drawing station if you wish. Try to complete some shading on the whole drawing during the allotted ten minutes. You will not have enough time to go into great detail for every fold, but the finished drawing should replicate the proportions of the arrangement, and the directional light source should be evident in the shading, as in Figure 7.17.

The Twenty-Five-Minute Drawing

Start the twenty-five-minute drawing in the same manner as the two-minute drawings. Then proceed exactly as you did for the ten-minute drawing, shading the folds and pleats of the fabric. Work the whole drawing rather than taking any one area to completion. If you stop at any point before the time is up, all the parts of the drawing should be roughly at the same stage of completion. Use the extra time you have for this drawing to carefully observe the light, shade, and cast shadows in the arrangement. You will notice at least eight levels of value: the base values, and the highlight, shade, and lowlight on the two different fabrics. Cast shadows especially on the darker fabric may appear even darker than the lowlight. Use the kneaded eraser and stomps to remove charcoal where necessary to clearly show the different levels of value in your drawing. The lightest value (most likely the highlight on the lighter fabric) will be the color of the newsprint, and the darkest will be as black as you can make the charcoal on the paper. The other values will be gradated between these two extremes.

EXERCISE 3: FIGURE DRAWING—THREE-DIMENSIONAL MODELING AND THE CLOTHED FIGURE

Soft vine charcoal is the preferred drawing medium for this exercise. Soft charcoal pencil, or very soft (9B) graphite pencil can be substituted for the vine charcoal if desired. Draw on 18 × 24″ newsprint using a full page for every drawing. You will need eighteen pieces of newsprint. Other materials needed for this exercise are a soft cotton rag, a kneaded eraser, a pencil or thin dowel six to seven inches long, and an angle guide. Take pictures of the model's poses with a digital camera (optional) so you can critique your work after the drawing session is completed.

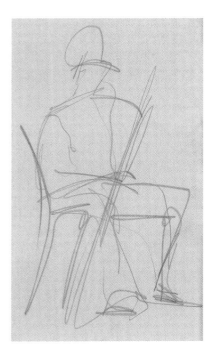

Figure 7.19 A twenty-second drawing of the clothed model.

Figure 7.21 A five-minute drawing of the clothed model.

Figure 7.20 A one-minute drawing of the clothed model.

The purpose of this exercise is to practice drawing as accurately as possible the movement and proportion of the model, the light and shade observed on the different planes of the body, and the drape

and fold of the model's clothing. An accurate portrait of the model's face is not a priority. The object is to draw the model as an accurately proportioned, three-dimensional form, with clear indication of the effects of the light source.

This exercise combines Exercises 1 and 2 using a clothed model. Ask the model to wear a combination of close and loose fitting clothing, perhaps a tight fitting top with a loose, unbuttoned shirt over top. As in Exercise 2, the clothing fabrics should have variety in value, have smooth texture, and be devoid of pattern. Set up a strong directional light source similar to the drapery arrangement. Adjust the light source as necessary so that one side of the model is clearly highlighted and the other side shaded. Proceed exactly as you did with Exercise 1 by using the same techniques used in the first two exercises.

This session will last approximately one hour to one hour and twenty minutes. As in Exercise 1, start by measuring the proportions of the model; give the

Figure 7.22 A twenty-minute drawing of the clothed model.

model a short break, and then warm up with ten twenty-second drawings. Continue the session with four one-minute and two five-minute drawings. Give the model another short break, and then do one twenty-minute drawing. If time permits, give the model a short break and then do an additional twenty-minute drawing (optional).

EXERCISE 4: DRAWING LIGHT BY ERASURE

The drawing medium for this exercise is very soft (8B or 9B) graphite stick, soft (8B) graphite pencil, and soft vine charcoal on 11 × 17″ white drawing paper. You will be covering your paper with the graphite, and then drawing a still life by erasure. For the beginning warm-up exercises, use soft vine charcoal on half sheets of your 18 × 24″ newsprint. You

will need three pieces of newsprint (for six drawings) and five pieces of white drawing paper. Other materials needed for this exercise are a pencil sharpener, a kneaded eraser, standard (pink or white) pencil eraser, an eraser shaped like a pencil, and an angle guide. Take pictures of the objects you draw with a digital camera (optional) so you can critique your work after the drawing session is completed.

The purpose of this exercise is to carefully observe how light affects a series of objects. When you draw with a dark medium such as charcoal or pencil on light paper, you are drawing shade and shadows and leaving the light colored paper to represent highlights. This trains your eyes to see shade and shadow. In this exercise, you will be adding highlight, rather than shade, by erasing graphite from your paper, training your eyes to see light.

This session will last approximately one hour. Begin by warming up with six two-minute drawings. Continue the session with four five-minute, and one twenty-five-minute drawing.

Setting Up

You will be drawing four objects of your choosing, first individually, and then as a still life. Select objects that are medium to light in value and have a reflective surface, for example, a ceramic teapot, a metal candlestick, a wine bottle, and a glass or metal vase with an interesting contour. This exercise, like Exercise 2, requires a strong directional light source. Set one of your objects on a table, and adjust the light source so that one side of the object is clearly highlighted and the other is shaded. The table should be set in front of a non-distracting, neutral background.

Before you begin drawing, prepare the white drawing paper for the erasing exercises. Using a very soft (8B or 9B) graphite stick, cover the entire surface of five pieces of white drawing paper. Heavy pressure is not necessary, but it is important to cover the paper sufficiently so that no white of the paper is visible.

The Two-Minute Warm-Up Drawings

Before you begin the erasing exercises, warm up your arm and hand by sketching the objects in vine charcoal on newsprint. Complete six two-minute drawings, one of each individual object you selected, and two of the four objects grouped as a still life. The erasure drawings will be 11 × 17″, and you should use approximately the same size newsprint for the warm-up drawings to familiarize yourself with the scale of the paper. One-half sheet of your newsprint paper will approximate the size of the white drawing paper. Your goals for these drawings are to fit the objects attractively on the paper, and replicate the contours and proportions of the objects. Use your angle guide as necessary to accurately replicate the lines of the objects. You are essentially creating six accurate line drawings, without any shading.

The Five- and Twenty-Five-Minute Drawings

After warming up, you are ready to begin the erasing exercises. Begin by setting one of the selected objects on the table and adjust the light source as necessary. You will remove graphite from your white drawing

Figure 7.23 The reflective surface of this object creates various interesting highlights.

Figure 7.24 A two-minute line drawing.

Figure 7.25 A five-minute erasure drawing.

Figure 7.26 A twenty-five-minute erasure drawing.

paper in three stages, first with the kneaded eraser, then with the standard pencil eraser, and finally with a pencil-shaped eraser. First use your kneaded eraser to carefully block in the largest areas of light, the side of the object facing the light source, and the surface of the table not affected by cast shadow. Remove the graphite by pressing down with the kneaded eraser, rather than by rubbing. The kneaded eraser will lighten the graphite but not completely remove it. The purpose of this step is to create a ghost image, without detail, of the object sitting on the tabletop.

Next, use the pencil eraser to further develop the contours and details of the object. The pencil eraser will remove more of the graphite, depending on the pressure you use. You should be able to easily remove the graphite almost completely, revealing the white of the paper. In the third erasing step, use the pencil-shaped eraser to add fine detail. Remember you are only drawing the highlights with the various erasers, not any shade or cast shadows. Finally, finish the drawing by adding shade and cast shadow as necessary with the 8B graphite pencil and soft vine charcoal. The vine charcoal will be much darker than the graphite, and should be applied to the darkest areas of your drawing.

Spend only five minutes on each of these drawings, even if you do not completely finish each one. Use the five-minute drawings to experiment with the materials and refine your technique. Take a short break when the five-minute drawings are completed, and then set up your four selected objects on the tabletop in an interesting still life arrangement. The twenty-five-minute drawing will be of the collected objects done using the same erasing techniques as in the five-minute drawings.

EXERCISE 5: EXPERIMENTING WITH LINE QUALITY

The drawing medium for this exercise is waterproof black drawing ink on 4-ply Bristol board, smooth illustration board, or hot-pressed watercolor paper. Trim the paper into three letter-sized pieces ($8^1/_2 \times 11''$). Other necessary materials include a .05 mm mechanical pencil; three different sizes of drawing nibs; a nib holder; a crow quill pen; water-soluble black drawing ink; a #4 or #6 watercolor brush; a small watercolor palette; two small water containers;

an eyedropper; a cork-backed metal ruler; a soft, lint-free rag; and paper towels. You will also need an assortment of small objects of your choice with simple but distinctive and recognizable contours. Some examples of appropriate objects are open matchbook, stapler, coffee mug, ballpoint pen, toothbrush, and banana.

Be careful to select drawing nibs, rather than calligraphy nibs, and make sure the nibs fit in the nib holder you purchase (see Figure 7.2). Nibs are inexpensive, but also fairly fragile. Purchase extra nibs in case a tine bends or breaks while you are drawing. If this happens, discard the nib and use a fresh one. You may choose to purchase multiple holders, so switching nibs is not necessary. A crow quill pen creates very thin fine lines. The drawing nibs create lines of varying thicknesses, depending on the nib and the pressure you apply to the paper.

The paper for this exercise was selected for its smoothness. Rough textured or fibrous papers will cause the pen nib to catch and spatter ink drops. It will also make the tines of the nib more likely to bend or break, rendering the nib useless.

This exercise is an exploration of lines and line quality. You will experiment by drawing using only lines, rather than shading as in the previous exercises. The effects of light and shadow, although addressed, are not a priority. An important goal for this exercise is to achieve a variety of line widths, not only within an entire drawing, but within individual lines. For this reason, rapidograph or fine point nylon-tipped pens are not acceptable, although, admittedly, they are easier to control than dip pens. They are designed to make lines of controlled width, while dip pens are designed to make lines that vary in width depending on the pressure of the nib on the paper.

This exercise will take about an hour and a half to complete. Rather than executing timed drawings, you will first experiment with the tools and materials, and then draw the objects you selected using contour lines, with a minimal application of diluted ink wash. A good follow-up to this exercise is to do some sketchbook drawings using pen and ink, copying the techniques of great masters of pen and ink drawing. A few artists you might want to copy are Michelangelo, Leonardo da Vinci, Corot, Van Gogh, and Daumier, among others.

Experimenting with Pen and Ink Tools and Materials

Begin by organizing all your tools and materials so they are conveniently at hand, and fill the two small containers with water. The format for your exploration of pen and ink is illustrated in Figure 7.27, and you will be replicating this diagram on your paper. Using the mechanical pencil and ruler, very lightly sketch six three-inch square boxes on one piece of paper, dividing five of the boxes into quarters. In one of the quartered boxes, very lightly draw a cone, a sphere, a cube, and a cylinder, one in each quarter.

A second piece of paper will be your scratch pad for testing each nib's ink flow and line width. Begin with the crow quill nib, which makes very fine, thin lines. Dip the nib in the ink and test the line width. It may take a new nib a few strokes until the ink starts flowing. Continue testing the line width of each of your nibs and organize them in order from thinnest to thickest. After use, dip the nibs in water, and then gently wipe off the ink and dry the nib with the lint-free rag to prevent the ink from drying on the nib. Dried ink on the nib can cause skipping and spattering.

Returning to the paper on which you have drawn the six boxes, trace over all the light pencil lines in ink with the ruler using a medium nib. Use a ruler with cork backing, as this will lift the edge of the ruler a bit off the paper and prevent the ink line from bleeding. Avoid crossing wet ink lines with the ruler because the cork backing will smudge the ink. Because you are drawing, and not drafting, it is perfectly acceptable to cross the lines slightly at the corners of the boxes. Variation in line thickness is also fine, although the ruler will prevent this to a certain extent. When the ink is dry, use the gum eraser to remove any visible pencil lines. Label each box according to the diagram in Figure 7.27.

Now you are ready to start experimenting. The basic pen stroke is called the hatch. Hatching is laying down a series of parallel lines that are a consistent distance from each other. This is how value

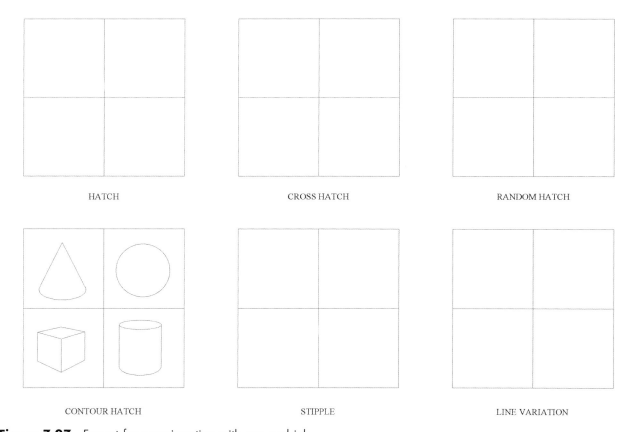

HATCH   CROSS HATCH   RANDOM HATCH

CONTOUR HATCH   STIPPLE   LINE VARIATION

Figure 7.27 Format for experimenting with pen and ink.

is created in a pen and ink drawing. The closer together the lines are, the darker the area will appear because less of the white paper is showing through. For each of the techniques in this exercise, you may choose to practice first on your scratch paper before drawing on the diagram. In the top left quarter of the top left box, practice hatching by drawing freehand lines using the thinnest nib. Start away from the direction your hand will be moving, and do not worry if the lines intersect the edges of the box. Always pull the pen toward you, rather than pushing away. Pushing the pen will cause it to catch on the paper and may damage the nib. Your lines may be vertical, horizontal, or diagonal, according to your preference. It may take some practice to lay down lines that are parallel and evenly spaced. If your pen spatters, or you are dissatisfied with your lines, just continue on; you will improve with practice. The object is to create an area of different value in each of the four quarters. Use a thicker pen nib for each successive quarter.

In the next four boxes, you will be experimenting with variations on the basic hatch stroke. The crosshatch stroke builds on the hatch by adding another layer of parallel, evenly spaced lines on top of the first hatch and at roughly 90 degrees. In the next box, practice crosshatching, creating a different value in each quarter as you did with the first box. Wait for the first hatch to dry before applying the crosshatch on top to prevent the ink from bleeding. Crosshatching is more challenging than the simple hatch, because you are going over areas of the paper that you have already dragged the pen across. If the pressure of the nib was hard enough to scratch the surface of the paper, the nib may catch on that area

when you apply the crosshatch. To avoid this, press lightly with the first hatch. Build darker value by using a thicker nib and spacing the lines closer together, rather than by pressing harder.

Another variation of the basic hatch is the random hatch. By now, you must be tired of straight, evenly spaced lines so this one will come as a welcome break. The random hatch creates value difference in the same way the hatch does, but the lines are squiggles rather than straight. Scribble with the pen, varying the scribbles, and avoid repeating the same marks. The size and density of the squiggles and the thickness of the lines will create varying levels of value. In the next box, create four different values in the quadrants using the random hatch technique.

The final hatch we will experiment with in this exercise is the contour hatch. With this technique, the hatch lines follow the surface contour of an object, creating the effects of light and shade. Practice the contour hatch on the geometric shapes on your paper, with the objective of making them appear to be three-dimensionally modeled. The highlight will be the white of the paper, and the hatch lines in the shaded areas will follow the contour of the shape. In the lowlight areas, experiment with a contour crosshatch to darken the value.

Another common pen stroke is the stipple. Stipple by touching the nib to the paper, and lifting up, creating a dot. The size and density of the dots create value variation in the same manner as the hatch. In the next box, practice stippling, creating four different value variations in the quadrants.

As mentioned previously, achieving variation in thickness within a single line is an important drawing

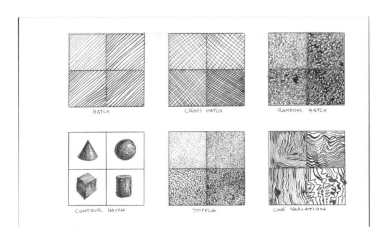

Figure 7.28 Hatches, stippling, and line variation.

aesthetic. For each of the quarters of the sixth box use a different nib, and practice drawing evenly spaced lines that contain thickness variation within the line. Space the lines fairly close together, but not so close that they touch. Create different thicknesses within each line by varying the pressure of the nib on the paper.

Although hatching and stippling create value variation in a pen and ink drawing, it is common to add shade and cast shadows, and to simulate the surface color of some objects by using washes. Washes often help to create focus in a pen and ink drawing, which without washes, has only two intrinsic values—black and white. Adding progressively more water to the ink lightens the value, and the diluted ink is brushed onto the selected areas of the pen and ink drawing. Using waterproof ink to execute the line drawing prevents the lines from dissolving when the washes are applied. In the next part of this exercise, you will produce line drawings of the objects you selected, and then add shade, cast shadow, and surface value with ink washes.

Begin by creating a series of ink washes, each different in value. Using the eyedropper, place a drop of water-soluble ink in each of four wells of your watercolor palette. Wash the eyedropper, and using clean water, add two drops to the first well, four to the next well, six drops to the next, and eight to the last. Stir each wash, avoiding cross-contamination, and with the watercolor brush, test each wash on your scratch paper. Wash the brush before dipping it in each successive wash. The washes should show a clear progression from darker to lighter. Adjust the amount of water in each wash, if necessary, to accomplish this.

On a fresh sheet of paper, lightly sketch line drawings of the chosen objects in pencil (at least four), placing them attractively on the page. The drawings should describe only the contours of the objects. Using your favorite pen nib, trace over the pencil lines with ink lines that have thickness variations. Use thicker line parts, created by pressing harder with the nib, for the parts of the objects that are away from the light source, and thinner line parts for the highlighted sections. As you look at an object, you will see that the lines that make up the outline of the object vary according to the light source and the inherent composition of the object. Emulate these observations in your contour drawing.

Allow the line drawings to dry completely, and then begin judiciously adding washes to your draw-

Figure 7.29 Pen and ink wash drawing of a matchbook.

Figure 7.30 Pen and ink wash drawing of a toothbrush.

ings. Leave the white of the paper to represent highlighted areas of the objects. Choose the dilution of the wash according to surface value of the object. For example if the object is very light in color (and value) the shaded areas should also be fairly light in value. For dark-colored objects, you may choose to apply a medium value wash to the whole object, except where the highlights are, and then add darker washes to describe the shade and lowlight areas. All the washes should be translucent, allowing the pen lines to show through.

The techniques used in this exercise will be used and expanded upon in the following exercise. They are also the basic building blocks of ink and watercolor painting, which will be discussed later in this book.

EXERCISE 6: HAIR TEXTURES

The drawing medium for this exercise is waterproof black drawing ink on 4-ply Bristol board, smooth illustration board, or hot-pressed watercolor paper. Trim the paper into two letter-sized pieces ($8^1/_2 \times 11''$). Other necessary materials include a .05 mm mechanical pencil; three different sizes of drawing nibs; a nib holder; a crow quill pen; water-soluble black drawing ink; a #4 or #6 watercolor brush; a small watercolor palette; two small water containers; an eyedropper; a cork-backed metal ruler; a soft, lint-free rag; and paper towels. You will also need six good-quality photographs or drawings that highlight distinctly different hairstyles.

The purpose of this exercise, which will take about an hour to complete, is the practical application of the pen and ink wash techniques, begun in Exercise 5, in thumbnail sketches of various hairstyles. It is necessary to complete Exercise 5 before beginning this exercise. In this session, you will draw six hairstyles. These will begin a collection of thumbnail references you can continue as part of your sketchbook sessions. Obviously hairstyles and the fabric textures sketched in the next exercise are most useful to costume designers, but collections of thumbnail technique sketches can also be tailored to scene and lighting designers (for scene designers, references for how to render different types of brick, stone, wood, or marble).

The same six-square format you used to experiment with hatch techniques in Exercise 5 will be used for the thumbnail sketches in this exercise. Do not quarter the squares, however. Each square is

Figure 7.31 *Examples of hairstyles.*

$3 \times 3''$. Draw the squares in waterproof ink with a cork-backed metal ruler as in Exercise 5. One sheet of paper will be used for hairstyles, and the other is for scratch paper. Set up your materials as in Exercise 5 as well as preparing the four ink washes. Remember to use waterproof ink with the pen and nibs and water-soluble ink for the washes.

The photograph or drawings you choose should include faces; emphasize the hairstyles, including the texture of the hair; and be large enough to clearly see the details of hair and face. Photos that have a directional light source are best. Avoid silhouetted heads or photographs that obscure the hair with text or other objects. The photographs can be pulled from magazines, if desired, and should be black and white. Color photographs can be scanned into a digital imaging program such as Adobe Photoshop, de-saturated, and then printed out on good quality paper. Choose drawings that have been done by artists or designers that you want to emulate. The photographs or drawings are the "real" or original things you will be copying, so do not copy originals that are not of good quality.

The $3 \times 3''$ squares on your paper are approximately the size you would normally draw the head and hair in your costume renderings. Include at least the contour of the face in your thumbnail sketches; features are optional, and if you include them, keep them simple. Determine the size of the face in the three-inch square by the hairstyle; that is, fill the square as if it were an entire piece of paper, making sure the head and hair fit in the box neither going off the edge, nor having too much empty space around the head.

The number one rule of drawing hair is to treat the mass of hair as a three-dimensional object, and not as thousands of individual hairs. Think of the observer's perspective as several paces from the figure, where individual hairs are not discernable from the mass. The second rule of drawing hair is less is more. Use the minimum number of lines to describe the contour and texture of the hair, and use the least amount of wash necessary. Avoid allover texture or allowing the texture to get too busy, as this will make the head look flat.

Contour Drawings

Begin by sketching lightly with the .05 mm mechanical pencil, practicing first on your scratch paper if you wish. First, draw the contour of the hair

Figure 7.32 Contour drawings of hairstyles.

Figure 7.33 Shade and lowlight added to contour drawings.

including any waves, curls, or wisps that break out of the collected mass, and are partially surrounded by negative space. For curly hair, take the time to describe the shape and scale of the curls in the contour drawing, but avoid drawing the curls in the interior of the hair mass. When you are satisfied with your pencil drawing, trace over it in pen and water-proof ink, using line variation to avoid outlining. When the ink is dry, remove any visible pencil lines with your gum eraser.

Shade and Lowlight

Next, add shading with your ink washes. The head and hair are three-dimensional and spherical and are affected by light accordingly—one side of the head will be highlighted, and the other in shadow. In this step, you are indicating the light source, but not the texture of the hair. Start with the wash lightest in value and build up to the darkest wash needed. Use the washes judiciously, leaving the white of the paper to describe the highlight (not color highlights specific to the hairstyle, but the highlight on the head and hair from the directional light source).

Texture

At this point, you should have a drawing that looks three-dimensional, but has no hair texture inside the hair mass. To finish the drawing, you will add any additional texture that is necessary for a specific hairstyle. Some hairstyles, like long, smooth, or very tightly kinked styles may need very little texture embellishment; some, such as loosely curled styles,

Figure 7.34 Texture added to shaded contour drawings.

may need more. Carefully observe the interior texture of the hair mass in your reference photo or drawings and add the least amount of texture needed to make the hair look realistic. Add texture with pen or wash, or both, using a contour hatch and/or brush strokes that follow the contour of the head and hairstyle.

Hair and faces in costume renderings are rarely foci, but well executed, they do help describe the characters' personalities and add professionalism to your drawings. Use the three simple steps outlined in this exercise to quickly add realistic hair to your figures: (1) draw the contour of the hair mass, (2) add shade and lowlight, and (3) add texture as necessary.

Continue compiling reference thumbnail sketches by occasionally using your sketchbook drawing sessions to execute another page of six hairstyles, experimenting with different mediums, if you wish. The sketches are much more useful than reference photos because you are working out how to render the various styles and textures. Take notes (for example, pen nib sizes or wash formulas) in the margins of the paper to help yourself remember how you achieved certain techniques.

EXERCISE 7: FABRIC TEXTURES AND PATTERNS

The drawing medium for this exercise is waterproof black drawing ink on 4-ply Bristol board, smooth illustration board, or hot-pressed watercolor paper. Trim the paper into two letter-sized pieces ($8^1/_2 \times$ 11"). Other necessary materials include a .05 mm mechanical pencil; three different sizes of drawing nibs; a nib holder; a crow quill pen; water-soluble black drawing ink; a #4 or #6 watercolor brush; a small watercolor palette; two small water containers; an eyedropper; a cork-backed metal ruler; a soft, lint-free rag; and paper towels. You will also need six distinctly patterned or textured fabric swatches, such as might be used for costume designs. Make sure the swatch is big enough to discern the repetition of the pattern.

Choose only fabrics that are heavily and distinctly textured or have a clear pattern. In a rendering, solid, smooth, matte fabrics like serge or percale sheeting are described by their color, drape, and the effects of a directional light source, none of which apply to this exercise.

The purpose of this exercise is to build on the pen and ink wash skills and techniques used in the previous two exercises, and to begin compiling a collection of reference thumbnail sketches of fabric textures and patterns. In this exercise, which will take about an hour and follow the same format as Exercise 6, you will render the textures and patterns of six fabrics in three-inch squares on your paper. You will be employing the pen and ink hatching and stippling techniques described in Exercise 5, and augmenting the drawings as necessary with ink washes.

Figure 7.35 Examples of fabric swatches.

Start by measuring and inking six three-inch square boxes on one piece of paper, and preparing four gradated ink washes, as in Exercise 5. Then, beginning with one fabric swatch, carefully analyze the details and value differences in the swatch. For a patterned swatch, is the background lighter or darker than the pattern? Does the ribbing or other surface quality of a textured fabric appear lighter or darker than the background? Does the texture appear linear, bumpy, swirled? Try to emulate the texture or pattern of the fabric on your scratch paper by making various hatching and stippling marks with various size pen nibs. The goal is to find a technique that is fast and simple to execute. Use the minimum amount of lines necessary to replicate an impression of the fabric. Add ink washes as necessary to simulate color value.

Consider that when you draw or paint these textures and patterns in a costume rendering, the observer will be at a distance from the figure, so the fabric details will be considerably scaled down.

It is recommended that you occasionally use your weekly sketchbook session to render another six fabric textures and patterns to add to your collection. Make notes in the margins of the paper of your process for each technique, and attach the fabric swatch to the paper for reference.

Figures 7.36 through 7.39 Some examples of fabric swatches rendering in pen and ink wash.

EXERCISE 8: PERSPECTIVE DRAWING TECHNIQUES

The drawing medium for this exercise is a .05 mm mechanical pencil on white 11 × 17″ drawing paper. You will also need a pencil eraser, a ruler, and a large 45-degree triangle. This is the most technical of these exercises, but the processes and techniques, once assimilated into your drawing lexicon, will make the execution of the freehand drawings in Exercises 9, 10, and 11 more straightforward. It may be helpful to review Chapter 4 before beginning this exercise.

This exercise explains common techniques used in perspective drawings. You will learn how to draw a square in perspective; find the center of a geometric plane; divide a plane into specific parts; draw an inclined plane; and draw circles, cylinders, and cones in perspective. By practicing and mastering these basic techniques mechanically, you will eventually be able to sketch relatively accurately in perspective without using vanishing points and rulers.

DRAWING A SQUARE IN ONE-POINT PERSPECTIVE

Every side of a square is exactly the same length as the other three sides, and it is simple to draw in plan or elevation view. However, as the square tilts in perspective, becoming a rhomboid, it becomes more difficult to determine how deep the shape should be and still remain perfectly square. The depth will be shorter than the true length of any one side, but how much shorter?

Following the diagram in Figure 7.40, first establish a horizon line and a center vanishing point. With your drawing paper oriented horizontally, draw a 10″ vertical line in the center of your paper. Make a

dot at the bottom of this reference line. Then, draw a 10″ horizontal line bisecting the first line in the center of your paper. This is the horizon line. The horizon line and the vertical reference line should intersect at their respective midpoints. Place a dot at this intersection. This is the center vanishing point. Next, using the ruler and 45-degree triangles, draft a 4″ square near the top center of the long side of your paper. The top center of the square should be aligned with the 10″ vertical reference line.

To determine the perspective depth of this square, connect each corner of the square to the point at the bottom of the vertical reference line, as illustrated in Figure 7.41. Then draw vertical lines from the points where each of these diagonal lines intersects the horizon line to the bottom of your paper. The side of the 4″ square that is closest to the horizon line will be the side closest to the observer in perspective, and appear longer than the receding sides.

Draw a horizontal line connecting the two vertical lines that are spaced farthest apart, creating Line AB, as in Figure 7.42. The vertical placement of this

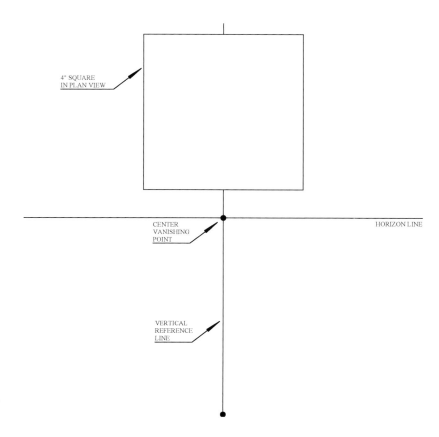

Figure 7.40 A square in-plan view with horizon line, center vanishing point, and vertical reference line.

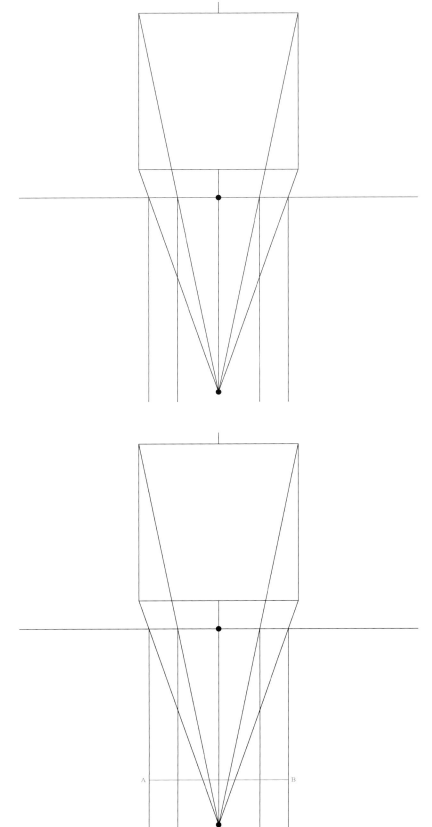

Figure 7.41 Connect the corners of the square to the reference point, and then draw vertical lines from the intersection of these lines and the horizon line.

Figure 7.42 Line AB is the side of the square closest to the observer.

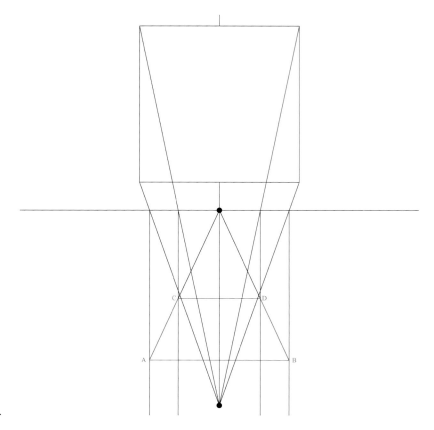

Figure 7.43 The square in perspective.

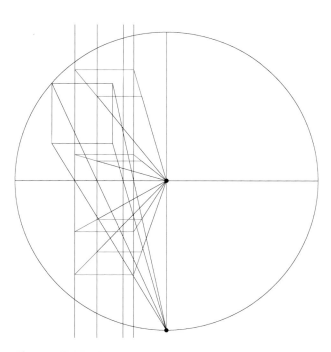

Figure 7.44 Perspective squares in various positions.

line on the page is arbitrary; it indicates the placement of the side of the square nearest the observer.

Next, connect the endpoints of Line AB to the center vanishing point. At the intersection of these lines with the two vertical lines that are spaced closest together, draw Line CD, as in Figure 7.43. The figure you have created is a true square in perspective.

If you drew a circle with the center vanishing point as center and the endpoints of the horizon line and vertical reference line as points on the circle, then you could draw a square anywhere inside or touching the edge of the circle and use this technique to determine its perspective placement. Practice drawing perspective squares in different positions as illustrated in Figure 7.44. This mechanical method is tedious and can slow down the creative process, but the purpose of practicing it is to become very familiar with the appearance of a true square in perspective. Practice until you can identify whether or not a plane in perspective has equal sides or not, and then practice drawing them using freehand techniques. Eventually the mechanical process will be unnecessary.

Drawing a Square in Two-Point Perspective

Follow the diagrams in Figures 7.45 through 7.48 to draw a perfect square in two-point perspective, where the square is centered anywhere on the vertical line perpendicular to the center vanishing point, and the left and right vanishing points are equidistant from the center vanishing point. This is a fairly rare occurrence, but it will help you see what a square should look like in two-point perspective and is useful for quickly drawing square tile floors. First, draw a 10″ horizon line across the center of the long side of your paper. Draw points at the endpoints and midpoint of this line, and label the left, center, and right vanishing points LVP, CVP, and RVP, respectively. Next, draw a perpendicular, vertical line in the center of your paper whose midpoint intersects the CVP, and connect the LVP and RVP to the bottom endpoint of this line. Beginning at the end-

point of the vertical line, and measuring left toward the LVP, tick off an arbitrary unit of measurement that represents the length of the square in perspective. Connect this point to the RVP. Finally, draw a line from the LVP from the intersection of the line

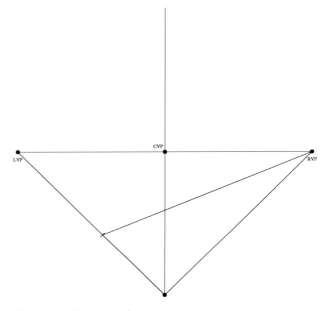

Figure 7.47 Step three.

Figure 7.45 Drawing a square in two-point perspective, step one.

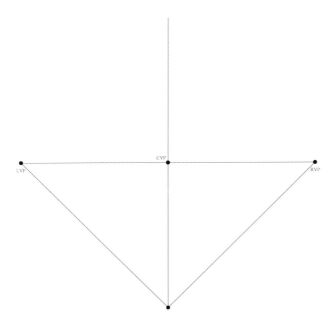

Figure 7.46 Step two.

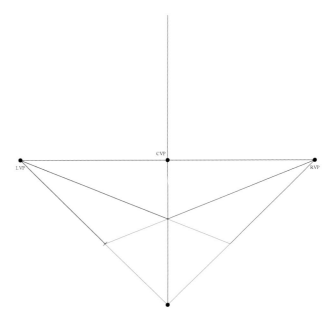

Figure 7.48 Step four, the square in perspective.

you just drew and the vertical centerline. The resulting shape is a true square in perspective. You can vary the size of the square by changing the length of the vertical centerline, and the distance from center of the equidistant left and right vanishing points.

To draw a series of perspective squares representing a tile floor, continue by drawing lines from the side corners of the perspective square to the CVP, as in Figure 7.49, and then draw lines progressively toward the horizon line where these CVP lines intersect the diagonal lines leading to the LVP and RVP, as illustrated in Figure 7.50.

Finding the Center of Planes in Perspective

This technique is simple, and is used countless times in every perspective drawing. For any rectilinear plane, find its perspective center by connecting its opposite corner points. The intersection of the crossed diagonals is the center point of the plane in perspective. In one-point perspective, find the centers of the sides of the plane by drawing a line through the center point that is parallel to the non-receding sides, and another line from the center point of the plane to the center vanishing point on the horizon line, as illustrated in Figure 7.51. In

two-point perspective, draw lines that intersect the sides of the plane from the center point of the plane to the right and left vanishing points, as shown in Figure 7.52. Find the center of the receding sides by drawing a line from the center point to the vanishing point. Each individual plane of complex objects will have its own center point, as illustrated in Figure 7.53.

Finding the Placement of Evenly Spaced Planes and Objects in Perspective

A classic one-point perspective drawing shows the posts and rails of a fence receding to a distant point on the horizon. The posts are, in reality, evenly placed a specific distance apart, but in perspective they appear progressively closer together as they approach the horizon line. Using the fence as an example, follow the procedure illustrated in Figures 7.54 and 7.55 to find the correct placement of the posts in perspective.

For this technique, you will need to place the first two posts in the series. First determine the height of the post closest to the observer relative to the horizon line and vanishing point (Line AB in Figure 7.54). Connect the top and bottom of this line

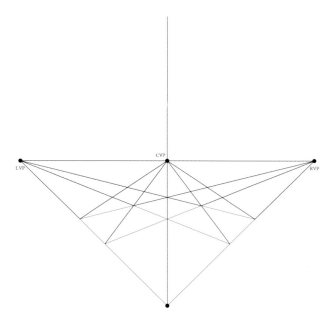

Figure 7.49 Drawing a series of perfect squares in perspective.

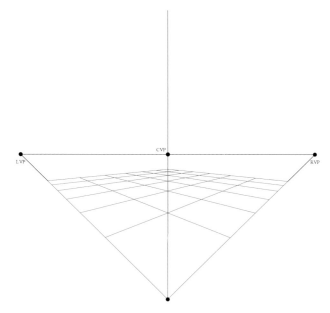

Figure 7.50 A grid of perfect squares representing a tiled floor.

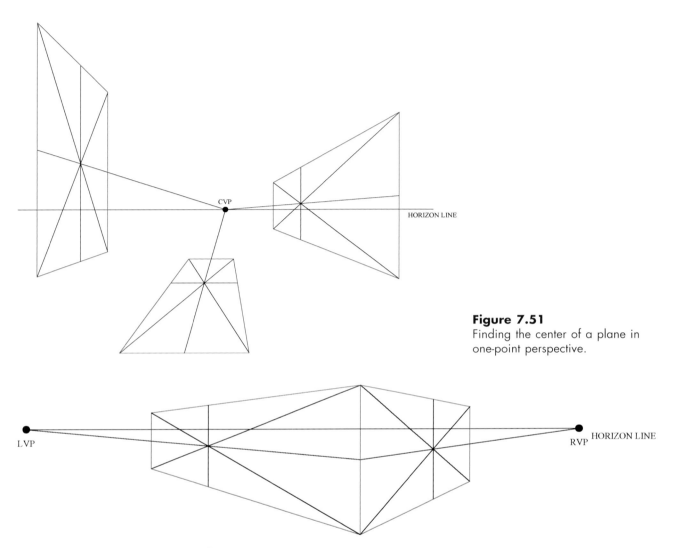

Figure 7.51
Finding the center of a plane in one-point perspective.

Figure 7.52 Finding the center of a plane in two-point perspective.

to the vanishing point. The top and bottom of each post in the series will intersect with these lines. Find the midpoint of the line, and recede that point to the vanishing point. This line will intersect the midpoints of all posts in the series. Then determine the width of the post, proportionate to its height (Line CD in Figure 7.54). Next, place the second post at an aesthetically pleasing distance of your choice from the first (Lines EF and GH in Figure 7.54). This second post should be slightly less wide than the first.

Find the placement of the third post by drawing a diagonal line through point A through the midpoint of Line EF to a point on the fence baseline,

and another line through point C through the midpoint of Line GH to a point on the fence baseline. Draw vertical lines from these points on the baseline to the top line. Continue this procedure until all posts in the series are completed, as in Figure 7.55.

Dividing a Plane into Specific Parts

Another way to divide a plane into equal divisions is to use the side of the plane closest to the observer as a unit of measurement that describes the entire receding length of the plane. Divide this line into equal units of a size appropriate for your drawing, and connect each of the tick marks to the vanishing

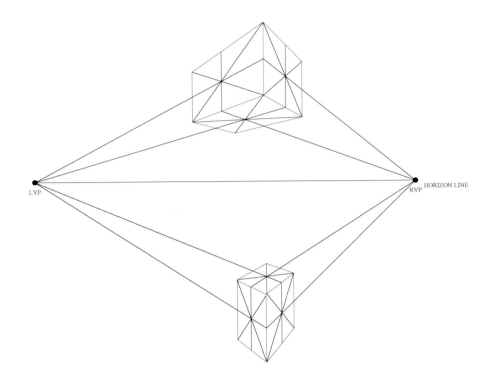

Figure 7.53
Each plane has its own center
point.

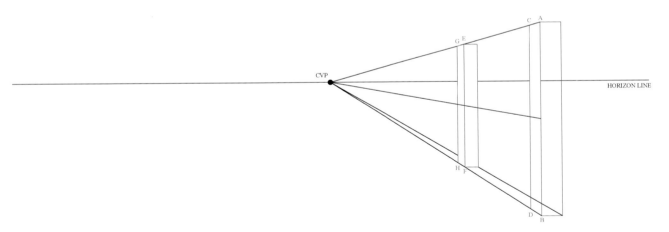

Figure 7.54 Placing the first two objects in the series.

point. Then draw lines connecting opposite corners of the plane, and draw verticals where the diagonal lines connecting the corner points of the plane intersect the lines that connect the tick marks and the vanishing point, as in Figures 7.57 through 7.59.

You can also use this technique to find uneven divisions in a plane. The illustration in Figure 7.58 shows a wall with unevenly spaced vertical divisions, and the same method is used to find the divisions in perspective. To find the placement of the vertical divisions in the plane, use the vertical line closest to the observer as a unit of measurement that describes the entire receding length of the plane. Divide this line into units of proportional size by placing pencil tick marks on the line and connecting each tick mark to

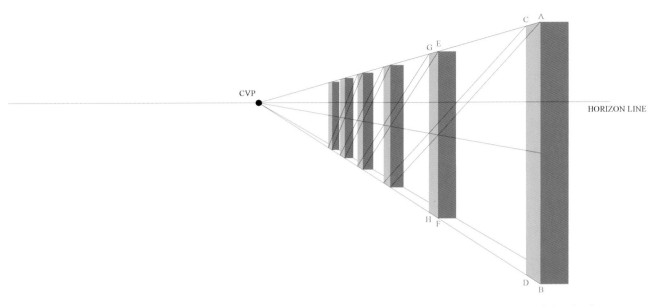

Figure 7.55 Connect the top of the first line through the midpoint of the second to find the base of the third.

Figure 7.56 Examples of evenly spaced objects in perspective.

the vanishing point. Next, draw diagonal lines connecting the opposite corners of the plane, and draw vertical lines where these diagonal lines intersect the lines from the tick marks to the vanishing point.

Drawing Inclined Planes in Perspective

Inclined, or ramped planes, in a perspective drawing need special vanishing points of their own. These points will be located on a vertical line directly above or below a vanishing point that already exists in the drawing. The simplest way to explain inclined planes is to refer to the inclined plane of a pitched roof of a building. Begin by drawing a rectangular solid

representing a barn-like structure in two-point perspective, as depicted in Figure 7.61.

Find the center of the right-hand plane by crossing diagonals, and then draw a vertical line from the base of the plane through the midpoint and up to a point appropriate for the peak of the pitched roof. Also draw a vertical line straight up your paper from the RVP that will intersect with the vertical vanishing point of the roofline, as in Figure 7.62. This line is a vertical horizon line of sorts. Draw a line from top left corner of the right-hand rectilinear plane, through the point representing the peak of the roof, to a point on the vertical horizon line. This is the roof's right vertical vanishing point, as illustrated in Figure 7.63.

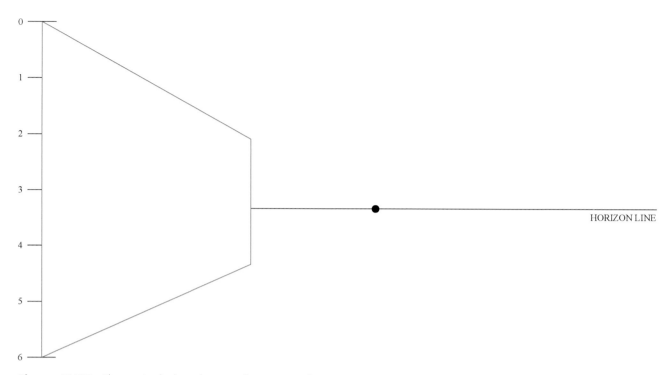

Figure 7.57   The vertical plane line used as a unit of measurement.

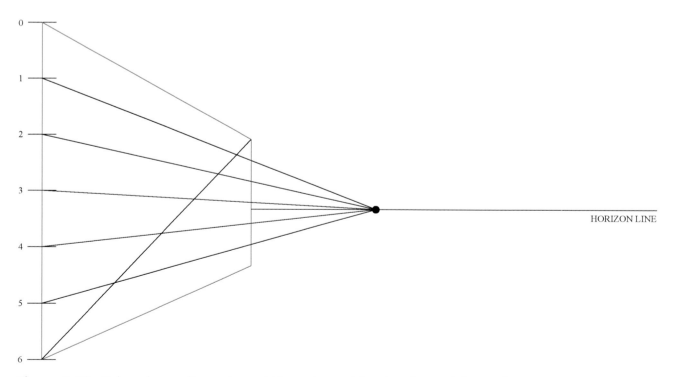

Figure 7.58   Tick marks receding to the vanishing point, and the plane bisected diagonally.

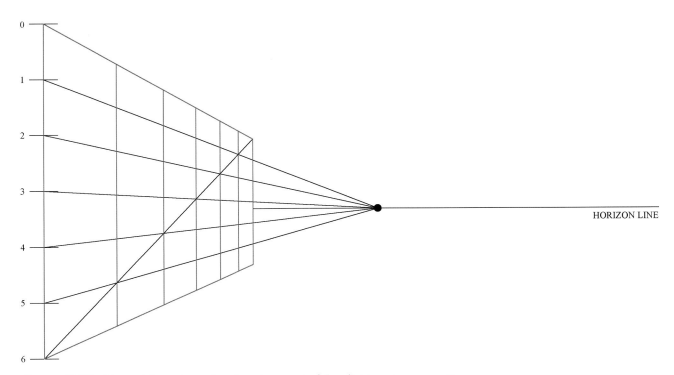

Figure 7.59 Vertical lines determine the placement of the divisions in perspective.

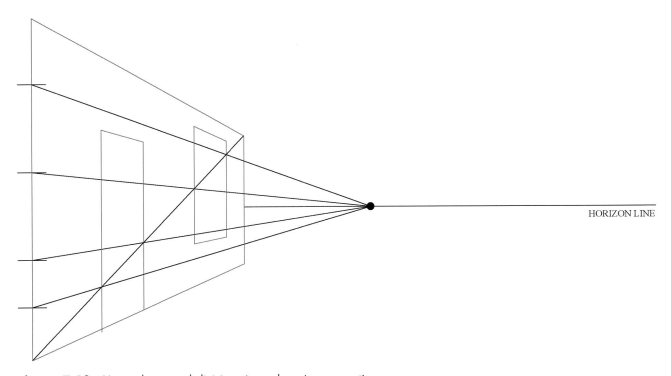

Figure 7.60 Unevenly spaced divisions in a plane in perspective.

Figure 7.61 A rectilinear solid in two-point perspective.

Figure 7.62
The peak of the inclined roof plane, and vertical horizon line.

Figure 7.63
Vertical vanishing point for the roof.

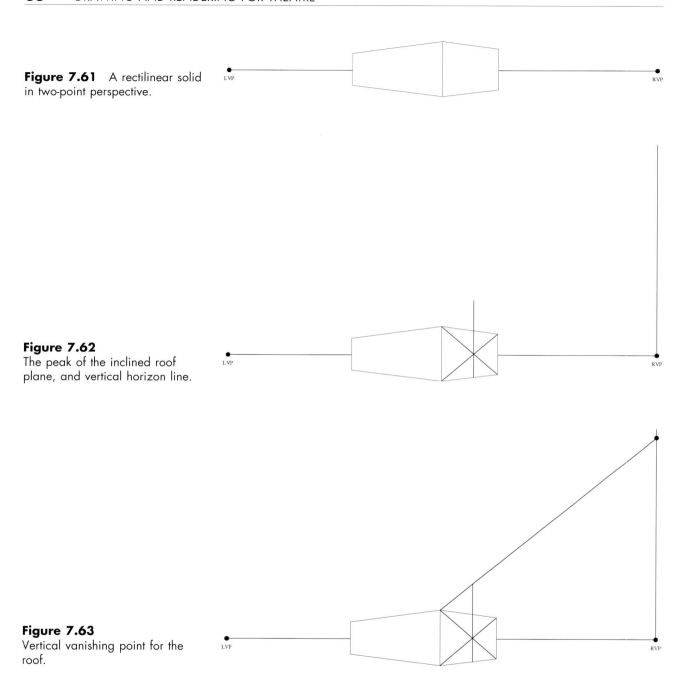

Next, draw a line from the top left corner of the left plane of the rectilinear solid to the roof's right vertical vanishing point, and draw another line connecting the peak of the roof with the LVP. Finally, draw a line connecting the point of the peak of the roof with the top left corner of the right-hand rectilinear plane, as depicted in Figure 7.64.

Circles, Cylinders, and Cones in Perspective

So far in this exercise you have drawn only rectilinear figures in perspective. With their curved surfaces, circles, cylinders, and cones create special challenges in perspective drawings. Just as in rectilinear perspective drawing, the square is the basic

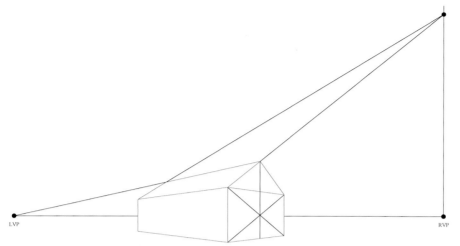

Figure 7.64
The inclined plane of the roof in two-point perspective.

building block, when drawing curved shapes in perspective, the circle is the basic unit. Cylinders and cones in a perspective drawing are basically foreshortened circles connected by straight lines. If you learn to draw a circle in perspective, you will be able to draw any shape with curved lines.

In Figure 7.65, a series of circles are inscribed on a horizontal plane and recede into the distance. From a top view, the circles would appear perfectly round, but in perspective they appear to be ellipses that get progressively narrower as they recede into the background. To accurately render the circles in perspective, you must first draw perfect squares in perspective, and then subdivide them into sections to create points on the sides of the squares. The points are used as a guide to correctly render the ellipses, as in Figure 7.66.

Creating a cylinder in perspective is done by the same method. Sketch it as a square or rectangle in perspective, depending on the configuration of the cylinder, subdivide the top and bottom planes and draw ellipses from the midpoints on the outer edge of the planes. Then connect the endpoints of the major axis of each ellipse with true vertical lines.

Similarly, draw a cone as a pyramid initially, and then create a perspective circle in the base plane of the pyramid. Draw a vertical line up from the center of the ellipse equal to the perspective height of the cone. Finally, connect the endpoints of the major axis of the ellipse with the top of the vertical height line.

The more you practice the techniques in this exercise, the easier it will be for you to draw accurately in perspective without the use of mechanical

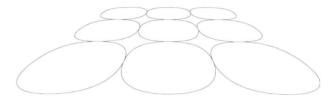

Figure 7.65   Circles in one-point perspective.

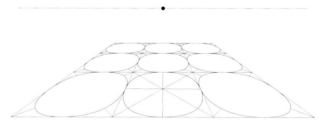

Figure 7.66   Drawing a perspective circle inscribed in a perspective square.

methods and measuring systems. The next three exercises employ the principles of mechanical perspective drawing in freehand drawing sessions.

EXERCISE 9: DRAWING THE FIGURE AS GEOMETRIC SHAPES

The drawing medium for this exercise is a graphite pencil on 11 × 17″ white drawing paper. Use an assortment of graphite pencils from very light

(4H) to very dark (7B or 8B). You will also need soft vine charcoal, half sheets of newsprint, an electric or manual pencil sharpener, erasers, and an angle guide.

The purpose of this exercise is to use the principles of perspective drawing to draw the nude human figure as a compilation of basic geometric solids. Details of any kind, including facial features, hair, fingers, toes, breasts, or genitals are not a priority in this exercise. You will be concentrating on the perspective of the figure.

You may be familiar with the easily posed, jointed, human-shaped figurines made of wood in various sizes that are ubiquitous in art stores and studios; a male example of which is pictured in Figure 7.69. These figurines replicate the proportions of the ideal figure in geometric solids. The drawings you produce in this exercise will look very much like this figurine. The goal of the exercise is to draw parts of the body as specific shapes, including spheres, cylinders, cubes, and rectangular solids. Use the photograph in Figure 7.69 to inspire you as to which geometric solids are most appropriate to represent the various parts of the body. As a rule of thumb, draw a distinct geometric shape for every place on the body that a joint or flexibility occurs. Geometric solids should represent the head, neck, chest, waist, torso, shoulders, upper arms, elbows, forearms, wrists, hands, pelvis, thighs, knees, lower legs, ankles, and feet. As in the wood figurine, it is fine to combine the small joints of the hands or feet as one shape jointed at the wrist or ankle. Keep the geometric shapes simple so you can concentrate on the foreshortening of the major volumes of the body without worrying about detail.

This exercise will take about one to one-and-one-half hours to complete. First, as in Exercise 1, ask the model to assume standing attention pose, and use the first twenty minutes to analyze and record the model's proportions. Use the time allotted for this pose, in addition to determining the number of head lengths tall the model is, to decide what geometric solid should represent each major body part.

Give the model a break, and then do ten twenty-second warm-up drawings with soft vine charcoal on half sheets of newsprint. Continue with four one-minute drawings, also using charcoal on newsprint. The twenty-second and one-minute drawings are necessary to warm up your drawing hand and arm, and should be executed as skeletons, exactly as in Exercise 1.

When you have warmed up, do two five-minute drawings with pencil on white drawing paper. Start by drawing the skeleton lightly with 4H pencil, and then blocking in the geometric solids of the body. Switch to progressively darker pencils to further

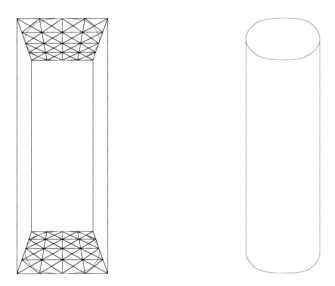

Figure 7.67 Drawing a cylinder in perspective.

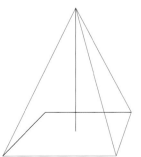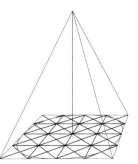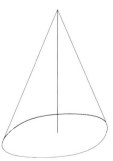

Figure 7.68
Drawing a cone in perspective.

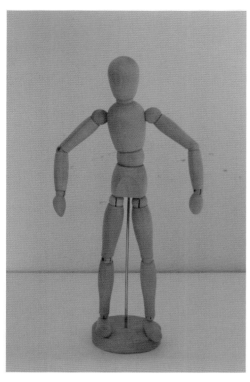

Figure 7.69 A jointed, easily posed wood figurine with the major parts of the body as geometric solids.

Figure 7.71 Another example of the figure drawn as geometric shapes: twenty-minute poses.

define the contours of the geometric solids and the effects of the light source on these shapes.

After the five-minute drawings are completed, take a short break and then execute at least one twenty-minute drawing. In the longer drawings, concentrate on the perspective and foreshortening of the geometric solids in the pose, and the highlight and shade on each of the major shapes.

EXERCISE 10: CREATING DEPTH WITH VALUE

The drawing medium for this exercise is artist's marking pens, and artist's colored pencils on 9 × 12″ heavyweight vellum or marker paper. You will need one black marker and a clear blender marker, and one black and one white pencil. You will also need a variety of gray markers and pencils. Gray markers and colored pencils are usually designated as neutral, warm, cool, or French (brownish gray). They are typically assigned a number representing a percentage on the value scale; 10 percent gray is the lightest (closest to white) and 90 percent is closest to black. At a minimum, purchase four gray markers and four gray pencils that represent the value scale: 20, 40,

Figure 7.70 One example of the figure drawn as geometric shapes: twenty-minute poses.

60, and 80 percent gray. All of the grays should have the same designation of neutral, warm, or cool. Other required materials are cotton swabs, cotton balls or makeup applicators, a portable electric or manual pencil sharpener, a .05 mm mechanical pencil, and a ruler. Denatured alcohol, which is the solvent that dissolves marker ink, is useful but optional.

The purpose of this exercise is to use gray scale values to create a sense of depth, or atmospheric perspective, in an abstract drawing. You will use the principles of perspective described in Chapter 4 and in Exercise 8 of this section, so you may want to review that material before beginning this exercise.

Experimenting with the Materials

For the first part of this exercise, you will be experimenting with the mediums on a scratch piece of paper. Notice that most art markers have two tips: a broad, often chisel tip and a fine tip. Experiment with the different tips, noting how they mark the paper, both by themselves and in combination with each other. Create a value scale strip from lightest to darkest. Markers tend to dry almost instantly on absorbent surfaces like drawing paper, but stay wet for a bit longer on slick, non-absorbent papers such as vellum or marker paper. Therefore, immediately after laying down a stroke of marker on your paper, you will have 15 or 20 seconds to manipulate the ink

as necessary for your purposes. Experiment with your clear blender and the cotton swabs to see how much time you have to work with the marker ink before it dries. Vellum and marker paper are both semi-translucent, and marker ink layered on the back of the paper will be seen through to the front, but with a frosted or ghosted appearance. Create another value scale strip on the back of your paper. Your clear blender will drastically soften, and perhaps nearly remove marker from your paper, but denatured alcohol applied to a cotton swab and rubbed on a marker line on your paper will react even more strongly. It is possible to achieve effects that emulate watercolor by manipulating marker with denatured alcohol.

Next, experiment with layering the pencils over the marker strokes. Using a pencil of the same gray percentage over an area of gray marker will soften the streaking effects of the marker. The black pencil is useful for creating crisp, dark cut lines, and the white pencil is excellent for adding highlights and zingers over dark marker. Continue playing with the materials in combination until you are familiar with the properties of the medium and the paper.

Drawing an Abstract Stage Space

After the experimentation phase, switch to a fresh piece of paper and begin the layout of an abstract stage space in perspective. To begin, using the .05 mm mechanical pencil, draw light lines that

Figure 7.72 Experimenting with the materials.

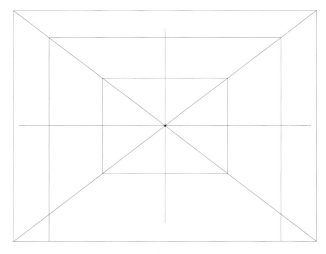

Figure 7.73 Setting up the abstract perspective drawing.

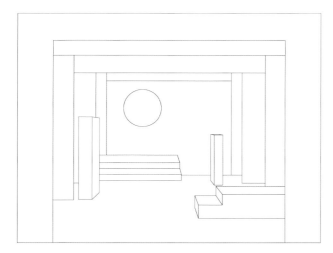

Figure 7.74 Geometric solids in perspective in the stage space.

bisect your paper vertically and horizontally, and place a dot at the intersection of these lines representing the center vanishing point. Then create crossed diagonals with lines by connecting opposite corners of the paper. Next, with your paper oriented horizontally, draw horizontal lines two-and-one-half inches from the top and bottom edges of the paper that end at the existing diagonal lines. Connect the endpoints of these lines with vertical lines. Draw a horizontal line one inch down from the top of the paper that terminates at the diagonal corner lines. From the intersection of these lines, draw vertical lines down to the bottom of your paper as in Figure 7.73. You have now created a sort of stage setting on which you will draw several geometric solids in perspective.

Draw several geometric solids in the stage space you have created. Elongated cylinders may represent

Figure 7.75 The proscenium arch, stage floor, and cyclorama in marker.

Figure 7.76 The geometric shapes rendered in marker and receding into space.

actors, while cubes and rectangular solids may evoke scenery. Use your imagination to create an interesting dramatic setting with geometric shapes. The shapes should appear to be staggered at various distances from the picture plane to the back of the "theater." Portray at least four levels of distance, or depth, with the objects from the proscenium line to the back wall of the theater. If you wish, some of the shapes may be floating in air above the stage floor. Remember that objects that are closer to the observer overlap, and are lower on the picture plane than objects that are farther away.

When your pencil drawing is complete, begin creating depth with value by using your black marker to make the proscenium arch a solid black shape. The lines between strokes of the maker can be softened by rubbing with cotton swabs and by going over the area with the black pencil. Cover the stage floor and the rectangle backing the stage with 20 percent gray, softening the marker lines as necessary.

Using the different shades of gray marker, model three-dimensionally the geometric solids in your stage space, assuming they are affected by one strong directional light source. The shapes toward the front of the stage will be rendered in the darkest gray shades and have crisp edges. As the shapes recede from the front of the picture plane, they will grow progressively lighter in value and less distinct, as in Figure 7.76. Blend and soften the edges of the shapes that are farthest from the proscenium line to create a sense of atmospheric perspective. Use the pencils to sharpen and define the shapes that are closest to the observer.

EXERCISE 11: PERSPECTIVE DRAWING—INTERIOR ARCHITECTURE DRAWING FROM LIFE IN ONE-POINT PERSPECTIVE

The drawing medium for this exercise is graphite pencils on white drawing paper. You will also need soft vine charcoal, half sheets of newsprint, a portable electric or manual pencil sharpener, erasers, angle guide, picture plane guide, cork-backed ruler, fine point dry erase marker, and digital camera. A laser pointer is useful, but optional. To construct the picture plane tool, you will need a piece of heavy mat or illustration board 11 × 17″, masking tape, and an Xacto or utility knife.

The purpose of this exercise is to accurately replicate the perspective and lighting in an interior architectural scene. First you will be constructing a picture plane tool, and then finding an appropriate vantage point from which to draw. After a few warm-up drawings, compose the picture by finding the horizon line and center vanishing point, sketching in the major verticals and receding lines. Finally, add detail, shading, and cast shadows, and photograph the scene. If, after working for about an hour, the drawing is not complete, finish at another time, using the digital image as a reference.

Constructing the Picture Plane Tool

Measure and mark in pencil a rectangular opening in the center of the mat or illustration board that is slightly smaller (by 1/4″ on all sides) than $8^{1}/_{2} \times 11″$. Using the cork-backed ruler and knife, carefully cut out the opening. The opening of the picture plane tool, slightly smaller than a letter-sized sheet of paper, is the exact size of the drawing you will be creating. You can easily create picture plane tools for any size drawing by altering the size of the opening cut from the center of the board.

Finding an Appropriate Subject

Choose a site that you can reasonably draw in about an hour. The object of this exercise is to accurately replicate the perspective of the scene. Avoid sites with an excess of elaborate furnishings or ornamented moldings and railings. When drawing, you must be able to get enough distance from your subject so that the effects of perspective are clearly apparent. Position yourself so you can see two parallel walls and at least some of both the ceiling and the floor. The wall farthest away must appear to be smaller than the nearer walls, and the lines of the walls at floor and ceiling should appear to converge toward the middle of your view. A long hallway with multiple doors or a large lobby is an ideal site.

Find a comfortable position that minimizes eye movement between the subject and the drawing paper. Have all necessary materials nearby, as you will need to maintain the same position during the execution of the pencil drawing. If it is necessary to move away from the subject during the session, take careful note of your position, mark it with spike tape, and resume the exact position upon your return.

Warming Up

As in the figure drawing exercise, a few quick sketches of your subject will loosen the muscles in your arm and hand and prepare your brain for the task. Using vine charcoal on half sheets of newsprint, complete two or three quick studies of the subject without concern for accuracy. Spend no more than one or two minutes on each sketch. Remember to orient the paper for a vertical or horizontal composition. During the warm-up period, you might identify sections of the site that are particularly challenging to draw, and you will be especially careful with these areas when you move to the pencil drawing.

Composing the Picture

Humans have peripheral vision. The eyes see a wide-angle view of the room that includes what is seen straight ahead as well as the sides of the room as they recede behind the viewer. Because you will be drawing only what you see straight ahead of you, it is necessary to find the edges of where the scene will cut off. Think of composing the picture as placing the part of the scene you want to draw on a stage framed by a proscenium arch.

Use the picture plane guide to frame the scene into a "stage picture." Place the guide over your drawing paper, lining up the edges, and trace the rectangular opening of the guide on your paper. This will be the size of your drawing. Hold the guide out toward the architectural subject with your arm at shoulder height and fully extended at the bottom edge parallel to the floor. Look directly through the center of the opening. What you see is what you will draw on your paper. If you are unhappy with the composition, reposition yourself until the view through the

Figure 7.77 The view down this hallway is a good site for an interior perspective drawing.

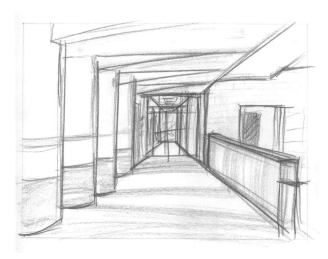

Figure 7.78 A warm-up drawing of the view down the hallway.

guide (held with arms at shoulder height and fully extended) is more satisfying. After deciding on the composition it is important to maintain the position of your head throughout the drawing session.

You are now ready to begin a pencil drawing of the architectural scene. You will be using several different lead weights to complete the drawing, but start with your lightest (4H) pencil.

Finding the Horizon Line and Vanishing Point

The horizon line is a horizontal line across the paper at your eye level. To determine the composition for this exercise your eyes were focused directly through the center of the picture plane guide, the opening of which is the same size as the drawing paper. Therefore, the horizon line is a horizontal line through the middle of your paper. Using the 4H graphite pencil and ruler, lightly draw in the horizon line.

Although it is obvious where the horizon line is on your paper (you have drawn it in), it is often difficult to locate exactly where the horizon line is in the scene you are drawing. A laser pointer can be very useful for this task. Point the laser at your eye level toward the subject.

A vanishing point is a point on the horizon line to which parallel lines appear to recede. In one-point perspective, all horizontal parallel lines recede to one point on the horizon line. For this exercise your eyes were focused directly through the center of the picture plane guide, so the vanishing point for all parallel horizontal lines in your drawing will be exactly in the center of your paper on the horizon line. Mark this point on your paper. Remember, if your eye level or side-to-side position varies, the horizon line and vanishing point in your drawing will no longer be accurate.

Sketching in Verticals and Horizontals

You can use your picture plane guide to find points of horizontal lines on the edge of the "stage picture." Hold the guide up in position with one hand, making sure the bottom edge is parallel to the ground. In pencil, lightly mark the top and bottom edges of the walls at the points where they intersect the frame of the guide. While marking the points, keep your eye level at the center of the opening of the guide and hold it with arms extended at shoulder height. Then, place the guide opening over your drawing and transfer the marked points to your paper. Use the ruler and 4H pencil to lightly connect these points to the vanishing point in the center of the paper.

The vertical lines in your drawing will be true verticals—parallel to the sides of your paper. If not,

Figure 7.79 The hallway as seen through the picture plane tool.

Figure 7.80 The horizon line and center vanishing point.

Figure 7.81 Guides drawn in pencil on the edges of the picture plane guide.

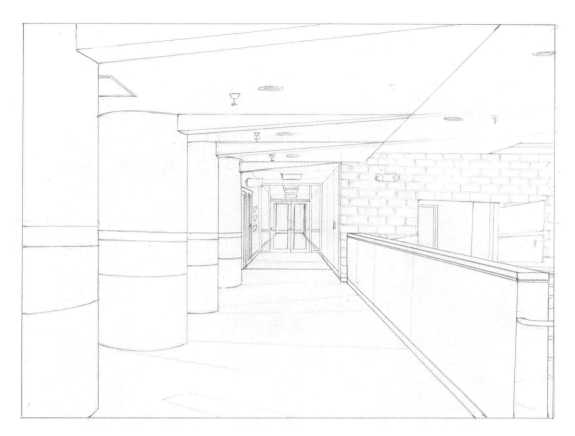

Figure 7.82 The drawing sketched in 4H pencil.

it will appear as if the building you are drawing is about to fall down.

Adding Detail

Continue adding detail to your drawing with the 4H pencil, using the picture plane tool to line up any points that intersect with the edges of the opening frame of the tool. Make sure all horizontal lines in your drawing, such as lines of floor or ceiling tiles, or the tops of door frames, recede to the center vanishing point, and that all verticals are true verticals.

It is not necessary to "draft" the drawing by constantly using the ruler. After the major verticals and receding lines are sketched in using the ruler, you can use these lines as guides and freehand detail lines. Pinpoint accuracy is not required, as long as the drawing looks right.

Shading and Cast Shadows

To finish your drawing, add gray scale value with the darker graphite pencils. It may be more convenient to photograph the scene and finish the drawing from the photograph.

Figure 7.83 The hallway drawing with shading and cast shadows.

EXERCISE 12: PERSPECTIVE DRAWING—EXTERIOR ARCHITECTURE

The drawing medium for this exercise is graphite pencils on white drawing paper. You will also need soft vine charcoal, half sheets of newsprint, a portable electric or manual pencil sharpener, erasers, angle guide, picture plane guide, ruler, fine point dry erase marker, and digital camera. A laser pointer is useful, but optional.

The purpose of this exercise is to accurately replicate the perspective and lighting in an exterior architectural scene. Use the same picture plane guide to create a drawing approximately the size of a letter-sized piece of paper. Proceed with this exercise exactly as you did with the interior perspective drawing, but draw in two-point perspective instead of one-point.

Finding a Vantage Point

Choose a spot to draw where you are looking at the corner of a building, and both visible sides of the building recede into the distance, one to a vanishing point somewhere to the left, and the other to a vanishing point somewhere to the right. Chances are likely that one or both of these vanishing points are too far to the left or right to fit on your paper, so use the picture plane guide to determine where the receding lines intersect with the opening frame of the guide and then transfer these points to your paper. Holding the picture plane guide at arm's length and shoulder height, reorient your position until your have framed an attractive two-point perspective composition where the receding horizontals intersect the interior frame of the guide (Figure 7.84).

Figure 7.84 The receding horizontals of the building in this composition intersect with the interior frame of the picture plane guide.

Figure 7.85 The drawing sketched in 4H pencil.

Figure 7.86 The finished drawing with shading and cast shadows.

Unless it happens to be a beautiful day to be outside, you may want to minimize the amount of time you spend drawing from life. Take a digital picture of the scene from the exact perspective you will be drawing and with the camera at your eye level (the horizon line). After lightly sketching the scene in 4H pencil and adding detail, finish the drawing from the photograph.

EXERCISE 13: DRAWING LIGHT

For this exercise, you will be using a variety of white mediums on black drawing paper, Bristol board, or illustration board. You will be using two or three pieces of paper about 9 × 12″ in size. You will need a white Prismacolor (or similar) pencil, white charcoal pencil, white soft pastel, and white conté crayon. Other materials needed include soft

(9B) graphite stick, a .05 mm mechanical pencil, stomps in various sizes, a portable electric or manual pencil sharpener, ruler, and a #4 or #6 watercolor brush.

This exercise builds on the seeing skills you studied in Exercise 4 by erasing light from a dark background. You will draw highlights with white drawing mediums and leave the black of the paper to represent the darkest values in your drawing. For the first twenty minutes of this session, you will experiment with the materials, and then, after warming up, you will execute a still life drawing with a strong directional light source. As in Exercise 4, you will draw objects that are medium to light in value and have a reflective surface; for example, a ceramic teapot, a metal candlestick, a wine bottle, and a glass or metal vase with an interesting contour. It will take longer to execute these drawings than it did to execute the erasure drawings, so you only need one or two objects, rather than four.

Experimenting with the Materials

Assemble all of your white drawing materials and one piece of black paper, and test the qualities of each medium by creating a value scale strip for each. Beginning with the Prismacolor pencil, compose a strip of pigment across the short side of the paper that gets progressively lighter with harder pressure of the pencil until the paper will accept no more pigment. Start out with as little pressure as you can, and see how many levels of value you can achieve with the pencil. Label the strip "Prismacolor Pencil." Create and label value strips for all the white mediums you have. Notice that some materials work better at creating soft gray values, and some are better at achieving bright, solid highlights. The most challenging part of drawing on black paper is getting the highlights as white as they need to be.

Next, experiment with layering the different mediums. Find the medium or combination of mediums that give you the brightest white possible. This is the lightest part of your drawing, reserved for the brightest highlights. The black of the paper is the darkest value, and you must create all the intermediate values using varying pressure of the tools on the paper. Experiment with softening and blending the white mediums using your stomps, your finger, and the watercolor brush. Control the blend, and keep the edges of the blended shape sharp by masking the area with a piece of paper.

Drawing the Still Life

Set up a directional light source and an object of your choice as done in Exercise 4. Place a clip light or table lamp at your drawing station so your paper is well illuminated, but the directional light source on the object should be the only other light in the room. The object should be very starkly lit with strong contrasts between black and white. This

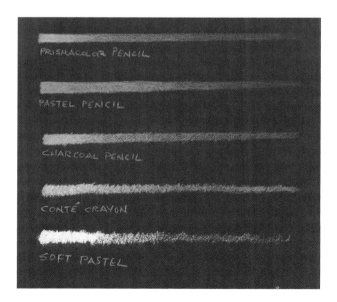

Figure 7.87 Value scale strips made with the white drawing materials.

Figure 7.88 Experimenting with blending.

lighting creates a minimum number of value levels, which makes it easier to draw. Warm up with a few two-minute drawings of the object in vine charcoal on half sheets of newsprint. Concentrate on drawing the shapes of the highlights that you see.

Now you are ready to start drawing with the white mediums. Lightly sketch out the areas of highlight and areas of gray with the mechanical pencil. If you cannot see the contour of the shaded side of the object, do not draw it. Draw only the shapes of white and gray, noting the number of value levels, in the still life. Starting with the darkest value, begin building up the white using the techniques experi-

Figure 7.89 The still life set-up.

Figure 7.90 The still life drawn in white on black paper.

mented with earlier. Continue building the light until the lightest areas of the still life are as white as possible.

If you have time for another drawing, increase the ambient light in the room by a small percentage. This lighting will create more levels of gray scale value on the object, therefore making it more challenging to draw.

Drawings done on black paper closely resemble theatrical stage lighting, where the lighting is often tightly focused on a particular area of the stage, and the rest of the space fades to darkness. In the next exercise, you will continue the exploration of drawing light by drawing a set rendering on black paper.

EXERCISE 14: DRAWING LIGHT— DETERMINING THE EMOTIONAL QUALITY OF A DRAWING

For this exercise, you will be using a variety of white mediums on black drawing paper, Bristol board, or illustration board. You will be using one or two pieces of 9 × 12″ paper. You will need a white Prismacolor (or similar) pencil, white charcoal pencil, white soft pastel, and white conté crayon. Other materials needed include soft (9B) graphite stick, a .05 mm mechanical pencil, stomps in various sizes, a portable electric or manual pencil sharpener, ruler, and a #4 or #6 watercolor brush.

In this exercise, starting with a black line drawing, or cartoon, of a set design rendering with actors, you will be creating an emotional mood by choosing a focal point and emphasizing it with light and gray values. This challenging exercise will take about an hour and a half to complete. Consider that the lighting designer deliberately chooses to illuminate certain areas of the stage, and not others; the rest of the space is dark and invisible to the audience. A good set rendering should also have this type of focus. A play is inherently about words, and the silent set rendering must attempt to capture the feeling of a particular moment of the play. In preparation for this exercise, study the set rendering in Figure 7.91, and decide what emotional mood you think should be depicted in the rendering. Decide what areas of the set should be lit and which should be in darkness. Choose one or more areas of focus. What do you think the audience should be looking at in this moment of the play?

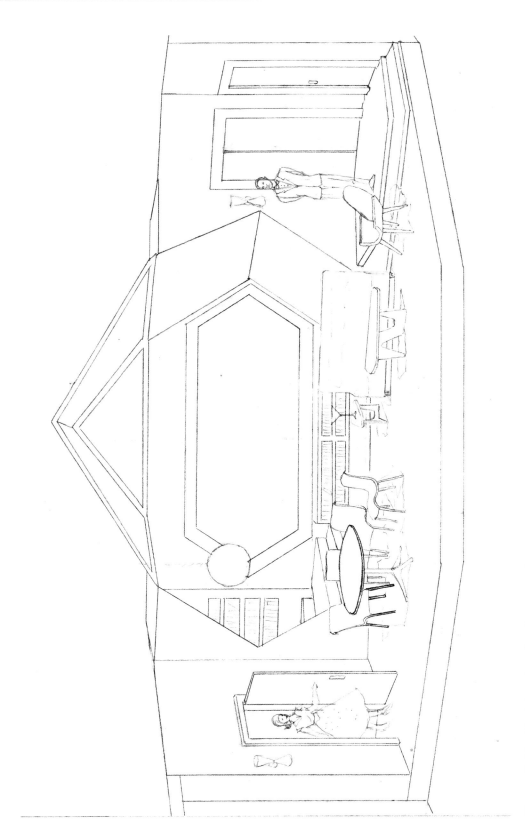

Figure 7.91 Black line drawing of a set rendering.

Prepare your drawing surface by photocopying the set rendering in Figure 7.91 and then rubbing soft (9B) graphite stick all over the back of the copy. Position the copy on your black paper and tape down the top edge. Carefully trace over all the lines with the mechanical pencil, pressing just hard enough to transfer the graphite to the black paper, but not so hard as to dent or score the black paper.

Up to this point, for the exercises in this section, you have mainly been drawing things that are affected by light. You can see the light, and only need to copy what you see. In this exercise, you are the lighting designer (but with no director, script, or other designers), and you must decide what receives light, what does not, and why. You must create a specific emotional mood. If you are having trouble getting started, it is usually a safe bet to illuminate any actors on stage, since they are there for a reason, and enough of the set for the scene to make sense to the audience. Beyond those basics, make up a story about the characters that explains their relationships to each other and how they feel about each other. Start out slowly with the darkest values, and build up to the brightest whites.

You may want to repeat this exercise in a later sketchbook session with the same cartoon, but create a different emotional mood by changing the focus of the light. You can also repeat this exercise with a cartoon of your own set design, or a tracing of a professional designer's rendering.

EXERCISE 15: FIGURE DRAWING— COSTUMING THE MODEL

The drawing medium for this exercise is graphite pencils on white drawing paper. You will also use soft vine charcoal, newsprint, an electric or manual pencil sharpener, erasers, and an angle guide. You will be drawing a nude model, as in Exercise 1. Begin by warming up with vine charcoal on newsprint for ten twenty-second, and five one-minute drawings.

The purpose of this exercise is to draw an accurately proportioned figure in a frontal standing pose, and then "dress" the figure drawing with a costume derived from a drawing or photograph of your choice. The costume could be taken from one of your own renderings, from a book or magazine,

or it could be a copy of a professional designer's rendering. This is a rendering exercise, not a design exercise; so do not spend time altering a costume design or making one up from your imagination.

After you have warmed up, take as long as you need to draw an accurately proportioned frontal figure in a pose appropriate for the costume. The figure's pose in the drawing or photograph need not necessarily match the live model's pose. Use a 4H pencil to create a contour drawing of the model, and erase any unnecessary lines as you go. You will add three-dimensional modeling after the costume is added, but even without shading the contour lines of the figure drawing should indicate the solid forms of the model's body (Figure 7.92).

When the contour drawing is complete, you can dismiss the model and begin "dressing" your drawing with the elements of the chosen costume. Continue working in light 4H pencil, and concentrate on making the clothing look like it is draped on a three-dimensional form. For example, sleeves, collars, necklines, and waistbands should curve slightly as they encircle the respective body parts, rather than drawn straight across. When you are satisfied with the lightly penciled drawing, erase any extraneous

Figure 7.92 A fifteen-minute contour figure drawing.

Figure 7.93 Clothing added to a nude figure drawing.

lines, and using the rest of your set of graphite pencils, shade the drawing. Use shade, lowlight, and highlight to further enhance the illusion of three-dimensionality.

VARIATIONS ON THE EXERCISES

Upon completion of these exercises you will have a solid knowledge base and a language with which to talk about drawing. The lessons learned in this chapter are necessary to continue with the next chapter, so it is a good idea to continue practicing the techniques and methods learned by occasionally repeating selected exercises in your weekly sketchbook sessions. Expand your comfort zone by working specifically on techniques that you find to be challenging. Vary the exercises by using different drawing mediums or by combining parts of two or more exercises.

Chapter 8

Introduction to Color

A good designer is a master manipulator of color. The color palette is an integral part of scenic, costume, and lighting designs. The effective use of color plays a major role in evoking period, time, and emotion. A deep understanding of color mixing and manipulation is the basis for the subtle and creative use of color for the stage. The following chapters include exercises intended to help the reader understand and explore color.

TALKING ABOUT COLOR

With literally millions of different colors available, it is necessary to have a vocabulary with which to talk about and analyze color. Some terms that are used when discussing color are defined below. We will discuss discretely individual colors, isolated from other colors against a white background, and two or more colors in relationship to each other.

When discussing a color, the words "color" or hue may be used interchangeably. Any individual color has a relationship to the spectrum colors of paint. The spectrum colors of paint are based on the pure color of visible light refracted through a prism (the colors of the rainbow) and include red, orange, yellow, green, blue, and violet. Of these red, yellow, and blue are primary colors of paint. It is impossible to create these three colors by combining any other colors. Orange, green, and violet are secondary

colors of paint, so named because you mix together two primary colors to create each secondary color. In the following chapters the terms "primary" and "secondary" will, unless otherwise noted, refer to the colors of paint, rather than light, the primaries of which are red, blue, and green. A visual diagram of the spectrum colors of paint is normally arranged on a color wheel with the primaries forming a triangle and the secondary colors arranged between the primaries according to which two primaries create them. Combining the three pure primary colors will theoretically yield black. Actually, mixing the primaries of most color media yields a dark brownish gray.

The six spectrum colors represent the purest, most intense version of these colors. They are said to be at full or highest intensity. Intensity is also referred to as saturation. The spectrum hue yellow contains nothing but yellow; that is, it absorbs all the other colors in the visible spectrum of light and reflects back only pure yellow. Mixing a pure primary color with one other primary color yields a secondary hue that also has full intensity. A hue created by mixing any two adjacent colors of the six on the color wheel also will have full intensity and is called a tertiary color. For example, mixing spectrum yellow and spectrum orange creates yellow-orange, a tertiary color with full intensity. Any two primary colors plus the secondary they create and the two tertiary hues created by mixing the secondary with

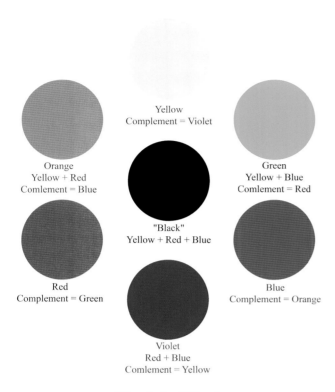

Yellow
Complement = Violet

Orange
Yellow + Red
Comlement = Blue

Green
Yellow + Blue
Comlement = Red

"Black"
Yellow + Red + Blue

Red
Complement = Green

Blue
Complement = Orange

Violet
Red + Blue
Comlement = Yellow

The Color Wheel

Figure 8.1 The color wheel.

each of the adjacent primaries are analogous colors. Mixing analogous spectrum colors creates high-intensity, harmonious hues. An analogous color scheme utilizes two primary colors in any intensity or value plus any hues that can possibly be created by combining those two primaries.

The slightest introduction of a third primary color to a hue will reduce its intensity thus creating a duller color. Adding a tiny bit of green to red, for example, will create a muddier version of red than is seen on the color wheel in Figure 8.1. This happens because green is composed of both yellow and blue, so the mixture of red and green contains some of all three of the primary colors. For each of the primary and secondary hues on the color wheel, only one other color will lower its intensity. Pairs of color that reduce each other's intensity are called complements. Besides red and green, the other two pairs of complements on the color wheel are yellow and violet and orange and blue. Helpfully, complementary pairs are directly opposite each other on the color wheel. Primary colors have secondary colors as complements, and secondary colors have primaries as com-

plements. Tertiary colors have other tertiary colors as complements. The complement of yellow-orange is blue-violet which would be directly opposite it on the color wheel pictured if it included tertiary colors.

Each of the hues on the color wheel has an intrinsic value. Value is a color's relationship to the gray scale with white at one end, black on the other, and a graduated range of grays in between. Of the spectrum colors, yellow is the lightest, followed by orange and then red and green. Blue and violet have the darkest value of the spectrum colors. Adding white pigment to a color lightens its value and produces a tint. Adding a color's complement or black pigment creates a shade.

Warm and cool are terms often used to describe color. Of the spectrum colors, yellow, orange, and red are considered warm, while violet, blue, and green are cool. Each of the colors can be mixed to be warmer or cooler by adding more of one of the two adjacent colors. For example, a yellow hue with a touch of orange mixed with it is warmer than a yellow with a touch of green mixed in. Although both red and yellow are warm hues, yellow is the warmer of the two, so a reddish orange is relatively cooler than a yellowish orange. A warm red hue can be created by adding orange and a cool red by mixing in violet.

Up to this point we have discussed the pure colors of the color wheel as absolutes. However, unlike pure colored light, color mediums used by artists are manufactured using ground pigments and binders and often vary between types of color media and by brand name within the same medium. Less expensive color media often include extra dyes or fillers that affect the intensity and quality of colors. More expensive paints, pastels, markers, and pencils tend to be so because of the quality of their ingredients. It is advisable to buy the best quality color media you can afford.

If it were possible to paint with pigments that precisely matched the yellow, red, and blue of the color wheel and white, one could theoretically mix any imaginable color. But the primary colors of most commercial pigments tend to be either slightly warm or cool. Yellow is fairly reliable, blue and red less so. For example, two popular blue pigments are cobalt and ultramarine. Cobalt is a warm blue hue that appears to be very slightly closer to green, while ultramarine, a cool blue, appears slightly more violet. The chemical composition of ultramarine blue pigment is such that some violet light from the visible spectrum is reflected back rather than absorbed. Mixing a green hue from yellow and ultramarine pigments then, will produce a less intense green than the green on the color wheel because trace amounts of red are present in the appearance of the mixed color. Practically, it is a waste of time for theatrical designers working on tight deadlines to hand-mix each color in a chosen palette. If the perfect hue is available straight out of the tube it should certainly be utilized. However, learning to mix color from a limited palette of primaries is an excellent way to explore color manipulation. Watercolor exercise 1 in chapter 12 uses warm and cool primaries to create a diverse palette.

An individual color has a specific hue, intensity, and value relative to its closest corresponding spectrum color. The first step in color mixing is identifying the closest match to the target color from among the available pigment colors. Then this closest match is adjusted for hue, intensity, and value to match the target color. The order of adjustment will depend on the properties of the target color. For example, if the target color is a very light tint, adjust the value first. Using specific wet or dry, opaque or translucent color media is discussed in detail in later chapters. Whatever color medium is used, the mixed and target colors should be compared against a white background because of the heavy influence colors have on each other when juxtaposed.

COLOR RELATIONSHIPS

The hue, intensity, and value of an individual color are relative to the color or colors that surround it. In general, in a field of different colors those lighter in value and/or more intensely saturated attract more attention and migrate to the foreground of the field, while dark and low saturation colors recede into the background. In Figure 8.2, the lighter more saturated blue color field draws the eye as the dark, low-intensity brown recedes. This effect is heightened as value and intensity contrast between adjacent colors is increased. Dark, low-intensity colors can occupy the foreground and be the focus of a composition even when juxtaposed with highly saturated color, such as the dark silhouetted trees against the bright blue sky as illustrated below in Figure 8.3, if the shape of the darker object is sufficiently interesting to command attention.

Figure 8.2 Colors with lighter value and more saturation draw the eye.

Figure 8.3 Interesting shape brings the darker, low-intensity brown trees to the foreground.

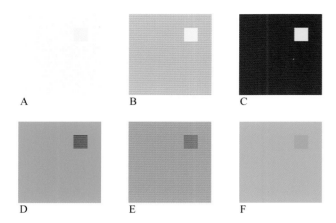

Figure 8.4 Color relationships.

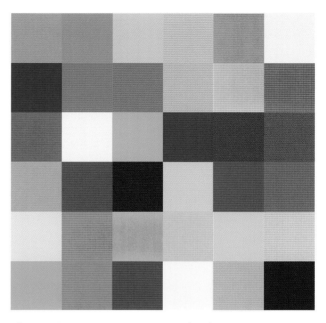

Figure 8.5 Too many saturated colors in a composition results in a lack of focus.

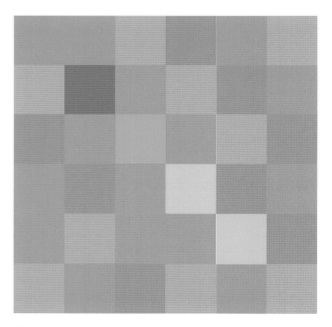

Figure 8.6 Creating focus with color intensity.

In Figure 8.4, squares A, B, and C contain identical smaller squares of the same yellow hue. Notice how the yellow square in A appears darker in value in contrast to the lighter field surrounding it. The yellow squares in B and C appear progressively lighter as the surrounding field gets darker in value. The yellow square in A is barely noticeable because the relative values and intensities of the field and square are very similar. In C it is impossible not to notice the yellow square because its value and intensity are in stark contrast to the field.

Squares D, E, and F in Figure 8.4 illustrate another phenomenon of color relationships. Complementary colors placed next to each other compete with each other for attention. This tension increases as the colors increase in intensity, while juxtaposed analogous colors coexist harmoniously. The highly saturated green field in D contains a highly saturated red square. The two complementary colors compete violently with each other, seeming to vibrate with energy. In E the same two complements vie for attention, but the effect is lessened by the decreased intensity of the colors. The analogous blue and green colors in F, while of high intensity, present a well-balanced appearance.

In Figure 8.5, colors of various hue, intensity, and value are grouped together. While squinting at the illustration, notice which colors catch the eye and jump to the foreground and which recede. Note also the interaction of adjacent hues. The many competing highly saturated hues make the composition chaotic. The judicious use of high intensity, light value, and extreme contrast is necessary to create focus in a composition. Notice how the four center squares running diagonally downward from left to right in Figure 8.6 move to the foreground of the picture against the neutral background. They are the same hues in the same positions as in Figure 8.5 in which they compete poorly for attention.

Color relationships are also affected by the degree of translucency of each color, and by extension, the color of the background on which the colors are applied. Watercolor paints are naturally translucent and usually applied to white paper because any other color would alter the applied pigments. When a wash of one watercolor is applied over another, the eye mixes the two hues together and creates a third. A layer of gouache pigment, an opaque medium, will completely obscure the color of the paint or paper it is applied on even if the top layer is lighter than those below it.

In summary, the properties of a color, its hue, value, intensity, and degree of translucency can be analyzed and defined in relationship to the color wheel using the properties of the colors of the spectrum as a constant. These properties fluctuate, however, when a color is juxtaposed with one or more different hues. The overall impact of the color palette of a composition is formed by the relationship of the various different hues in the palette. Color relationships (with the other elements of design) help create an emotional impression, define distance and depth, and determine the focus of a composition. Exercises designed to explore the use of color in several different color mediums are included in the following chapters. Each chapter concentrates on a particular medium, beginning with the easiest to use and progressing toward the more challenging. Chapter 14 explores the use of two or more mediums used in combination.

TOOLS AND MATERIALS

The following is a list of tools and materials you will need to complete all of the exercises in this section. Specific tools and materials needed for each exercise are listed at the beginning of each exercise, as well as specific instructions on how to use each item. Most of these items are available at art or craft and hobby stores. You will also need a carrying case for your supplies. Art stores carry hard plastic cases in a variety of sizes designed to hold art and craft supplies. Hard- or soft-sided fishing tackle boxes are typically much less expensive, but just as useful.

Art supplies are expensive, but do not be tempted to buy cheaper supplies not intended for professional artists and designers. Inexpensive art

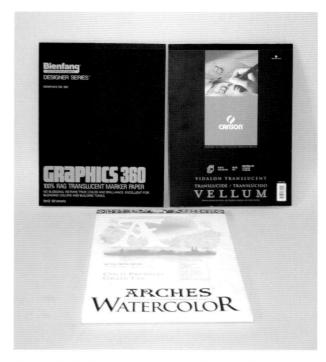

Figure 8.7 Watercolor paper, vellum, and marker paper.

supplies are usually of poor quality, and can impede your progress by producing disappointing results. Never buy art supplies at a grocery store, supplies designated as "student" or "scholastic," or supplies designed for elementary school art classes. Buy the best supplies designed for professional artists and designers that you can afford, but shop around for sales and bargains. The Internet is a great place to find discounts on art supplies, such as at *dickblick.com*.

One pad or block of heavyweight watercolor paper approx. 12 × 18″, at least eight sheets
One pad of heavy weight vellum pad 9 × 12″
One pad of marker paper 9 × 12″
Several pieces each of black and white vellum finish illustration board or heavyweight drawing paper approximately $8^1/_2 \times 11''$ such as Canson Mi-Teintes
One or two pieces of vellum finish heavyweight colored (midtone) drawing paper approximately $8^1/_2 \times 11''$ such as Canson Mi-Teintes

Figure 8.8 Black, white, and midtoned heavyweight drawing paper.

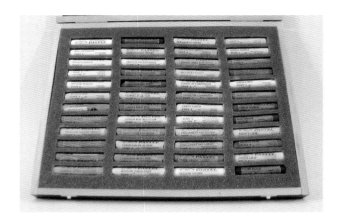

Figure 8.10 Soft pastels.

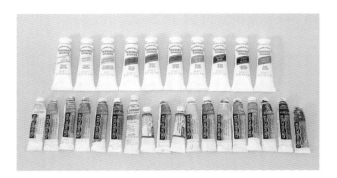

Figure 8.9 Gouache and watercolor paints.

Figure 8.11 Pastel pencils.

Watercolors:

Artist quality such as Da Vinci, Grumbacher, Holbein, Prismacolor, or Winsor & Newton

The following is a basic palette that includes a cool and warm hue of each of the primary colors plus gray and brown. If desired, supplement this list with your own favorites.

Cadmium Yellow Light or Lemon Yellow
Cadmium Yellow Medium
Cadmium Red Light or Cadmium Red Medium
Carmine or Alizarin Crimson
Ultramarine Blue
Cobalt Blue
Payne's Gray
Ivory Black
Burnt Sienna
Burnt Umber

Gouache:

Winsor & Newton introductory set containing Zinc White, Yellow Ochre, Ultramarine, Spectrum Red, Primary Yellow, Primary Red, Primary Blue, Permanent Yellow Deep, Ivory Black, and Brilliant Green.
Waterproof black ink

Pastels:

One set of 12 or 24 soft pastels, such as Winsor & Newton
One set of 12 or 24 pastel pencils, such as Faber-Castell or Derwent
Colored pencils (artist quality such as Prismacolor)
At a minimum, a set of 24 different colors

Figure 8.12 Colored pencils.

Figure 8.13 Markers, including a variety of colors plus metallic gold and silver, and opaque white.

Figure 8.14 Watercolor brushes including, from top, 1″ wash brush, #12 round, #6 one stroke, #10 round, #6 round, and #3 round.

Figure 8.15 Stencil brush, assorted Conté pencils and crayons, dip pen holders and nibs, kneaded and gum erasers, brass pencil sharpener, assorted stumps, sandpaper block, graphite stick, cotton swabs, and make-up applicators.

Markers:

Artist/Designer quality such as Prismacolor or Chartpak

One 24 or 25 color, a clear blender, metallic silver and gold, opaque white

Watercolor brushes:

Sable or synthetic sable

Four pointed round brushes, sizes 3, 6, 10, and 12

One flat or one stroke brush in size 6 or 8

One square wash brush 1″

Hard toothbrush or small stencil brush

Crow quill pens or nib holder with assorted nibs, or a fine point fiber-tipped pen

One bottle of black waterproof drawing ink

Assorted Conté pencils or crayons (Sepia, Burnt Sienna, White)

Soft graphite stick or graphite transfer paper

One small handheld pencil sharpener

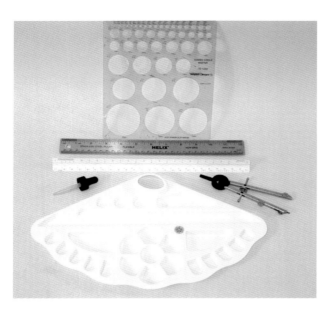

Figure 8.16 Circle template, cork-backed metal ruler, architect's scale, eyedropper, bow compass, and plastic palette.

One kneaded eraser
A gum eraser
Several stumps in assorted sizes
Sandpaper block
Spray fixative
12″ ruler
One white plastic or enamel palette
Masking tape

Figure 8.17 Denatured alcohol, spray fixative, masking fluid and masking fluid pen, water containers, waterproof black drawing ink, masking tape, and sponge.

Soft cotton rags or paper towels
Two cups or containers for water
Small sponge
Eyedropper
Masking fluid (frisket)
Bow compass or circle template
Architect's scale rule
.05 mm mechanical pencil
Denatured alcohol
Cotton swabs, make-up applicators, and cotton
    balls

Chapter 9

Colored Pencil

Colored pencils are an excellent medium with which to begin to explore color mixing and color relationships. The medium is clean, portable, and naturally intuitive to use for anyone who has ever held a pencil. Dozens of different hues are readily available and, compared to watercolor or gouache paints, are relatively inexpensive. By varying the pressure of pencil on paper, the value of each pencil's hue can easily be manipulated, and color mixing is as easy as layering one color on top of another.

For designers the one big drawback in using colored pencils is the time required to complete a drawing. A costume rendering may take three or four hours to complete, and a set rendering much longer. The tiny size of the pencil point constrains the area that can be covered in one stroke, and layering color over color is a time-consuming business. Pencils are inherently a drawing medium and the structure of the tool dictates that the color will be applied to the paper as lines. It takes only a few seconds to lay down a smooth wash of color on watercolor paper with paint and brush. Covering the same area in a solid coat of color with colored pencils takes much more time than most designers have. However, mastering the use of colored pencil is well worth the effort as it is extremely useful when combined with other color media such as watercolor wash or marker.

The basic technique of colored pencil painting is to use short, light, crosshatched strokes, building up from light to dark. Pressing too hard will create permanent linear dents in the paper. Avoid rubbing the pencil with long strokes in one direction, as this will create a visual texture that negatively affects the composition of your drawing. You can use a contour hatch (see Exercise 5, Chapter 7) as a directional stroke, but it must follow the outlines of the object you are drawing. Draw on a smooth hard surface with no texture, as any bumps or imperfections in the tabletop will transfer to your drawing paper. Sharpen your pencils frequently.

There are two colored pencil exercises included in this chapter. They are an introduction to colored pencils that will familiarize you with basic techniques, while at the same time explore the use of color in general. Colored pencil by itself is not the optimal medium for theatrical rendering because it is extremely time-consuming, so there are no rendering exercises in this chapter.

TOOLS AND MATERIALS

The tools and materials you will need for these exercises include:

Several pieces of vellum finish white illustration board or heavyweight drawing paper approximately $8\frac{1}{2} \times 11''$

One piece of heavyweight colored midtone drawing paper approximately $8\frac{1}{2} \times 11''$

One small handheld pencil sharpener

A ruler
A kneaded eraser
A clear blender marker
Denatured alcohol
Cotton swabs, such as Q-tips brand
Bow compass or circle template
A set of artist quality colored pencils

Prismacolor offers colored pencil sets in a variety of sizes from 12 to 120 pencils. A set of 24 is a good size to start with, and is sufficient to complete the exercises in this chapter. The paper you choose should have a smooth texture; a rough texture will make it difficult to fully conceal the white of the paper with the colored pencil pigment. Canson Mi-Teintes drawing paper is an excellent choice, with a slightly different finish on each side; one side has a vellum finish and the other side has a flat finish. The colored drawing paper can be of any hue, but must be of medium tone to effectively complete the three-dimensional modeling project in Exercise 2. You will use the color of the paper as a color in the drawing to which shades and tints will be added. Choose a paper color that corresponds with colors in your pencil set. For example, if you choose a medium red paper, you must have a pencil that closely matches the basic hue of the paper but is darker in value and one that is lighter in value. A quality brass or metal manual pencil sharpener is more effective than an electric one, because the force of the motor of some electric pencil sharpeners may break the relatively soft, fragile tip of the pencil. Colored pencils, in general, do not erase well from paper, so do not expect to fully remove a pencil stoke. Instead you can lighten dark areas with a kneaded eraser. Press repeatedly on the area with the eraser to pick up pigment from the surface of the paper. Use the clear blender marker to dissolve and smooth the pigment, filling in areas where the paper is showing through as white speckles. You only need a tiny amount of denatured alcohol to clean the tip of the clear blender marker. Denatured alcohol is available in gallons at hardware stores, or in smaller quantities at drug stores for a higher price per ounce.

COLORED PENCIL EXERCISE 1: COLORED PENCIL TECHNIQUE

The purpose of this exercise is to explore the potential of colored pencils as a medium and to create an accurate color wheel and gray scale for use as a reference for this and the other color medium exercises in the following chapters.. This exercise will take approximately two hours to complete. If you prefer, you may want to divide the exercise into two one-hour blocks of time.

Working with Hue

Begin by practicing the basic technique of drawing with colored pencils on a blank sheet of paper. Create a chart of small patches about 1-inch square of each of the colors you have, organizing them according to color in a logical manner. Practice crosshatching with light, short strokes of consistent pressure, layering the color until it is as intense as you can make it. Keep the pressure light to avoid denting the paper, and build up layer upon layer of color. Sharpen the point of the pencil frequently. Using the clear blender marker, blend a portion of each patch of color. Between colors, apply some denatured alcohol with a cotton swab to the tip of the marker to clean off any pigment. You now have a chart to which you can refer when choosing colors for the rest of the exercises in this chapter.

Next, duplicate the blank color wheel in Figure 9.1 on a fresh sheet of paper. Photocopy or scan and print the diagram and transfer it to your paper, or simply draw it using your lightest gray pencil and a bow compass or circle template. To transfer the diagram, cover the back of the photocopy with your lightest gray colored pencil, and then trace over the circle lines with the bow compass.

From your available selection of colored pen-cils, choose the closest matches to the primaries yellow, red, and blue and the secondary colors orange, violet, and green. Refer to the diagram in Figure 8.1 for color matching. Fill in the corresponding primary and secondary colors on your color wheel diagram. Make short, crosshatched strokes using steady light pressure to layer the color, continuing until no white of the paper is discernable in the color fields.

In the smaller circles labeled with the names of the tertiary colors, layer the corresponding primary and secondary hues that create each tertiary. The goal is to generate a hue that is a balance between the primary and secondary. For example, red orange should appear to contain equal parts of red and orange. In reality the red pencil may have a stronger pigment than the orange and equal amounts of each may produce a red orange that appears more red

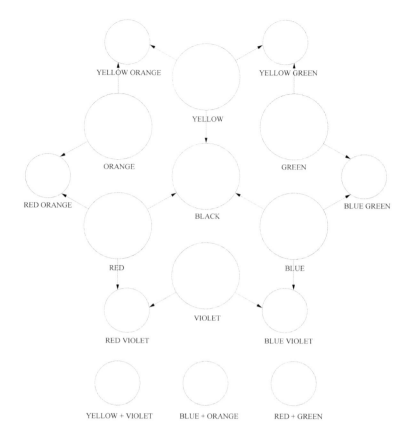

Figure 9.1 The color wheel.

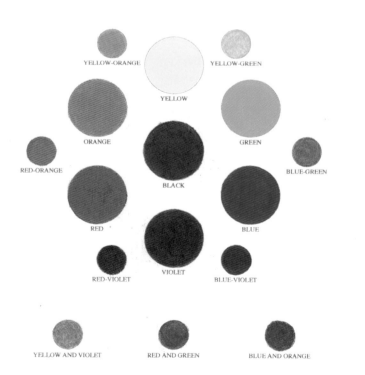

Figure 9.2 Colored pencil color wheel.

than orange. Lightly layer the more dominant color first with the weaker hue on top. Continue lightly layering, alternating between the two colors, until the white of the paper is not visible, and the hue appears to be halfway between the primary and secondary colors that create it.

In the circle labeled "black," layer the darkest hues of red, blue, and green at your disposal. (Green contains yellow, and the naturally light value of yellow is not conducive to creating black.) After one set of layers is applied, the hue will probably resemble the last color applied. Continue layering the colors, alternating the order applied until the color is as intense as you can make it.

Layer the designated pairs of complement in the corresponding circles at the bottom of the diagram. Use the same procedure used when mixing the tertiary colors. The goal is to produce a hue that resembles neither of the complements but is an even mix of both. The resulting hues will be shades of brown.

You have now created a color reference tool useful for identifying complementary colors. Although most of us have committed to memory the pairs of primary and secondary complements, a visual reference of the tertiary complements is often quite useful.

After completing this exercise, it becomes clear why most designers do not use colored pencils as an exclusive medium. Creating the color reference in watercolor would have taken a fraction of the time as it did using colored pencils. However, the hues of good quality colored pencils are very pure and are available in colors quite close to the colors of the spectrum, which makes your color reference chart more accurate.

COLORED PENCIL EXERCISE 2: VALUE, INTENSITY, AND THREE-DIMENSIONAL MODELING

The purpose of this exercise is to use colored pencils to experiment with color value and intensity and three-dimensional modeling. This exercise will take about two hours to complete. The value and intensity projects and three-dimensional modeling drawing may also be broken into two drawing sessions, if you prefer.

Value and Intensity

You can regulate value with colored pencils either by adding white, black, or a combination of dark colors to a hue, or by varying the number of layers applied to the paper. Using the gray scale in Figure 9.2 as a guide, create a ten-step value scale on a fresh sheet of paper using one of the darkest hues in your palette (blue or violet) and white. Lay out the diagram on your paper using the lightest gray pencil you have and a ruler. The first square should be the white of the paper and the last the full-strength color of the pencil. In the middle squares, layer the color and white adding enough layers to cover all of the white of the paper. Next, create another ten-step value scale using the same color without the addition of white. Apply more layers of light strokes the closer you get to the #10 value. The tenth square should be the full-strength pigment with nearly no white paper visible.

Now make a gradient ranging from full-strength red pigment to "black." Draw a small (about $3/4$" high by 3" long) rectangle with red pencil on your paper, as in Figure 9.3. Apply as many layers of color as necessary until the entire rectangle is red. Then, starting at the right side of the rectangle, layer your darkest brown and darkest blue colors. The first layer will end about a half inch from the left side of the rectangle, leaving an area of pure red color. Continue layering the brown and blue colors, ending each layer a bit farther to the right, until you have a gradient from red to black. Smooth the transition with an additional light layer of red that starts at the left side and tapers off toward the darker edge. If you wish, further smooth the gradient with the clear blender marker.

A wide variety of hues in a range of values and intensities are available in colored pencils. If you purchase a large set, chances are good that any color you desire will be available or require only slight modification of hue, intensity, or value. If the intensity of a hue needs to be lowered, put a light coat of its complement on the paper first, then layer the color on top. Subsequent layers of the complement may be added as necessary.

Three-Dim ensional Modeling with Colored Pencils

The next step in your experimentation with colored pencils will be to draw some actual objects affected by a light source. Taking into consideration the time-

Figure 9.3 The gray scale.

consuming nature of colored pencil drawing, these will be simple geometric shapes, drawn on your midtone colored drawing paper. The base color of the shapes will be the color of your paper, to which you will add shade and highlight. Completing the drawing will be much faster than if you had to lay in the base color with pencil as in the red-to-black gradient exercise. The basic techniques of trompe l'oeil drawing and three-dimensional modeling are described and terms are defined in Chapter 5. Review this chapter before beginning this project.

Duplicate or copy and transfer the diagram in Figure 9.4 to your midtoned paper. If you transfer the diagram, cover the reverse side of the copy with pigment using a colored pencil close to the color of the paper, then trace the outlines of the shapes onto your paper. Be careful not to dent the paper with hard pressure of the pencil. You want to be able to barely see the cartoon outline, especially in the cast shadow areas. If the cartoon seems too dark, lighten it by pressing on the lines with your kneaded eraser.

Next, select the pencils you will use to execute the drawing. Optimally, you would have five or six different pencils to render shade, lowlight, cut line, highlight, zinger, and cast shadow. The shade color should be the same basic hue as the color of the paper, but one step darker in value. The lowlight color is the same basic hue and two steps down in value. Use black or very dark brown or blue for the cut line. The highlight is the same basic hue as the paper but one step lighter in value. The zinger is a very pale tint of the paper hue, or white. The cast shadow color is dark blue or brown and could be the same pencil that is used for the cut line. If your base color is warm, use blue for the cast shadow, and brown if the base color is cool. At a minimum, you need an accurate shade color that you can deepen for the lowlight with an appropriate dark color, a very dark color for the cut line and cast shadow, and white for the highlight and zinger.

Figure 9.4 Red to black gradient using Crimson Red, Dark Umber, and Indigo Blue Prismacolor pencils.

Decide on the placement of a light source that will determine where to put the shade and highlight, and then begin modeling the shapes, starting with the shade color. The illustrations accompanying this project depict the light source as above, in front of, and to the right of the object. The left sides of the geometric solids will be shaded, and the right sides will be highlighted.

In the drawing of the cube, the top plane is lightest, the front plane is mostly the base color, and the right-hand plane is shaded. Layer the shade color on the appropriate plane using short, light, crosshatched strokes. In addition, put a little shade at the base of the front plane and the receding edge of the top plane, feathering the strokes out so no hard line is visible. Apply the shade color to the left one-third of the cylinder, tapering off at the right-hand edge and at the receding edge of the top plane. Apply a thin strip of shade to the very edge of the right-hand side of the cylinder to convey the impression of roundness. Either crosshatch the strokes or follow the contour of the object with your strokes using a contour hatch. Apply shade to the cone in the same manner as you did the cylinder, tapering the shaded area to a point from the base to the tip of the left side of the cone. For all the solids, apply more layers

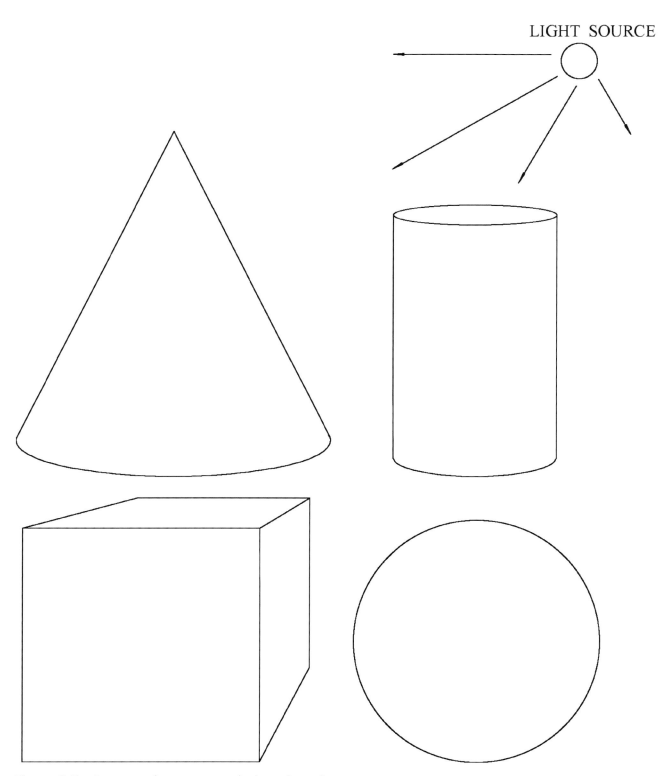

LIGHT SOURCE

Figure 9.5 Geometric shapes: cone, cylinder, cube, sphere.

Figure 9.6 Midtoned paper and Prismacolor pencils in Light Umber, Dark Umber, Sepia, Deco Orange, White, and Indigo Blue that will be used to render shade, lowlight, cut line, highlight, zinger, and cast shadow, respectively.

of shade as necessary to the parts of the objects away from the light source that are receding in space.

The next step is to apply the lowlight color in the areas of shade that are farthest away from the light source. In your drawing, this area is to the extreme left and bottom edge of the cube, and just a bit away from the left edges and at the bottom edges of the cylinder and cone. Apply the first layer of lowlight very lightly, and then continue layering until the desired affect is visually apparent. If the first layer is too dark, you can make it somewhat lighter by pressing on it with the kneaded eraser, but it is best to start out very lightly, and then layer as necessary. Remember, you cannot completely erase colored pencil from your paper.

Next, using the freshly sharpened dark brown, dark blue, or black pencil, draw in the cut lines at the edges where the objects intersect the cast shadows. Re-sharpen the pencil frequently to keep the tip very pointy. The cut lines should be slightly thicker in the center of the cast shadow and taper out at the outer

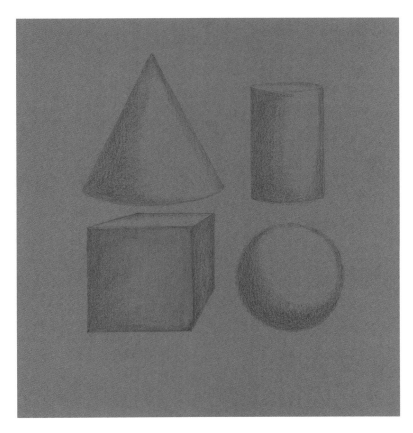

Figure 9.7 The placement and color of shade on the geometric objects.

edges of the cast shadow. You attain this line quality difference by varying the pressure of the pencil on the paper. In addition to the intersection of object and cast shadow, add a tapered vertical cut line to the left side of each object beginning with harder pressure at the left bottom corner and feathering out to a stop about one-third of the way up the left side. Switch to the shade pencil, and apply cut line to the rest of the contour of each object, varying the line thickness, as you did with the darker cut lines. This step is necessary to define the outer edges of the objects, since so much of the objects' color is actually the color of the paper. Using the shade color, rather than the darker cut line color, and varying the thickness of the lines prevents an outlined appearance.

With the lowlights accurately rendered, the geometric solids begin to appear three-dimensional. The highlight is the next step toward completing the drawing. Beginning at the bottom edge of the top face of the cube, layer the highlight color lightly, fading the color toward the receding edge of the plane. The highlights on the cone and cylinder closely mirror the shade shapes for these objects. Continue layering color until the highlight areas and the shade

areas have equal visual importance. When you look at the drawing as a whole, you should not see "shade" or "highlight" distinctively; you should see a three-dimensional object.

Using your lightest value pencil, add zingers of bright light at the forward edges of the top faces of the cube and cylinder, and the points of the cylinder and cube that are closest to the light source and within the highlight areas. Vary the line thickness of the zinger as you did for the cut line.

Lightly lay in the cast shadow color, adding layers of color close to the object, and feathering out to the extreme edges of the shadow shape. The shadow should look translucent and slightly dark where it meets the object.

Finally, look critically at your drawing and check that each individual step you applied appears to be in balance with the others. The highlights and shade should be an equal number of value steps away from the base color. The objects' contours should be noticeably defined on the page, but not look outlined. The intersection of the three planes of the cube should clearly show three value levels. The transitions from shade to base color and base color to highlight on the cylinder and cone should be soft and gradual.

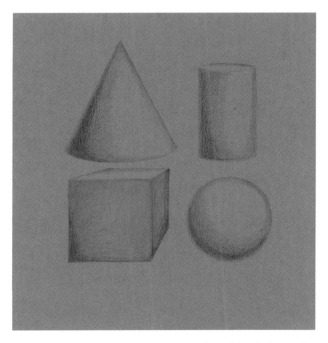

Figure 9.8 The placement and color of lowlight on the geometric objects.

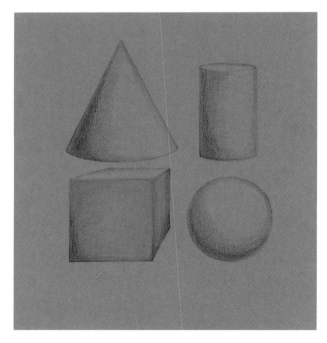

Figure 9.9 The placement and color of cut line on the geometric objects.

Figure 9.10 The placement and color of highlight on the geometric objects.

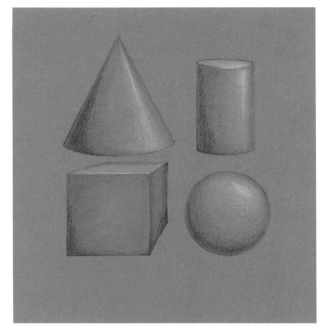

Figure 9.11 The placement and color of zingers on the geometric objects.

Figure 9.12 The placement and color of cast shadow on the geometric objects.

Colored pencils as a medium have many quality features: clean, portable, the color is vibrant and available in dozens of hues, and the techniques are easy to master. But colored pencil renderings often look like a child's crayon drawings with visible pencil strokes and too much white paper showing through the pigment, because accurately rendering in colored pencil is so time-consuming. Adding color pencil details to fields of color created with a faster to apply medium is an excellent way to combine the best features of colored pencils with the designer's need to execute renderings quickly. The following chapters include exercises in mixed media such as marker and colored pencil and watercolor and colored pencil.

Chapter 10

Marker

Marker is an obvious choice of color medium for creating theatrical renderings. Like colored pencils, they are clean, portable, vibrantly colored, and intuitive to use. The medium is versatile enough to mimic both the translucent washes attainable with watercolor paints, and the opacity, if not the texture, of acrylic paints. Like watercolor, you can cover large areas of paper quickly, but still create fine details such as intricate fabric patterns. Art markers are available in dozens of different hues. Chances are good that, provided you have a large set of markers, you will find exactly the right color you need, eliminating the need to mix color. This really speeds up the rendering process. With practice, you can expect to be able to easily finish a costume rendering in marker in under an hour, and a set rendering in a couple of hours.

TOOLS AND MATERIALS

Markers (artist/designer quality such as Prismacolor or Chartpak)
One 24 or 25 color set and a clear blender
One pad of heavy weight vellum pad 9 × 12″
One pad of marker paper 9 × 12″
Denatured alcohol
Cotton swabs, make-up applicators, and cotton balls

Several fabric swatches with interesting patterns and colors

About Markers

Art markers are pens with felt or nylon tips that dispense permanent pigment suspended in a solvent, usually alcohol. Most brands of markers have two tips, one at each end of the pen. One tip is broad, for maximum coverage, and the other is thin for small, detailed areas. Prismacolor markers have a chisel tip on the broad end, which makes it easy to execute a variety of strokes and line widths. At about three dollars per pen, markers are relatively expensive. Sets are available at a savings over individual pens, and large discounts are generally available on the Internet. If you are not sure if you will be using markers to do your renderings on a regular basis, buy a basic set of colors to begin with, plus a variety of gray values, black, and a clear blender. If you do use markers often, buy the biggest set you can afford for the convenience of always having the perfect color available.

One drawback is that markers have a short shelf-life relative to other color mediums. The alcohol solvent that allows the pigment to flow freely from the tip of the marker will evaporate over time, making the pen useless. Protect your investment by storing your markers in airtight plastic bags or containers. Sets of markers often come packaged in practical cases that prop up and allow easy access to each marker. Seal up the entire case in plastic when not in use.

Marker Paper

Paper is the most critical material in successful marker technique, because marker pigment dries very fast after it is applied. On an absorbent surface, such as drawing paper, the marker's solvent and pigment will soak into the paper and dry as you apply it, making blending impossible. The results are streaky, dark, and wholly unsatisfying. Working on a surface with little absorbency, the colors are more translucent and stay wetter longer, allowing you a short period to manipulate the pigment to the desired effect.

Marker paper, specially designed to work with this medium, is an excellent surface. These papers typically have either a translucent or a bleed-proof white finish. Bienfang Graphics 360 Marker Paper is a good example of the translucent variety, and Canson Pro-Layout Marker Paper an example of the opaque type. The advantage of the translucent paper is you can create interesting effects by working on both sides of the paper. Marker applied to the reverse side appears soft and diffused from the front side. Drafting vellum is another good surface for marker rendering. Depending on the smoothness and translucency of the paper, drying time can be several minutes, permitting watercolor-type techniques, and nearly total erasures. Clearprint 1000 H Drafting Vellum and Canson Vidalon Vellum are good choices in this category. The Vidalon Vellum has such a slick surface that you may find the marker dries too slowly for your taste. You should try a broad range of different papers and choose the one that works best for your particular needs. Whatever paper you choose, make sure it is 100% rag or archival to prevent the color from bleeding and fading and the paper from yellowing over time. As a theatrical designer, even though you do not create your renderings as fine art, you should take care to preserve your work for the best possible portfolio presentation.

Blending and Layering

Cotton swabs or make-up applicators are excellent tools for blending markers just after color has been applied to the paper. How much time you have to manipulate the color depends on the slickness of the paper, but you should have at least ten seconds. You can prevent the streak marks of overlapping marker strokes by blending them with the cotton swab while the marker is still wet. You can also use the swab to soften blends between colors laid down side by side, and to lighten the value of a color by rubbing some of it away, allowing more of the white of the paper to show through. Because the blending must be done while the marker is still wet on the paper, apply only as much color as will stay wet while you are blending.

Another way to blend markers is to apply a solvent that dissolves the pigment, which allows you to move it around on the paper. Clear blender markers are pens containing only solvent, usually alcohol, and no pigment. With the clear blender, you can do all of the blending techniques as with the cotton swab, even if the marker appears dry on the paper. The marker pigment will transfer to the tip of the clear blender, but you can remove the color with denatured alcohol to keep the tip clean. For additional thinning and blending, apply denatured alcohol with the cotton swab directly to marker strokes on the paper. On very slick paper, denatured alcohol will nearly completely remove most marker colors.

All marker colors are at least somewhat translucent, which means that the color will get darker in value as successive layers are applied. You can clearly see this effect when laying down adjacent and overlapping strokes of the same color. At the point of overlap, the color is darker. Similarly, if you do the same with two different colors, the overlapping area will appear as a third color, a mix of the original two. Although some people find the streaking caused by overlapping strokes in a single field of color an annoying aspect of the medium, this layering property also makes the marker a very versatile medium.

MARKER EXERCISE 1: MARKER TECHNIQUE

In this exercise, you will be experimenting with marker to test the limits of its possibilities. This exercise will take about an hour to complete. First, make a color chart of small squares of your available markers, organized logically by color, on a piece of the marker paper. For each square, blend the streaks from the overlapping strokes with a cotton swab or make-up applicator before the marker dries on the paper.

Figure 10.1 Marker color chart.

On another piece of marker paper, lay down a 1-inch square patch of color, and using the cotton swab or make-up applicator, blend the color out toward blank paper as far as it will go. Make another square of the same color next to the first, and thin the color out as far as it will extend with the clear blender. Do the same with another patch of color and a cotton swab dipped in denatured alcohol.

On the same piece of paper, experiment with darkening the value of a color by applying successive layers. Lay down a long horizontal single stroke of color with the broad tip of a marker. A short distance from the left end of this stroke, make a vertical stroke of the same color that overlaps the first. Move to the right and apply two vertical strokes, one on top of the other. Allow the first of these to dry before applying the second. Continue with three strokes of color, and then four on different areas of the horizontal stroke of color.

Practice layering analogous colors by laying down a vertical stroke of one color and a horizontal stroke of the second color that crosses the first. Test the translucency of the marker paper by applying

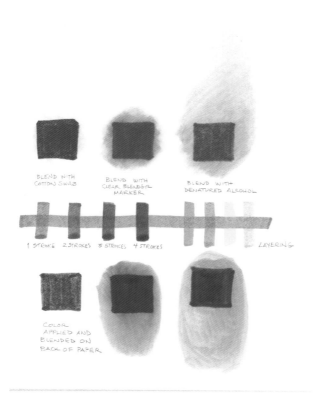

Figure 10.2 Blending and layering on marker paper.

Figure 10.3 Blending and layering on vellum.

color to the reverse side of a blank section of the paper. Experiment with the cotton swab, clear blender, and denatured alcohol on the back of the paper. Finally, repeat the blending and layering exercises on heavyweight vellum.

MARKER EXERCISE 2: EXPERIMENTATION

The purpose of this exercise is to experiment with marker techniques that would be useful in your own renderings. For example, if you are a scene designer, you may choose to experiment by rendering various surfaces such as brick or wood. Use either marker paper or vellum, whichever you prefer. Have a scratch piece of marker paper or vellum handy to practice your technique before rendering the fabric on another piece of paper. As you experiment with different techniques, note on your paper

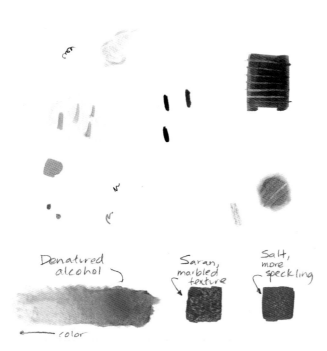

Figure 10.4 Experimenting with plastic wrap, salt, and wax resists.

Figure 10.5 Experimenting with skin tone and hair rendering technique.

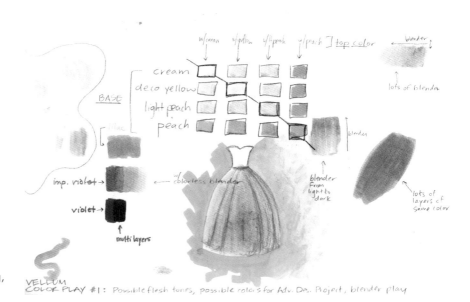

Figure 10.6
Experiments in layering, blending, and mixing skin tones.

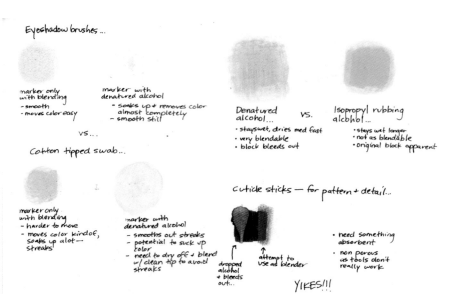

Figure 10.7
Experimenting with various blending methods.

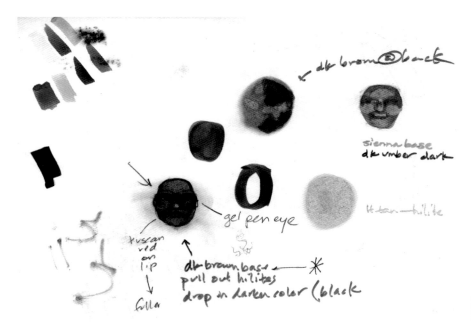

Figure 10.8
Experiments in mixing skin tones.

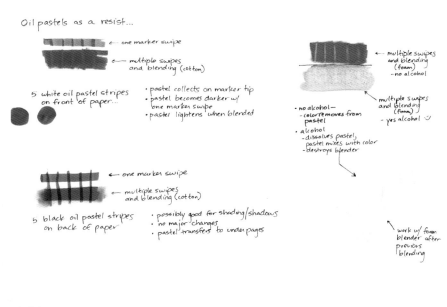

Figure 10.9
Experimenting with various resists.

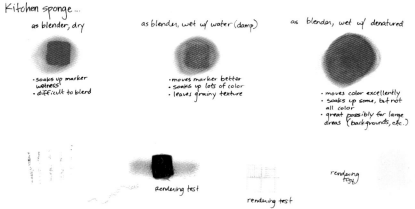

Figure 10.10
Experiments in blending with a sponge.

the colors you used, in sequence, to achieve the result. Include any special layering or blending techniques in the notation.

The illustrations that accompany this exercise were done by a costume design student who was experimenting with layering and blending techniques, and using various mediums as resists, within the context of costume rendering. This type of experimentation and the accompanying notations are valuable reference tools.

Chapter 11

Pastels

Pastel is an excellent medium for lighting design renderings. The colors are intensely vibrant, and the medium, used correctly, creates a sense of immediacy and freshness perfect for describing a dynamic moment in time. Using black or dark colored paper as a base, the designer builds a cue by painting the intensity and color of the light, illuminating only those scenic elements and actors that will be visible to the audience in that cue. A lighting design rendering in pastel can evoke an accurate sense, in miniature, of what the audience will experience visually in a given moment of a play.

Pastels are made of ground pigment, like those used to make artist's paints, combined with a medium that holds the grains of pigment together. Soft and hard pastels are available in square or round sticks, and hard pastels are available in pencil form. Soft pastels contain less medium, crumble into grains of pigment more readily, and lose a sharp edge more quickly than hard pastels, but the colors are more vibrant. They are best used for large color fields and when very intense color is necessary. Hard pastels in stick and pencil form are good for detail work and crisp lines. Oil pastels are altogether a different medium. They are similar to crayons, but with an oily rather than waxy base, and will not be discussed in this chapter. Make sure you purchase hard and soft pastels, and not oil pastels for the following exercises.

The technique of pastel painting involves laying down strokes or dabs of color on paper that has a slight tooth. The texture of the paper abrades the grains of pigment from the pastel stick or pencil, and holds the grains to the paper. If too much pastel is applied to the paper and the tooth is obscured, the excess pigment will not adhere to the paper, but will fall off as dust. Color mixing is achieved either by laying different colors side by side and letting the eye mix them together, or by layering colors on top of each other. The strokes of pigment can be softened and blended with a variety of tools.

TOOLS AND MATERIALS

You will need the following tools and materials to complete the two pastel exercises in this chapter.

One set of 12 or 24 soft pastels, such as Winsor & Newton
One set of 12 or 24 pastel pencils, such as Faber-Castell or Derwent
Several pieces of black vellum finish illustration board or heavyweight drawing paper approximately 8½ × 11″ such as Canson Mi-Teintes
One pointed round brush size 12
Several stumps in assorted sizes
Sandpaper block
One kneaded eraser
12″ ruler with metal edge
Several sheets of notebook or photocopy paper

Masking tape
Cotton rag
Spray fixative

Pastels are available in dozens of different colors, and having just the right color saves time in rendering. However, good pastels are also expensive, and cheaper pastels have disappointingly small amounts of pigments, which compromises their vibrancy. You will have better results if you buy fewer good quality pastels and mix whatever color you need, than if you buy a huge set of inferior pastels.

You will use the sable or imitation sable pointed round brush and the stumps to blend the pastel colors together. The sandpaper block is used to create a hard edge on the pastel stick and to sharpen the tip of the pastel pencil. The kneaded eraser is useful for picking up excess or unwanted grains of pigment on your paper. Stick pastels will quickly transfer to your fingers as you use them, so it is helpful to have a cotton rag handy to clean your hands. Pastel paintings must be sealed with fixative or the grains of pigment will smear and fall off the paper. You will use the notebook or photocopy paper for masking certain areas of your painting to create sharply defined lines, and the masking tape to hold the paper in place. Seal your paintings in the same manner described for charcoal drawings at the beginning of Chapter 7. To avoid smearing your pastel paintings, keep the heel of your hand and your arm elevated above the paper. Only the pastel stick or pencil should touch the paper, unless you are blending color. It may help to work with your paper on an angled surface.

PASTEL EXERCISE 1: PASTEL TECHNIQUE

In this exercise, you will experiment with using soft pastel sticks and hard pastel pencils, explore the medium, and learn specific techniques useful for lighting design renderings. This exercise will take about two hours to complete.

Creating a Color Chart

On one piece of white pastel or drawing paper, create a chart of all of the colors in your soft pastel set. Organize the colors logically, and lay down 1-inch square patches of each color, starting at the top left

corner of your paper and moving across the top of the page if you are right-handed and the opposite if you are left-handed. Be careful not to let your hand brush against the work you have already completed. Take note of the coverage and vibrancy of each color.

Figure 11.1 Soft pastel color chart.

Figure 11.2 Pastel pencil color chart.

Then, do the same with your set of pastel pencils. If you purchased large sets of soft pastels and pencils, you may need to use another sheet of paper for the pencil swatches. Note that the pigment in the pencils is much harder, and the intensity of color is less than the soft pastels. Seal the color chart or charts with fixative before moving on to the next step.

Color Mixing

Setting strokes of color side by side is one way to mix colors with pastels. Even though you have not physically blended the colors together, your eye will see them as combined into a third color. To illustrate this phenomenon, choose two analogous colors such as blue and green from your soft pastel set. Using the edge of the stick, lay down several broad strokes of blue creating a small field of color. Draw another field of color the same size next to, but not touching, the second by alternating small strokes of blue and green. The alternating colors should touch, but not overlap each other. Draw a third field of color the same size next to, but not touching, the second by using just the green pastel. Examining the three fields of color, you will see that the one consisting of alternating strokes of blue and green reads as blue-green and is distinct from the two colors on either side. Experiment with color mixing in this manner using various colors from your set. Vary the size and contour of the strokes as you experiment, try stippled, angled, and curvilinear strokes.

Another method of mixing colors with pastels is by layering one or more colors on top of each other. The pigment granules of each color mix, and a new color is created. First one color is laid down in strokes, and then the next is applied on top of the first. The strokes applying the second color may be in the same direction as the first or hatch over the first in the opposite direction. Experiment with color mixing by layering using both soft and pencil pastels in combination with each other.

Blending

Blending pastels with various tools softens the edges of hard lines, changes the value of the pigment by revealing some of the black color of the paper, and creates seamless transitions from one color field to the next. Stumps are made of soft gray paper that is perfect for blending pastels. The paper is tightly rolled into a stick with a point at each end, and the pointed ends do the blending. Stumps are available in a variety of sizes; choose the size that is appropriate for the area you want to blend. Tortillons are tools similar to stumps but are rolled to a point at only one end. Other tools effective for blending include cotton swabs, make-up applicators, your fingertip, and soft brushes such as watercolor or make-up brushes.

To experiment with blending, repeat the blue and green alternating stroke exercise using soft pastels, blending the colors together with a stump. Compare the results with the unblended drawing. Repeat the exercise with pastel pencils, and compare the results with the soft pastel drawing. Soft pastels blend more readily than hard pastels.

Figure 11.3 Color mixing by alternating adjacent colors.

Figure 11.4 Color mixing by layering.

Figure 11.5 Blending with a stump.

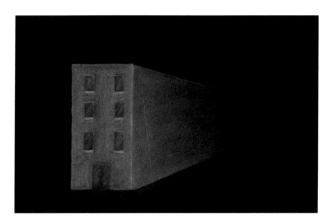

Figure 11.6 Fade to black.

Working with Black Paper

Dynamic lighting renderings are characterized by crisp shifts from contours of objects brightly illuminated by colored light to the jet black of the paper, and by soft transitions from colored light to black. This section of Exercise 1 explains how to create a fade to the black of the paper.

Lay down a vertical rectangular field of color, such as gray, with soft pastel. Accentuate the contour of the rectangle using a sharpened gray pastel pencil and a ruler. Spray the rectangle with fixative and allow it to dry. Then, on the right edge of the rectangle, draw short light lines angled back in perspective from the top and bottom corners of the rectangle. Mask the area between the angled lines with two pieces of notebook or photocopy paper and tape the paper in place with masking tape. Do not tape the black paper, if possible, because removing the tape may cause the paper to tear. Apply a broad stroke of gray pastel to the paper off the right edge of the rectangle between the angled lines. Create a gradation from light to dark value by blending out gradually with a large stump or your fingertip from the right edge of the rectangle toward blank paper. Continue blending out with the stump until no more color transfers from the stump or your finger to the paper. The rhomboid shape to the right of the rectangle should be darker in value than the rectangle at the intersection line between the two shapes. The resulting drawing should resemble a building front and side in perspective with the side of the building in shadow. This gradual "fading to black" technique is very useful in lighting design renderings.

PASTEL EXERCISE 2: PAINTING THE FIGURE IN SPOTLIGHT

In this exercise you will paint an actor illuminated by three distinctly different light cues. The first rendering is an actor standing in a single white spotlight. The second is an actor illuminated by side light in contrasting colors. In the third light cue, the actor is in silhouette.

To begin, transfer the illustration in Figure 11.7 to three pieces of black pastel or drawing paper as follows. Photocopy the illustration. Make a second copy at about 60 percent the size of the first. Apply light gray pastel to the back of the full size copy. Position it face up on a vertically oriented piece of black pastel or drawing paper, and carefully trace the contours in mechanical pencil. Place the copy on another piece of vertically oriented black paper and retrace the figure, but omit the spotlight beam and cast shadow at the actor's feet. Apply light gray pastel to the back of the 60 percent copy and place it on another piece of horizontally oriented black paper. Trace the figure, omitting the beam and shadow.

Actor in White Spotlight

For the first rendering, the actor is standing in a single spot; the lighting instrument is in front of and above the actor and illuminates his entire body. Using white pastel pencil, render the highlighted parts of the body and the pool of light hitting the floor, as illustrated in Figure 11.7. The shaded parts of the body and the cast shadow of the figure will remain the black color of the paper. Notice that there

Figure 11.7 Cartoon of figure standing in spotlight.

Figure 11.8 Actor in white spotlight.

Figure 11.9 Actor in side light.

Figure 11.10 The actor in silhouette.

is some variation in the value of the white pigment on the body, and that thin white lines between the shaded areas of the body and the black void behind the body accentuate the actor's contour.

Actor in Side Light

For the second rendering, the actor is illuminated by blue light from the left, and amber from the right. Apply blue pastel to the left sides of all of the parts of the body, limbs, torso, and head and yellow pastel to the right sides of the body. Let the black of the paper describe the shaded areas of the body.

Actor in Silhouette

In the third rendering the actor is in silhouette with just a bit of dark gray pastel defining his body. The background is a very saturated yellow-orange field that fades to black, and the stage floor is dark gray.

The outline of the actor is obvious because of the value contrast, but be careful to render his contour carefully, or he will look out of focus. Paint the yellow-orange right up to the outline of the figure, and make sure the color intensity is maintained at the juncture of body and color field.

Lighting designers often choose to render on black paper so they can draw the "light," rather than drawing shadows. However, keep in mind that any rendering must be appropriate for the particular production it is portraying. For a light musical comedy, or a play with a set that is very light in value, it may be more appropriate to use a lighter colored paper, rather than black paper. Do not hesitate to experiment with different tools, materials, and techniques, according to the needs of the production. If you always execute your renderings in the same style, on the same paper, with the same color range, it may be difficult to differentiate between dramatic productions when looking at the body of work in your portfolio.

Chapter 12

Watercolor

Watercolor is a wonderful medium for theatrical design renderings. Good techniques combined with "happy accidents" caused by the mixture of water and pigment on paper, lend a spontaneous and fresh appearance to the renderings. Once mastered, you can quickly execute the basic techniques from broad washes to fine detail. Mastering watercolor is challenging, however. This is the first medium discussed that is not applied to paper with a pencil-like object. Although brushes are, at first, more difficult to control than pencils, markers, and pastels, learning a few basic techniques will enable you to create convincing watercolor renderings.

TOOLS AND MATERIALS

The following is a list of tools and materials you will need to complete the watercolor exercises in this chapter.

One pad or block of heavyweight watercolor paper, such as Arches or Strathmore, approximately 12 × 18″
Small (5 ml) tubes of artist-quality watercolor paints such as Da Vinci, Grumbacher, Holbein, Prismacolor, or Winsor & Newton

The following is a basic palette that includes a cool and warm hue of each of the primary colors plus gray and brown. If desired, supplement this list with your own favorites.

Cadmium Yellow Light or Lemon Yellow
Cadmium Yellow Medium
Cadmium Red Light or Cadmium Red Medium
Carmine or Alizarin Crimson
Ultramarine Blue
Cobalt Blue
Payne's Gray
Ivory Black
Burnt Sienna
Burnt Umber

Zinc White gouache (from your set of gouache paints)
Watercolor brushes: sable or synthetic sable
Four pointed round brushes, sizes 3, 6, 10, and 12
One bright or one stroke brush in size 6 or 8
One square wash brush 1″
Hard toothbrush or small stencil brush
One white plastic or enamel palette
Masking tape
Soft cotton rags or paper towels
Two cups or containers for water
Small sponge
Masking fluid (frisket)
Gum eraser
Circle template
.05 mm mechanical pencil

Watercolor Paper

Watercolor paints are applied thinly, and are always mixed with some water before using. Used correctly, the paint does not build up thickly on the surface of the paper, but rather soaks in. The paper used for watercolor, therefore, is absorbent, and may or may not have a visible tooth. Textured watercolor paper is called "cold press," and smooth watercolor paper is "hot press." A medium to light texture or a smooth texture is best for theatrical renderings so that detail is not obscured by the tooth of the paper. The paper is available in various thicknesses, designated by pounds. Buy the best paper you can afford in the 95- to 140-lb range. It comes in a variety of sizes and in single sheets, pads, or blocks. The sheets in the blocks come glued together on the edges of all four sides, except for a small bit at the top of the block. The finished rendering is removed from the block by inserting a long thin knife in the unglued slot and carefully working the paper free from the block. Watercolor paper has a tendency to buckle and curl when you apply water to it, so if you did not purchase a block, it will be necessary to tape down all four sides of the paper before beginning to paint.

Tools

You will need a surface on which to mix water with your watercolors and create different colors. This surface, a watercolor palette, must be white. Any other color will interfere with the appearance of the pigments. Typically, a palette is made of white plastic or enamel. It has recessed compartments, or wells, that are used to segregate the colors and provide shallow bowls for mixing quantities of pigment and water. It usually has a flat area, as well, for mixing colors together. Some people prefer a large flat palette with no wells. A small white plastic or enamel bowl, or even a white ice cube tray is useful for mixing a quantity of wash to cover a large area of paper.

If you purchased single sheets or pads of paper, you will need masking tape to hold your paper securely to a board or table. You must tape the paper down along every inch of each side to prevent the water from buckling it. Heavier paper and paper of better quality buckles less than thinner, cheaper papers. You will also need two containers for water: one is for cleaning brushes, and the other holds a supply of fresh, clean water for mixing. You will use a small natural sponge, available in drug stores at the makeup counter, to create texture in one of the exercises, and cotton rags or paper towels will be used to remove paint and water from the brush and paper. The eyedropper is handy for adding precise amounts of water to pigment. Masking fluid, or frisket, is liquid latex. It is used to mask out areas of the paper that you do not want to get wet or receive paint. Masking fluid is available in bottles and pens. You apply the bottled liquid latex with a brush, whereas the pen is quite useful for small details. After the latex has dried, apply washes to the paper as desired and allow the paint to dry completely. The gum eraser removes the latex without damaging the paper.

Watercolor Brushes

Watercolor brushes have thin, soft hairs that hold water well and apply paint smoothly to the paper without noticeable brush strokes. They are traditionally made of sable hair, but are widely available in synthetic materials that mimic the properties of sable. The round brush is the workhorse of watercolor painting. It has a round ferrule and the hairs taper to a narrower or pointed tip at the end. Round brushes are great for washes and details, and allow you to create thick or thin lines depending on whether you use the whole brush or just the tip, and how much pressure you apply. Three or four different sizes of round brushes will allow you to do most watercolor tasks. A flat or one stroke brush has a flat ferrule and a squared-off tip and is perfect for architectural details. The wash brush is your largest brush, holds a good quantity of paint, and is used to lay down large areas of thinned color. The toothbrush or small stencil brush with stiff hairs will be used for spattering color onto your paper.

Watercolor brushes are available in a variety of other shapes with which you might want to experiment. For example, a fan brush has bristles that extend out sideways in a fan shape from the ferrule. The hairs are separated from each other and create feathery, dry-brush strokes. An angled brush (similar to an American sash brush used for painting windows, but scaled down for watercolor painting) is perfect for cutting tight corners and precision work. Many watercolor brushes are sold blocked into shape with water-soluble glue. Before using them, just rinse the glue out with water. It is a good idea to have a special carrying case for your brushes to protect the hairs from bending. Always thoroughly wash your brushes with water after use, and never leave them sitting tip down in a container of water.

Watercolor Paints

You can buy watercolors in either tubes of wet paste or dry cakes. Both varieties are completely water-soluble. A blob of dried tube watercolor on your palette can be reactivated as viable paint by simply adding water. The cakes typically come in a boxed set and are useful for outdoor painting because they are very portable. You will probably find that the tubes are more convenient, especially for mixing large quantities of wash paint. The tubes are available in bigger sizes, but for the exercises in this book, you will not need more than the smallest tubes available (about 5 ml).

Good quality watercolor paints are expensive. If you use them often for your renderings, it saves time to have your favorite colors available straight out of the tube, but you can create many different hues with about ten different colors. These include a warm and cool version of each of the primary colors, plus black, blue-gray, and a couple of browns, one warm and one cool. Opaque Zinc White gouache is useful for adding bright highlights.

Watercolor Technique

Two qualities of watercolor paints dictate how you must use them to the best effect. First, watercolors are translucent. White is not used to create tints of color in watercolor painting. You make any color lighter in value by adding water. The pigment remains vibrant, but when applied, the white surface of the paper is revealed, more or less, depending on the amount of water you mix with the paint. For example, to make a pink color, instead of mixing red and white paint, you mix red paint with a quantity of water. When brushed on, red plus the white of the paper equals pink. You can create different colors by mixing on your palette, by mixing wet colors together on the paper, or by layering wet pigment over dry pigment. However, the translucent quality of the paint excludes the possibility of successfully layering a light value over a darker one. A light-colored top layer may slightly alter the appearance of a dark color field, but you cannot layer a light-colored recognizable object over a darker one. Second, watercolors are water-soluble, even after they dry. Layering a wash of color over a previously painted area of your rendering will blur and obscure the image, and the colors will intermingle. Plain water also dissolves and smears dry paint previously applied to the paper. That is useful when your aim is to correct a mistake, as you can nearly totally remove color from the paper with large quantities of water and strong pressure with a brush. Nevertheless, it is disheartening when an area of detail you have spent effort on suddenly becomes a puddle of unrecognizable mud because you washed wet paint over it. These are the qualities that make watercolor painting challenging. It takes a good deal of experience to know exactly what the paints and water will do and to effortlessly anticipate the sequence of steps you must follow to successfully execute any particular rendering.

For best results, first paint the largest areas of your rendering, and then proceed systematically toward the areas of smallest detail. For a costume rendering, you will paint the skin color and base colors of the clothing, including the effects of light and shade, before adding the details of facial features and fabric pattern. If parts of the pattern are very light in color, apply masking fluid to these areas before beginning the base painting. Paint a set rendering by protecting foreground objects, light-colored details and beams and pools of light with masking fluid. Then paint from upstage to downstage, removing the masking fluid to paint individual objects.

Always have a scrap piece of watercolor paper handy for testing paint color and consistency, as well as for trying out various techniques. Frequently, unhappy accidents occur due to overloaded brushes. If there is too much water and pigment in your brush, the result will be a runny blob when you touch the brush to paper. Conversely, if you do not have enough water in the brush you will see visible brush stokes on the paper as the hairs separate. Always test the brush load on scrap paper until you have gained the experience necessary to recognize a correctly loaded brush. Finally, do not be alarmed if water and pigment mix and run on your paper in an unexpected, but satisfactory way. Part of the joy of watercolor is the spontaneity in the interaction of pigment, water, and paper. If you require a painting medium over which you have total control that you can apply with absolute precision, see Chapter 13.

WATERCOLOR EXERCISE 1: WATERCOLOR TECHNIQUE

Cut one piece of watercolor paper in half, and tape the two pieces separately to your board or table with masking tape. Make sure the tape goes all the way around the edges of the paper. Organize your paints

Figure 12.1 Watercolor paper taped to the table with tools and materials ready for painting. Twelve circles drawn in pencil on one piece are filled in with masking fluid.

Figure 12.2 Watercolor wash applied to wet paper.

and supplies, and fill two containers with water. Have handy some paper towels or cotton rags and a scrap piece of watercolor paper. You will be experimenting with masking fluid, wet and dry washes, color mixing, layering, detail painting with the round brushes, texturing with the sponge, and spattering. This exercise will take approximately 90 minutes to complete.

On one of the pieces of paper taped to the table, lightly draw 12 circles with the bow compass or circle template and mechanical pencil, as in Figure 12.1. Apply the masking fluid to the circles with a round brush completely filling in each one. You should keep one brush dedicated for masking fluid, and clean it well with running water after use.

Wet and Dry Washes

Washes may be applied to either dry or wet paper. Dry washes are more controlled and have crisp edges. They may be slightly streaky at the areas where brush strokes overlap. A hard edge is impossible to achieve with a wet wash, and the overlapping stokes are smooth and soft with minimal streaking. You will execute a wet wash on the blank piece of paper and a dry wash on the one with the circles and masking fluid.

To prepare, choose a color from those available, and squeeze out a pea-sized amount of color onto your palette. Ultramarine Blue was used for the wash

in Figure 12.2. Moisten a medium-sized round brush with water, and pick up some of the paint and transfer it to a large mixing area of your palette, a large well, or small bowl. You will apply the wash to paper with the 1″ wash brush, so the container or area of your palette must be large enough to accommodate the width of the brush. You need enough wash to completely cover one of your pieces of paper. Use the eyedropper to gradually add water to the paint, mixing them together with the brush between additions. Keep adding water and paint until you have at least a couple of ounces of wash. Test the wash on your scrap paper; it should be translucent enough so that, when dry, it will act as a background for other deeper colors.

Wet the paper with the wash brush using enough water so that the entire sheet is glistening with moisture, but there are no visible puddles. The next step happens quickly; you must apply the wash to the paper while it is still moist. Load the 1″ brush with the mixed color. The brush should be full, but not dripping. Apply the paint to paper using the flat side of the brush. If you are right-handed, start at the top left corner of the paper (the top right if you are left-handed) and pull the brush across the paper horizontally. Start the stroke with very light pressure, increasing the pressure as you move the brush across the paper. You should have enough paint in the brush to complete at least one pass from one side of the paper to the other. When you reach the edge of the paper, reload the brush if necessary. If the brush is still charged with paint at the end of the stroke, flip the brush to the other flat side and complete another pass across the paper, slightly overlapping the first stroke. Continue applying adjacent horizontal strokes, zigzagging down the paper and recharging the brush as necessary. The wet paper helps to keep the pigment moving freely, and blends the strokes together. Each stroke should slightly overlap the previous one, but avoid going over any of the strokes twice. Applying a second coat of paint over a stroke will result in a darker wash in that area. When the entire paper is covered with paint, you can rinse the brush clean and even out the wash if necessary with the damp 1″ brush. Do this with smooth long strokes in the same manner as you applied the wash, without scrubbing at the paper with the brush. Using this technique, you can also create a wash that gets lighter as you move up the paper. Starting with a full load of pigment, lay a horizontal stroke across the bottom of the paper. For each successive pass, dip the brush in water (without rinsing) and apply to the paper.

While the wet wash dries, create a dry wash on the paper with the circles. Mix slightly more pigment than you did for the wet wash because the paint will soak into the dry paper. Use the same application technique as you did for the wet wash, stroking right over the masking fluid covering the circles. Notice that the brush drags less smoothly than on wet paper and the overlap of strokes is more visible. When the paper is covered, smooth the wash with your clean damp 1″ brush using long smooth strokes without going over any particular area more than once.

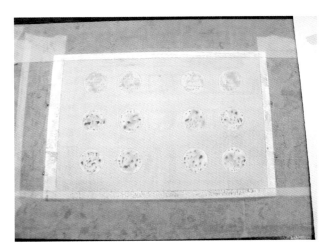

Figure 12.3 Watercolor wash applied to dry paper.

Brush Techniques

Continue with this next part of the exercise after the wet wash is completely dry. The paper is still wet if it is cool to the touch, even though it may appear to be dry. You will be experimenting with the potential and limitations of each of your brushes, and learning the proper amount of paint with which to load each brush to achieve clean, controlled strokes.

Squeeze a small amount of Payne's Gray onto your palette, and using a medium round brush pick up some of the pigment and transfer it to a palette well, scraping off on the edge of the well as much pigment from the brush as possible. Dip it in water (without rinsing or sloshing the brush) to wick some water into the brush, and mix this into the paint.

Continue adding water until the paint is liquid enough to apply smoothly to the paper, but is still nearly opaque. Remove as much paint as you can from the brush by scraping it on the edge of the palette well, and then reload the brush and test the consistency of the paint on scrap paper. Experiment with various strokes with this brush on your good paper, and then do the same with each of your round brushes and bright or one stroke brush. You should be able to make smooth, almost opaque lines and shapes with clean edges. If the strokes have a dry-brush appearance, there is not enough water in the paint and/or there is not enough paint on your brush. If the paint puddles as you first touch the paper with the tip of the brush, there is too much paint on your brush.

Add a little bit more water to the paint well to create a slightly thinner, lighter version of Payne's Gray, and practice various strokes with each of your brushes with this pigment. Repeat the process again, after adding more water to the paint. The brush strokes, although lighter in value and more translucent, should still have clean edges. Finally, try spattering some Payne's Gray on your paper using the toothbrush or small stencil brush. Dip the brush in the diluted paint and wipe most of it off. Hold the brush in one hand, and draw the thumb of the same hand across the bristles over an area of scrap paper. Adjust the amount of paint in the brush and the pressure of your thumb so that the spatter is fine and even. This technique is very useful when creating paint elevations. When you have finished this portion of the exercise, clean your brushes and palette and put fresh water in your containers.

Figure 12.4 Brush techniques.

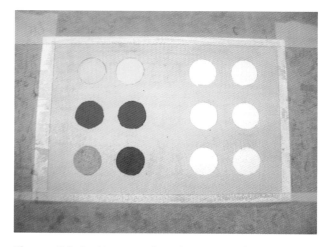

Figure 12.5 Warm and cool primary colors.

Color Mixing

When the paper with the 12 circles is dry, remove the masking fluid by dabbing it with your gum eraser. The frisket will stick to the eraser and lift off. Alternately, you can gently rub the frisket with your finger until it peels off. Put a dab of each of the six (three warm and three cool) primary colors on your palette. The warm yellow is Cadmium Yellow Medium; the cool is either Cadmium Yellow Light or Lemon Yellow. The warm red is either Cadmium Red Light or Cadmium Red Medium, and the cool red is Carmine or Alizarin Crimson. Cobalt Blue is the warm blue and Ultramarine is the cool version. Mix each color down separately with a little water so that the paint is liquid and brushes on smoothly, but the colors are as vibrant as possible. Apply these colors to the circles on your paper as shown in Figure 12.5. For each set of primary colors, the warm is on the left side and the cool is on the right.

Next, mix warm and cool versions of the secondary colors orange, violet, and green. You will be mixing warm primaries with other warm primaries and cool with cool. Keep in mind that because the paints, unlike spectrum colors, are slightly diluted with other hues, the secondary mixes will not be as vibrant as if you used commercially prepared colors in true secondary hues.

When mixing two or more colors together, always start by mixing down with water the less potent of the colors, usually the one that is lightest in value, and then add small amounts of the stronger color until the mix is satisfactory. Place a bit of the

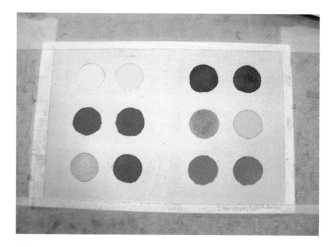

Figure 12.6 Warm and cool primary and secondary colors.

warm yellow (Cadmium Yellow Medium) in a palette well, and mix it down with a little water. Touch the tip of your brush to the warm red (Cadmium Red Medium) and add this tiny amount to the yellow. Continue to add small quantities of the stronger red until you have created the best possible approximation of true orange. If you accidentally add too much red, add more yellow until the orange hue is a good balance between the two primaries. Add more water as necessary to keep the consistency liquid but the color vibrant. Paint the appropriate circle on your color wheel the warm orange color as seen in Figure 12.6.

Mix a cool orange in the same manner, starting with the Cadmium Yellow Light or Lemon Yellow and add the cool orange hue to the color wheel. Continue mixing warm and cool versions of violet and green until the color wheel is complete. Start with red for the violets and yellow for the greens.

WATERCOLOR EXERCISE 2: PAINT ELEVATION

For this exercise, you will be copying a watercolor paint elevation. For best results, read the exercise through before beginning. Transfer the cartoon in Figure 12.7 to your paper, re-scaling it as you prefer, and emulate the watercolor techniques as shown. Each element of the painting was base-coated with a light wash, and then glazes of darker colors were layered on top. All of the washes were applied to dry paper. The lightest highlights were accentuated with white gouache.

Base Coats

Use masking fluid to protect the gold curtain trim, the flowers and stems (but not the vase), the chair legs, and the fireplace andiron. Begin painting by basing in all the non-masked elements of the painting with very light values of color. Mix each color in a separate well with a minimum amount of water, removing some of it to a mixing area of your palette, and thinning it out to the desired consistency as needed. As you add layers, you will be using the same base coat colors but in darker values. Test each color's value and intensity on a piece of scrap paper before applying it to the rendering. The style of this rendering is tight and controlled. To achieve this you must carefully regulate the amount of water and pigment in your brush; as little as possible to make the stroke on the paper without dry brushing.

Mix a tan color using cool yellow and red to make orange, and then add blue to reduce the intensity. Add enough water to make a light-valued wash, and paint the French door (going around the door handle), the wall that contains the French door, and the floor. Apply a light wash of Payne's Gray and black to the fireplace screen, and to the dark area of the mirror. Use a Cobalt Blue wash to base in the upholstered part of the chair, leaving the white of the paper to indicate the highlights on the arms and

top of the chair. Use the same blue to apply a wash to the sky seen through the door, painting around the foliage. Mix Alizarin Crimson with a bit of Payne's Gray to make the curtain base. Base the candlestick, mirror frame, and door hardware in a light wash of Cadmium Yellow Medium. When the sky is dry, use a light wash of Lemon Yellow to base in the foliage. Apply a bit of Lemon Yellow to the flower stems in the vase. While the paint is still wet, brush on a glaze of Cobalt Blue, mixing the colors on the paper to a light green. The vase was painted with Phthalo Turquoise. Make a greenish-blue with Cobalt and a bit of Lemon Yellow to approximate this color, and apply it to the vase as a light wash. Make sure the flower stems are dry before glazing the greenish-blue color over them.

To paint the marble fireplace, dab on some of each of the foliage, fireplace screen, wall, and sky colors in diagonal strokes, leaving some of the white paper showing. The washes on the fireplace should be mostly water, with just a touch of pigment in the wash. Paint the books with a bit of the wall color, leaving some of the white paper showing. Leave the masking fluid in place. The masked-out areas of the painting will be addressed later, after the wall, curtain, floor, and fireplace screen are completed.

Adding Shading and Detail

Notice in the finished rendering that the light source in the room is situated above and to the left of the picture, and the objects are shaded on their right sides. The sunlight coming in through the door is an additional source that casts a shadow from the chair onto the floor. Apply a darker value of the Cobalt Blue to the shaded areas of the chair, and a darker value of the Alizarin Crimson and Payne's Gray mix to the shaded areas of the curtain. Remember that shade is distinct from cast shadow. The cast shadows are added later in a separate step. Mix darker values of the curtain and chair colors by adding a bit of Payne's Gray to each, and apply lowlights in the deepest part of the shaded areas. Wait for each previous layer to dry before adding another glaze. Mix a darker value of the fireplace screen color and shade the right side of each fold. Add an even darker value of the color in the deepest part of each fold. With the same color, paint the crosshatching texture on the screen by squeezing your round brush at the base of the bristles to separate the hairs. With very little

Figure 12.7 Paint elevation cartoon.

Figure 12.8 Finished watercolor paint elevation.

paint in the brush, apply diagonal, dry-brushed strokes to the paper. You can also use a fan brush to create this texture.

Mix a medium-value brown color by combining Burnt Umber and Burnt Sienna. With a small, round brush, paint the grains in the wood floor as individual lines going in the direction of the planks. Thin this color out with some water, and paint a few veins in the marble fireplace by touching the tip of the brush to the paper and dragging the brush away from you. The value of this color should be only slightly darker than the base coat on the fireplace. When the floor graining is dry, glaze some of the individual planks with the watered down graining color. Create another slightly different brown color by adding more Burnt Sienna and glaze the rest floor planks. Use water to vary the value of these two colors to emulate the variety of hue in a real stained wood floor. You can also pick up wet color from the paper with a small sponge, paper towel, or cotton rag to lighten the value in some areas.

With a watered-down version of the fireplace screen color, paint the shaded areas of the marble fireplace: the right-hand planes of the protruding parts and underneath areas of the mantle. Shade the small and large recessed details and the right sides of each carved detail. This glaze should be thin enough to see the marble veins showing through. With the same thin color, shade the right side of each book and the right one-third of the candle. Using a very small brush, paint a thin line of this color along the left edge of the candle. Apply this color to the shaded areas of the glass vase. Paint the color along the left edge of the vase, at the base, and a broader stroke a bit away from the right edge. The lip of the vase should have some shade on the right side as well as under the lip.

Add texture to the door and wall with a darker value of the tan base coat. For the door, brush the wash on in the direction of the grain of the door, going around the door handle; that is, brush vertically on the vertical parts of the door and horizontally on the crosspieces. The brush strokes on the wall can be more random and applied with a nearly dry brush. The wall area is the largest open space in the picture, and a dry brush technique will allow the texture of the paper to add interest to this area. You can also use this tan color on the trunks of the foliage seen through the door. Using the watered-down fireplace screen color, add some shade to the

bottom edge of the door. The left side and bottom reveals of the muttons and mullions. With your 1″ wash brush, dry brush some of this color on the wall, getting darker toward the top of the picture, and where this wall meets the fireplace wall.

Mix a thin green color with yellow and blue and apply this with leaf-shaped dabs of the brush to the foliage, then leave some of the yellow base coat showing through. Paint the front of the upright book on the fireplace with this thin wash, and leave the inset panel as the wall color. Mix a small amount of Cobalt Blue with this color and paint the reflection of the flowers in the mirror as a very thin wash. When the green on the foliage is dry, apply more dabs of a darker version of the same color. Mix a bright orange color with Cadmium Yellow Medium and Cadmium Red Light or Medium for the door handle, candlestick, and mirror frame. Dab the color on with a small round brush, and leave some of the yellow base coat showing. When this layer is dry, mix a thin wash of Burnt Umber and apply it to the shaded areas of these objects.

At this point, remove the masking fluid from the flowers and andiron. Paint the andiron in the same manner as you did the door handle, candlestick, and mirror frame, beginning with the Cadmium Yellow Medium base coat. Paint the stems and leaves of the flowers with a thin wash of the green foliage color, and the flowers with light Lemon Yellow, leaving some of the white paper showing through on the petals. Add a layer of darker green foliage color with a bit of added Ultramarine to the flower stems and leaves, and add some dabs of Cadmium Yellow Medium and bright orange to the flower petals. With a watery Lemon Yellow color, add the reflection of the flower petals to the mirror.

Highlights and Cast Shadows

Squeeze some Zinc White gouache, which will cover a darker layer beneath it, onto your palette and transfer a small amount on your brush to a mixing area. Add some water and mix until the paint is slightly translucent. Brush this mix onto the left side of the vase lip in one stroke, and down the left side of the body of the vase just left of center. Add more Zinc White gouache to your mix until it is opaque but still brushes on smoothly, and add a zinger to the lip and body of the vase. Add zingers to the door handle, andiron, candlestick, mirror frame, and raised carved areas of the fireplace.

Mix a translucent wash of Payne's Gray for the cast shadow, and test its consistency by washing over an area of dry paint on your scrap paper. You should be able to see through the wash. Cast shadows appear in the rendering on the wall to the right side of the curtain, on the curtain below the tie back sash, and on the curtain below the valance. This shadow conforms to the curves of the folds of fabric. There is a cast shadow on the floor beneath the chair and on the fireplace screen cast from the andiron. Additional cast shadows appear on the chair, on the book lying open on the chair, beneath the mantle and protruding parts of the fireplace, and on the fireplace wall from the vase. The vase shadow also hits the books stacked on the mantle. Brush the shadow color on the floor around the chair, leaving some of the brown color of the floor showing to indicate an area of sunlight streaming through the French door. Glaze this highlighted area with a light wash of Cadmium Yellow Medium when the shadow color has dried.

Now you are nearly done. Remove the masking fluid from the curtain and the chair legs and brush a light wash of Cadmium Yellow Medium on the curtain trim. Accentuate the fringe and tie back details with Burnt Umber applied with a small round brush. Base-coat the chair legs in a light wash of the wall base color. When dry, glaze over the legs with a light wash of Burnt Umber mixed with a small amount of Payne's Gray. Add shading and detail to the legs with a darker version of this color. Accentuate the claw feet and carved detail with Payne's Gray, and finally, apply subtle highlights with Zinc White gouache.

Chapter 13

Gouache

Like watercolor, gouache is water-soluble, not water-resistant, and dries to a matte finish. Dry gouache will reactivate to malleable wet paint when water is added. Despite these similarities, the technique of painting with gouache is very different than that of watercolor.

Gouache is opaque and much thicker than watercolor. Whereas a layer of watercolor reveals and visually blends with a layer below it, a layer of gouache completely conceals all layers underneath, because gouache sits on the surface of the paper and other paint layers rather than soaking in. A layer of gouache applied over the same color paint will look exactly like the first layer, while a second coat of the same color will darken the value of the hue when working with watercolors. This opaque quality allows you to paint light colors over dark, so it is not necessary to work from light to dark, or to mask out light areas with frisket before applying a dark layer or cut around them with a darker color.

Watercolor paintings are typically produced on white paper because any other color will show through the paint and affect the appearance of the finished work. With gouache, the paper color is not visible where paint has been applied. This is a useful trait that can be exploited by choosing a paper color that will complement the rendering color scheme. You can choose paper that will be an attractive background color for a costume design rendering, for example, or a midtoned value of a dominant color in your rendering.

There are two basic differences between the technique of gouache painting and that of watercolor. First, gouache paint is applied to the paper in solid layers, not as translucent glazes. Although gouache can be diluted to a glaze with enough water, the paint is grittier than watercolor and may contain white pigment, making it unsuitable for translucent techniques. Second, watercolors are diluted with water allowing the white of the paper to lighten the value of a color, while white paint is added to gouache to create light values.

When first beginning to work with gouache, the most important thing to master is the ability to create completely flat, smooth fields of color with the paints. Good technique is achieved by understanding the proper amount of water to add to the paints and the correct quantity of paint to load into the brush. To obtain perfect color fields, the consistency of the paint must be thick enough to be as opaque as possible, but thin enough to flow easily. To minimize brushstrokes, the brush must be loaded with enough paint to cover the paper efficiently, but not so much that ridges of paint are visible in the color field. Your ability to produce flat, richly colored surfaces will be impaired if you use inexpensive brands of gouache.

Most cheaply made brands do not contain enough concentrated pigment to be truly opaque. Usually white paint is added for better opacity, but the white paint lightens the value of the pigments and reduces intensity. Buy Winsor & Newton paints as described in the list in the Tools and Materials section.

Scenic paint is quite similar to gouache, especially the casein formulas such as Iddings Deep Colors, distributed by Rosco. It dries to a flat, non-reflective surface, and, like gouache, it is not water-resistant. Off Broadway, made by Rosco, and Artist's Choice, made by Sculptural Arts Coating, Inc., are scenic paints that also dry to a matte finish, but have a vinyl acrylic binder and are water-resistant when dry. Iddings, Off Broadway, and Artist's Choice are all available in test kits that include from 23 to 30 different colors packaged in 1-ounce plastic jars. These paints can be used like gouache or watercolor. They are perfect for rendering paint elevations, because you can work out painting techniques in miniature with the same paint that the scenic artists will be using when they paint the set.

TOOLS AND MATERIALS

An introductory set of gouache paints made by
  Winsor & Newton containing Zinc White,
  Yellow Ochre, Ultramarine, Spectrum Red,
  Primary Yellow, Primary Red, Primary Blue,
  Permanent Yellow Deep, Ivory Black, and
  Brilliant Green
Waterproof black ink
One pad or block of heavyweight hot press or
  lightly textured cold press watercolor paper, such
  as Arches or Strathmore, or illustration board
  approximately 12 × 18"
Four pointed round brushes, sizes 3, 6, 10, and 12
One flat or one stroke brush in size 6 or 8
One white plastic or enamel palette
Masking tape
Soft cotton rags or paper towels
Two cups or containers for water
Eyedropper
12" ruler
.05 mm mechanical pencil
Circle template

GOUACHE EXERCISE 1: BASIC TECHNIQUES

A smooth surface is best for gouache rendering. You can use the same paper as you did for watercolor if it is lightly textured or smooth. If your watercolor paper is heavily textured, you will need to purchase smoother watercolor paper or use illustration board. Illustration board is heavy enough that it remains flat without assistance, but if you are using watercolor paper you will have to tape it down as you did for the watercolor exercises.

Gouache Color Chart

On one piece of paper or board, lightly draw ten rectangles with the ruler and mechanical pencil as shown in Figure 13.1. Paint a $1/_8$-inch wide stripe of waterproof black ink perpendicularly across one end of the set of rectangles. Use a cork-backed ruler as a lining stick. It holds the ruler edge a bit off the paper and prevents the ink from bleeding underneath the ruler. The ink will dry permanently, and, when painted over with gouache, will indicate the opacity of your color fields.

Below the rectangles, draw two 2-inch squares and one cube in two-point perspective as shown in Figure 13.1.

Squeeze some pigment from your tube of Zinc White gouache into a palette well. You will need more paint for the same area of coverage than when painting with watercolors. Add a few drops of water to the paint and mix. Remove excess paint from the brush on the edge of the palette well, and test the consistency and quantity of paint in the brush on a piece of scrap paper. The paint should brush on smoothly, and the paper should not be visible beneath the strokes. Adjust the amount of water and the amount of paint in the brush, if necessary.

Using your one stroke or bright brush, paint in the far left rectangle. Continue painting the rectangles from the left side of the paper in order of lightest to darkest value: Primary Yellow, Permanent Yellow Deep, Yellow Ochre, Spectrum Red, Primary Red, Primary Blue, Brilliant Green, Ultramarine, and Ivory Black. If you are left-handed, you may choose to begin with the darkest value and work toward the right. Check the opacity of your color fields by examining the ink stripe. Notice that some colors are inherently more opaque than others. Keep in mind that the paint will appear lighter in value when it is dry, and that if gouache is applied too heavily to the paper it will crack when it dries.

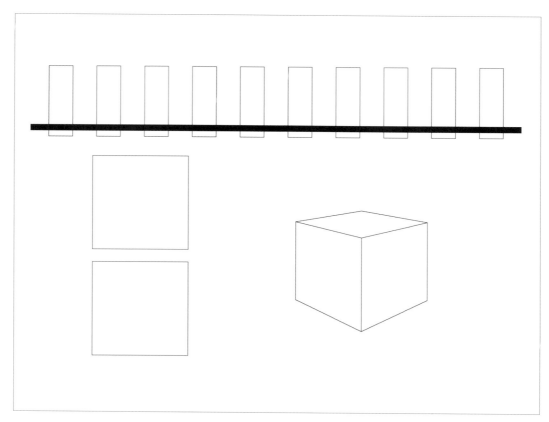

Figure 13.1 Gouache Exercise 1 layout.

Figure 13.2 Gouache color chart.

Mixing and Layering

Using Ivory Black and Zinc White, mix three values of gray—#2, #4, and #6 on the gray scale. Use the same mixing and application techniques as you did in making the color chart. Paint the top face of the cube the #2 gray with your bright brush or one stroke, and the other two faces the #4 and #6 values, respectively.

Next, paint one of the squares Ultramarine and the other Yellow Ochre. Make sure to mix enough paint to cover the area inside the squares, plus some extra paint for layering. When the Ultramarine is dry and no longer cool to the touch, lightly draw a one-inch circle in the center of the square using your pencil and circle template. Paint the circle Yellow Ochre using one of your round brushes. The paint should be applied with light pressure to create a layer

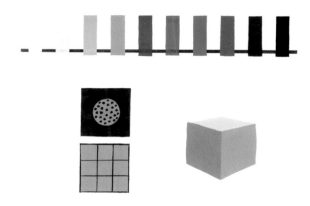

Figure 13.3 Squares and cube painted in gouache.

of paint that sits on top of the Ultramarine layer. Heavy pressure may reactivate the under layer and cause the two colors to blend. When the square painted Yellow Ochre is dry, trisect the square vertically and horizontally with pencil lines using the ruler. With a small round brush, paint the lines and outline the square in Ultramarine gouache. Returning to the square with the circle painted Yellow Ochre, apply small dots of Ultramarine paint, as in Figure 13.3.

GOUACHE EXERCISE 2: COSTUME RENDERING

In this exercise you will be copying a costume rendering of the character Marcellus from William Shakespeare's *Hamlet*. The original rendering was executed on Crescent 300 cold press medium weight illustration board. Any smooth-surfaced, heavyweight paper or board is suitable for this exercise. Lighter weight papers or boards tend to curl as the thick paint dries on the surface.

Transfer the cartoon in Figure 13.5 to your paper, resizing it if you wish. Apply soft graphite to the back of the cartoon or back it with graphite transfer paper. Tape the cartoon in place on the board carefully tracing over the cartoon with a mechanical pencil; alternatively, the designer recommends a fine point ballpoint pen that has run out of ink. With pencil and ruler, draw a rectangle around the figure about an inch from the edges of the board so as to form an attractive composition with slightly

more paper space under the figure's feet than above his head. Taping the outside of the rectangle with masking tape, if you wish, will keep the border of your rendering straight and clean. Add the trees, ground, and moon that appear in the finished rendering, lightly sketching them in pencil on your board. Have a scrap piece handy of the same type of paper or board you are using for the rendering to use for testing paint consistency and color.

Paint the backgrounds first, beginning with the sky. Mix a medium-dark gray with Zinc White and Ivory Black, making sure to mix enough paint to cover the whole area of the rendering (except the figure). You will generate the paint for the trees and ground from this original color. Test the consistency of your paint for smoothness and opacity on the scrap piece of board before applying it to the rendering. Then, starting at the top of the board, paint the sky, carefully painting around the figure, trees, and moon.

Next, mix the ground color by adding enough Zinc White to the original color to make a new color that is several steps lighter in value. Paint the ground in the same manner as you did the sky, keeping the color fields distinct from each other. As the sword blade is the same color as the ground, paint it in now while the color is handy. The highlight on the blade can either be painted in with Zinc White, or you can leave that area unpainted, letting the white of the paper create the highlight. Now mix a new color by adding a bit of Yellow Ochre to the left over ground color, and use it to paint the base color of the trees and the moon. When the trees are dry, paint the bark details with Ivory Black.

Start the figure by painting the face and hands. Mix a flesh tone for Marcellus with Zinc White and small amounts of Yellow Ochre and Spectrum Red. If the color appears too bright, add a tiny amount of Winsor Blue to reduce the intensity. Paint the hands as solid color fields. Paint the face by going around the eyes, nose, and mouth. Put some of the flesh color into a separate well in your palette. Add more Zinc White to create a tint that is about two steps lighter than the original color, and paint in the nose and eyelids. Add a tiny bit of Spectrum Red to this tint and paint in the lips.

Now add detail to the face. Mix a warm, reddish brown with Yellow Ochre, Winsor Blue, Spectrum Red, and Ivory Black. Shade the contour of the left cheek with the brown hue, feathering the color out toward the nose. Outline the lower edge of the

Figure 13.4 Cartoon of Marcellus for *Hamlet*. Costume design and rendering by Al Tucci.

Figure 13.5 Finished rendering of Marcellus.

upper eyelid and define the lower lid. Paint the pupil, the nostrils, and the inside of the mouth, going around the teeth. Mix some Primary Blue and Zinc White with a bit of the warm brown to create the beard color. Brush this color into the lower face. You can also use this color to outline the lips and, when the beard is dry, stipple it onto the beard area. Paint the eyebrows in with Ivory Black. Also use the black to add shade to the insides of the nostrils and mouth. Finally, add a dot of Zinc White to the pupils.

Next paint Marcellus' garment. The lighter, fur-like area of the garment is based in a color very similar to the original flesh color, but with a bit more Yellow Ochre added. Mix up a good amount of this color and paint the furry areas of the coat, hat, leggings, and boots. Mix some Primary Blue into what is left of this color, and paint the darker ochre areas of the garment, going around the brown trims and details. Mix a warm medium brown as you did for the shading on the face, but without the addition of Ivory Black, and paint the trims and buttons on the coat, the stripes on the hat and scarf, and the hilt of the sword. Make this color darker by adding a bit of Ivory Black and add shading to trims and buttons. Mix a medium gray with Zinc White and Ivory Black. Add detail to the fur with this color by touching the tip of a small round brush to the board and lifting up quickly making hair-like marks. Use this color to add wrinkles and pleats to the garment, and to define the boots. Finally, add more hair-like marks to the fur with Zinc White.

Chapter 14

Mixed Media

Many designers prefer to render with a variety of color mediums simultaneously. The advantages to mixing media are greater speed of execution and the ability to choose particular techniques in which you are proficient. For example, if you enjoy watercolor washes but become frustrated with detailed brush-work, you can achieve faster and more accurate results by putting in large areas of color with water-color wash, and then using colored pencil or marker for the details.

The exercises in this chapter each combine at least two different color mediums that have been previously discussed in this book. For each exercise, black line cartoons and finished color renderings of either set or costume designs are provided, or, if you prefer, you can use your own designs. If you use the provided renderings, you can scale them to the size you prefer.

MIXED MEDIA EXERCISE 1: SET DESIGN RENDERING IN MARKER AND COLORED PENCIL ON VELLUM

The basis for mastering the combined use of these two media are the notions that colored pencil has excellent coverage over a base of marker, and that markers can dissolve colored pencil pigment. As discussed in Chapter 9, it takes time and effort to cover a large area of paper with colored pencils. The broad

tip of a marker, however, can accomplish this quickly. Using the two media in combination you can lay down a base of marker for large color fields and then tone them, add highlights, shading, and fine details with colored pencils. You can also smooth and blend the pencil strokes with a clear blender marker or denatured alcohol.

It is recommended that you practice combining the media first on a piece of scrap vellum before beginning the rendering. Experiment with layering and blending, and the degree of coverage you can achieve with different colors over others. You will need the tools and materials listed for both colored pencils and marker.

Photocopy the black line drawing and scale it to the desired size. Tape the copy in place on the table and place a piece of translucent vellum over it. Tape one edge of the vellum to the table to prevent it from shifting. There is no need to transfer the drawing to the vellum because you can see the cartoon through the paper. To create the set rendering depicted in Figure 14.2, the scenic elements were base-coated in markers using light tints of yellow and orange and light to medium tints of cool and warm gray. The yellow and orange were used for the translucent roof, practical lamps, the areas of wall and set illuminated by the lamps, and the front edge of the stage. The rest of the set including walls, floor, and furniture were based in light to medium warm and cool grays. Remember that a clear blender or denatured alcohol

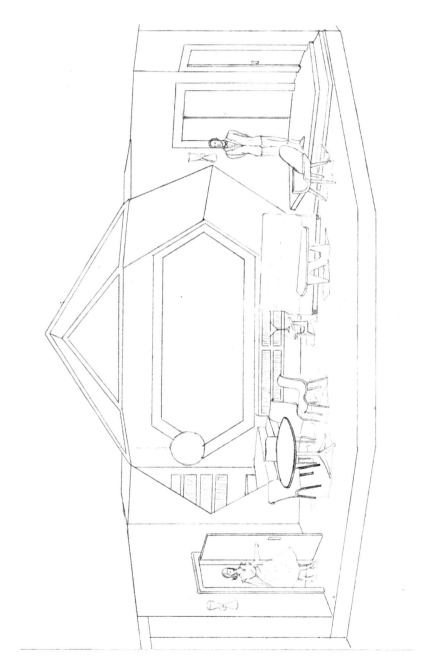

Figure 14.1 Black line drawing of set rendering designed by Clare Rowe for *Rain, Some Fish, No Elephants.*

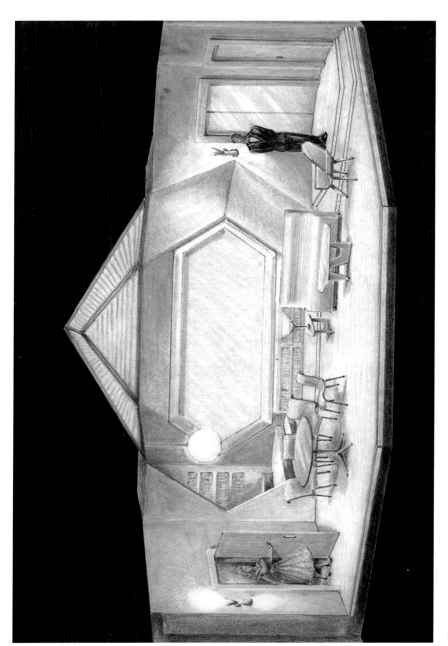

Figure 14.2 Finished set rendering in marker and colored pencil designed by Clare Rowe for *Rain, Some Fish, No Elephants.*

can create a lighter tint of a darker one. If you have only a dark red marker, you can thin it out to a tint by picking up some of the color with the clear blender or cotton swab dipped in alcohol. Alternately, you can apply a saturated coat of color to the back of the translucent paper, which will diffuse and soften the color when seen from the front.

Colored pencil was then added over the marker base and smoothed with the clear blender. Cut lines were put in last with the fine point of a dark gray marker. The figures were rendered similarly, although most of the detail is colored pencil. The surrounding black off-stage space is indicated with black marker.

MIXED MEDIA EXERCISE 2: COSTUME DESIGN RENDERING IN MARKER, COLORED PENCIL, AND INK ON VELLUM

This exercise, in addition to marker and colored pencil, also incorporates the use of very fine point ink pens in red and black.

Photocopy the black line drawing and place it under a piece of translucent vellum. Have another piece of vellum handy on which to test colors and techniques. Create the skin tones by putting down a Dark Umber base and then pull the highlights out with a cotton swab dipped in a small amount of denatured alcohol. Use Tuscan Red to color the lips, and shade the contours of the face, neck, and arms with Sepia colored pencil. The eyes are Sepia and Black colored pencil.

Color the apron, starting with the lightest hue, Peach, and then add the broader stripes in Light Umber. The very thin stripes in the apron pattern are red ink applied with a fine point pen, which is also used to define the bottom ruffle on the apron. Red ink is also used, along with Sepia colored pencil, to outline the figure and add detail in the face. Red and black ink creates the wisps of hair at the neck.

The dress (except for the Peach marker on the color) hair, and shoes are base-coated on the front of the paper with Sienna Brown and then darkened by applying Black to these areas on the back of the paper. Texturing and shading is done with Sepia colored pencil.

Finally, the background floor is put in on the back of the paper with 60 percent French Gray and

blended out to the sides with a foam eye shadow brush moistened with denatured alcohol.

MIXED MEDIA EXERCISE 3: COSTUME DESIGN RENDERING IN GOUACHE, WATERCOLOR, COLORED PENCIL, AND SILVER GEL PEN ON WATERCOLOR PAPER

This exercise combines gouache, watercolor, and colored pencil and includes the use of a silver gel pen (available at art and craft stores) for the metallic details. If you do not have a silver gel pen, you can use a silver or light gray colored pencil or light gray marker. The gouache was used to make the rich, dark color field and dark linear details of the skirt. Watercolor washes were used for the skin tones and the shading and shadows in the skirt. Details were defined with colored pencil and gel pen.

Transfer the black line drawing to a piece of watercolor paper by applying graphite to the back of a photocopy of the drawing, place it over the paper, and lightly trace over the image with a .05 mechanical pencil. Paint the violet watercolor background square first. Use frisket to create the sharp edges of the background by applying a strip of the masking fluid on the outside edges of the square. Also, mask the upper body of the character and the contours of the skirt with frisket. It is not necessary to mask the eyeglasses in the figure's right hand or the eyeglass chain. When the masking fluid is dry, create a wet wash with violet watercolor by wetting the background area with water, apply a small amount of pigment toward the sides of the square, and then blend out the paint with your 1″ wash brush saturated with just water and no pigment. Allow the background to dry completely before removing the frisket with a gum eraser and continue with the rendering.

Using watercolor, mix a very light wash for the skin tone with Cadmium Yellow Medium, tiny amounts each of Cadmium Red Medium and Ultramarine, and water. Apply the wash to the face and arms. While the skin color is drying, mix a dark navy color with Ultramarine and Ivory Black gouache. Apply this color to the solid panels of dark blue on the sleeves and skirt. The highlights in these dark areas will be added later. Using a small round brush, use the dark navy gouache to paint in the line work in the skirt and bodice, including the horizontal, vertical, and diagonal lines defining the ruffles

Figure 14.3 Black line drawing of costume design by Adam Dill of Mattie for *Joe Turner's Come and Gone*.

Figure 14.4 Finished costume design rendering by Adam Dill of Mattie for *Joe Turner's Come and Gone.*

Figure 14.5 Black line drawing of costume design by Kyle Schellinger of Miss Trafalgar Gower for *Trelawny of the "Wells."*

Figure 14.6 Finished costume design rendering of Miss Trafalgar Gower by Kyle Schellinger for *Trelawny of the "Wells."*

and the line work in the rosettes. Use the same color to outline and crosshatch the hair net.

Next, put the details on the face, shading with a darker value of the skin tone. Mix small bit of Alizarin Crimson for the lip color, and paint the lips in with your smallest brush. Outline the lips with a dark value, and create a highlight on the lower lip with a lighter value of the color. The mousy brown color of the hair can literally be dirty water from your rinse container applied with a brush, or a very light wash of Burnt Umber and Ultramarine watercolor. Using this same color, either rinse water or mixed color, paint in the eyebrows and wrinkles in the face with your smallest round brush.

Next, create the shading and cast shadows in the skirt. With a medium round brush loaded with nothing but water, draw the brush across the horizontal divisions between the ruffles in the lower skirt. The water will slightly reactivate the gouache line work, creating a shadow effect. Continue using water to add shadows and shading to all of the ruffled areas to emulate the finished rendering in Figure 14.6. Notice that the light source is situated above and to the left of the figure so the skirt is more deeply shadowed on the right side. To re-create this, start the shading on the left side of the figure and work toward the right without rinsing the wet brush. The shading will become increasingly darker as it reactivates the gouache paint. With the same brush containing reactivated gouache, put some navy blue shade into the shawl and handkerchief.

Now, finish painting the dress. Mix a lighter shade of your original navy blue gouache by adding more Ultramarine, and paint some streaks of this color as a highlight into the dark color fields of the skirt. Use a brush loaded with only water and pull away some of the color in the dark navy fields to create zingers in the dress, mopping the water up with a small sponge, paper towel, or cotton rag. When this step has dried, add the white swooshes with Zinc White gouache.

To finish the rendering, use colored pencil to add definition as necessary. Use black pencil to define the hand holding the handkerchief, around the eyes, and to color in the pupils. Color the eyeglasses and chain, bracelet, and necklace with the silver gel pen, and add highlights to these areas with Zinc White gouache.

Try all the different mediums described in this chapter, and others you are interested in that are not mentioned here. When using a medium for the first time, experiment with all the things it can do. As in many of the exercises in this chapter, make a color chart and then test the translucency and opacity of the medium, its layering capacities, and experiment with the specific tools used to apply the medium. Find your own best medium or media, and create your own style by experimenting with different combinations. Do not hesitate to change mediums according to the play you are designing. Different mediums naturally seem right for different plays or musicals.

Chapter 15

Designer Renderings

This chapter contains numerous examples of student and professional costume, set, and lighting design renderings. As a supplement to the detailed exercises in this book, it is recommended that, after completing the drawing and painting sections, you copy some of these renderings to enhance your own rendering skills.

Of all the theatrical design areas, costume design remains the one that utilizes the least technology. Although this may change in the future, computer software for creating costume designs is not particularly popular with many costume designers. Therefore, it is crucial for costume designers to hone their skills in figure drawing and figure painting, fabric illustration, and the techniques of illustrating how various fabrics drape on the human body.

Unlike costume rendering, advancements in computer software have revolutionized the way many scenic designers create renderings and paint elevations. The time-consuming process of manually generating a three-dimensional sketch from a two-dimensional ground plan has been simplified and speeded up by the capabilities of drafting software such as Vector-Works. VectorWorks enables you to easily draw and print a three-dimensional black line drawing of your set in perspective and creates the cartoon for your hand-painting rendering or paint elevation.

Lighting designers are dependent on scenic designers to provide three-dimensional draftings of the scenery to create lighting design renderings. Many contemporary lighting designers prefer to use computer software to generate lighting design renderings, but some still prefer to render in conventional color mediums. I recommend first learning the traditional painting techniques to create lighting renderings before switching to computer-generated images, because this progression will enhance your ability to manipulate color and understand value and intensity of color, three-dimensional modeling, and depth of field.

Figure 15.1 Set rendering by Peter Beudert for *Pygmalion*.

Figure 15.2 Costume rendering of Esmeralda by Patrick Holt for *Camino Real*.

Romeo and Juliet V, i
LD: Kalliope Vlahos

Figure 15.3 Lighting rendering for *Romeo and Juliet* by Kaliope Vlahos with scenic design by Courtland Jones.

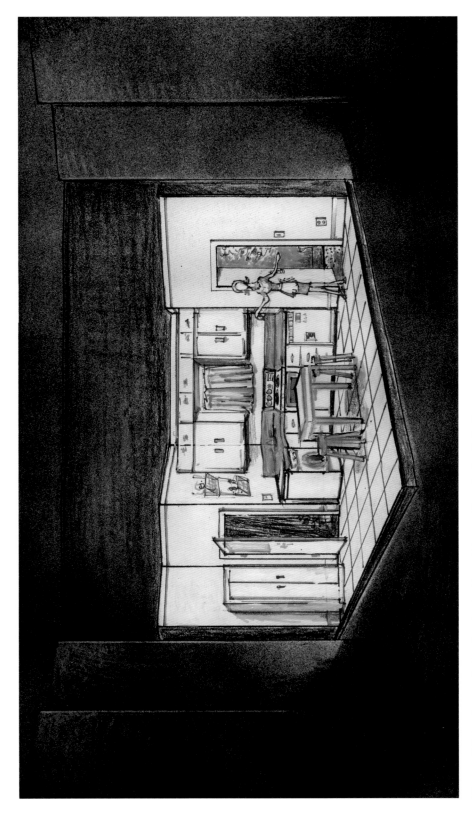

Figure 15.4 Set rendering for Act I, *Absurd Person Singular* by Sally Day.

Figure 15.5 Set rendering for Act III, *Absurd Person Singular* by Sally Day.

Figure 15.6 Costume rendering by Adam Dill.

TWELFTH NIGHT II v.   WHAT EMPLOYMENT HAVE WE HERE?

Figure 15.7 Set rendering for *Twelfth Night* by Clare Rowe.

Figure 15.8 Costume rendering by James H. Hopkins.

Figure 15.9 Costume rendering by James H. Hopkins.

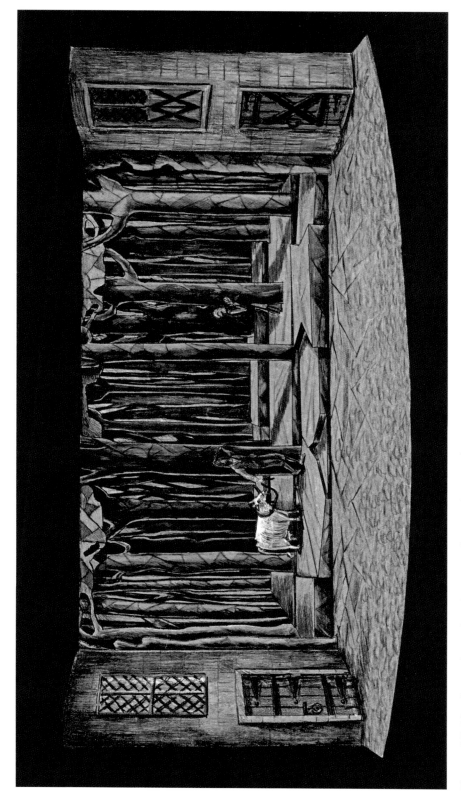

Figure 15.10 Set rendering by Clare Rowe for *Into the Woods.*

Figure 15.11 Costume rendering by Al Tucci.

Figure 15.12 Preliminary sketch by Peter Beudert for *Miss Julie.*

Figure 15.13 Costume rendering by Eugenia Furneaux-Arends.

Figure 15.14 Lighting sketch by Derek Warrick.

Figure 15.15 Set rendering by Melanie Rentschler.

Figure 15.16 Set rendering by Bruce Brockman for *Three Sisters*.

Figure 15.17 Costume rendering of the Gravedigger by Patrick Holt for *Hamlet*.

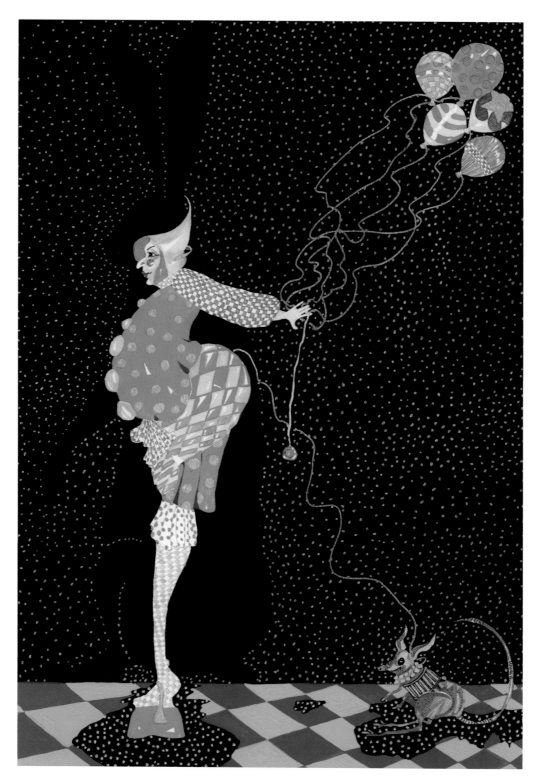

Figure 15.18 Costume rendering by Al Tucci.

Figure 15.19 Set rendering by Peter Beudert for *Guys and Dolls.*

Figure 15.20 Paint elevation by Clare Rowe.

Figure 15.21 Costume rendering by Kyle Schellinger.

Figure 15.22 Paint elevation by Bruce Brockman for *Oklahoma*.

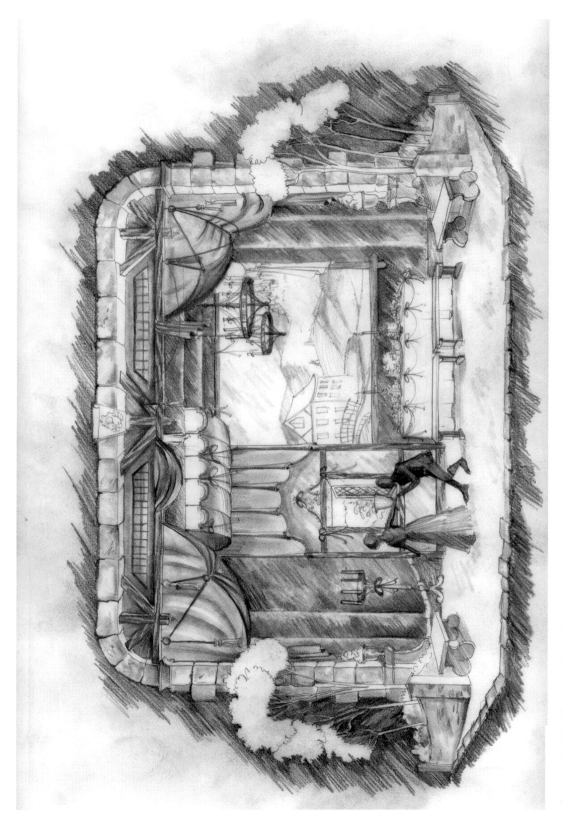

Figure 15.23 Sketch by Bruce Brockman for *The Elixir of Love.*

Figure 15.24 Costume rendering of Richard for *Richard III* by Patrick Holt.

Figure 15.25 Lighting rendering by Julie Mack for *Romeo and Juliet.*

Figure 15.26 Lighting rendering by Julie Mack for *A View From the Bridge*.

Figure 15.27 Lighting rendering by Julie Mack for *A View From the Bridge.*

Figure 15.28 Drop paint elevation by J Branson for *Stones in His Pocket.*

Chapter 16

Digital Drawing

The art tools used to create and communicate a stage designer's visual idea have changed radically within the span of a generation. New digital drawing tools are widespread in all fields of theatrical design as well as many fields of art. These digital tools are new to us not having undergone centuries of gradual development. Using today's digital tools requires learning the tool itself as well as how to draw or paint. It also means that digital tools can (and they will) change significantly from year to year. Pencils have changed little in my career; however, I cannot say the same for the software I use.

Some theatrical designers have thoroughly accepted digital computer-based drawing as a satisfying and useful means to generate paint elevations, renderings, and models. Some theatrical designers consciously reject using digital tools. The presence of the computer in a studio as an artistic tool is difficult for some to accept, but the computer is a presence that will not disappear. Like it or not, the computer is here and the ability to use it efficiently and effectively is a marketable skill, just like traditional drafting, model-making, and rendering.

Computer tools have replaced traditional drawing tools for many artists. It is one of the most profound and rapid changes to how artists express their ideas. Digital drawing tools remove the "barrier" of drawing for some artists and opening alternative methods of self-expression. This is most

obvious with student artists who find a computer is a much easier means to an end. The thorough integration of computer-aided design (CAD) for lighting designers, scenic designers, and technicians into the industry is the clearest example of how profoundly the computer has changed how individuals approach drawing. Many students and professionals see traditional drafting as a quaint, archaic, and somewhat bothersome craft.

This change poses several challenges for educators. Many believe that traditional drawing is an irreplaceable skill and that work done on computer is less artistically valid. Many students feel that using a computer is the only way to work and traditional drawing is unnecessarily difficult and limiting. For some, the act of teaching digital drawing is challenging because they need to fully educate themselves in a new medium before being able to teach digital drawing. Instructing those on a computer requires new classroom techniques and new classrooms as well. For others, the very expense of digital tools is an impossible barrier.

Nothing replaces traditional drawing and painting. These skills are necessary for theatrical artists, particularly when learning to harness a computer into a useful tool. Beginning to use a computer as a drawing tool is infinitely easier and more successful if you have good fundamental art skills. Poor drawing skills are not improved by using a computer, and it is more difficult to learn to draw on a computer than by hand. The skills of drawing and painting are still requirements for making good art no matter the medium.

There was a time when digitally created rendering and paint elevations were not appreciated by scenic artists, and for good reason. Few scenic designers could match competent traditional work on the best computer equipment. Many young designers took to computers in lieu of traditional tools with poor results thus giving digital work a bad reputation. Inevitably, the equipment required for good digital work became much more affordable and many talented, established theatrical designers were drawn to the benefits of digital drawing. Digital work was common by the beginning of the 21st century and, by the second decade, will probably be ubiquitous.

Digital drawing and painting has great strengths. Digital drawing for a theatrical designer is so convenient that it is no surprise that many designers prefer to work with a computer instead of with conventional drawing tools. Anything created on a computer can be very easily duplicated and shared. Making a change or an alteration to a digital drawing is infinitely easier than with a traditionally made drawing or painting. Do you have a backdrop paint elevation that is slightly too small, too dark, too green, too pale? It is far easier to digitally change it than re-paint it. Need to send a copy from Miami to a director in San Francisco and a shop in Connecticut? That can be done instantly over e-mail. If you wish to change a single color or all the color, move an object, add or delete lines, or remove an error, it can all be done easily on a computer. With vector-based images objects can be manipulated in space with ease. Objects can go from foreground to background, appear closer, rotate to reveal another surface, or move in any way the artist wishes. Mistakes can be eliminated instantly from a digital drawing as well. In theory, every digitally generated drawing should be absolutely perfect and remain perfect when stored.

The irresistible appeal of digital drawings lies not only in the conveniences just mentioned as much as it does in the artistic tools it provides the scenic designer. The ability to make a collage image is extremely effective and simple with digital tools. Collages further benefit by virtue of adjustable transparency between layers and visual elements. Any element within a drawing can repeat itself with great ease and total accuracy. The use of text and lettering

in digital images is infinitely more accurate and convenient than by traditional means. Once one understands the powerful ability to layer drawings in Adobe Photoshop and other applications, a new approach to "painting" begins to coalesce in the artist's imagination.

Computer drawing and painting has great drawbacks though. One of these is the relatively great expense of the equipment and software. A good set of digital drawing tools is far more expensive than a good set of traditional drawing tools. One needs significantly more technical knowledge to get a good set of digital tools than with more conventional tools. After all, it is pretty easy to buy a pencil, a few brushes, and a Rosco Supersat paint sample kit without getting something useless, let alone spending thousands of dollars. It is not so easy when getting started with digital tools. The initial investment is sizable and the need to keep up-to-date with software can be a significant additional expenditure. The first computer and software purchase involves many important decisions that may take a bit of research on the buyer's part. If you do not have an adequate working knowledge of some of the applications you wish to use then you have to take time learning them, which can be a great challenge while trying to generate paint elevations for a production. Rarely does one have a lot of time to spend to learn software, and it often does take a good amount of time to truly learn it.

There are much more profound drawbacks to digital drawing and painting beyond issues of cost and convenience. Digital drawing is limiting in many crucial artistic ways. A mouse or trackball are awful drawing tools. A digital drawing tablet is a big step forward, but still very awkward relative to a pencil or a brush. Pastel or charcoal on paper has a wonderful textural connection to drawing no computer can give, yet. No printer can match the range of colors possible from a good set of watercolor or gouache. Computer-generated images are very deceptive to the viewer in terms of scale. It is far easier to sketch a scenic design on a sheet of paper than to try to start from scratch on a computer. I find I understand scale intuitively on paper. No computer, yet, gives an artist the equivalent of a pencil and blank paper. Simple pencil and paper is still, for me, the tool to create and dream. Turning a sketch into something more presentable can be easily done on a computer. Creating that sketch, especially when working in scale, is very difficult on a computer.

This book is about the acquisition of skills. We hope to give a good starting point for training and working in digital media for theatrical artists in the discussion of what tools to use for the best results in digital drawing and how to put these tools to work.

DIGITAL DRAWING EQUIPMENT

Digital rendering requires a considerable investment in computing equipment such as hardware, peripherals, and software. The investment is much greater than buying paint and brushes. Digital tools are convenient, but not inexpensive. You may easily spend as much for a software upgrade in a year as you would for all other traditional drawing and painting tools combined. Such expenses are common and unavoidable and the artist must be prepared to fully commit to the costs of the necessary tools. This is especially true because of the very convenience that digital tools offer: the ability to easily distribute and share work. It is essential to remain as up to date with the equipment and software as all potential collaborators.

Extremely good quality computing hardware and peripherals are increasingly affordable and constantly improving. This allows the buyer to get much more "bang for the buck," but the expense is still considerable. Software costs have not lowered in the same manner for full versions of high-end applications. In fact, software prices are generally higher than they were 5 or 10 years ago whereas computers are much better for less. Upgrading any software is not a minor expense. The initial purchase of drawing, drafting, and modeling applications is certainly more costly than the computer equipment itself. The initial cost of software is the greatest because the purchaser is entitled to subsequently purchase a less costly upgrade to maintain a current version.

Not only is the investment onerous it is ongoing. No computing system can be expected to last more than five years. It is not because the computer itself wears out, but because the computer's operating system and processor become outdated relative to the current software. Digital drawing software tools require an efficient operating environment. As operating systems developers improve and update their product to most efficiently use new hardware, software developers keep pace. Compare any widely used computer or piece of software to its equivalent from five years ago. My drafting software has changed three times, painting software at least as many times, modeling software also three times and any five-year-old computer cannot adequately drive the newest versions of any this software. A drawing made with five-year software might need some translation if sent from a designer to a scenic studio that had up-to-date computing tools. Owning current software is a professional necessity.

Computers

There is a fundamental decision to make when choosing a computer, which is between Apple products and their operating system and the more widely accepted PC Windows environment. Apple, which manufactures Macintosh computers, has created a range of computers that are widely used by many artists. The Apple operating system is proprietary and only Apple hardware can drive it. This means that less software is available for Macs than Windows machines, but most software aimed at artists is available for the Mac, if not developed for the Mac. The popular belief is that Macs are for artists. This is a drastic oversimplification of a complex discussion. It is true that Apple has developed a successful combination of hardware and software to make formerly very expensive digitally-based artistic practices (digital photography, film-making, music-making, and painting to name a few) available and easy at a very affordable cost. But Apple by no means has a monopoly on the artist's computer market. For some computer users the choice between which computer platform to adopt is a matter of aesthetics and comfort with the operating system.

Windows-based equipment is made by a large number of manufacturers including Dell, Gateway, Hewlett-Packard, and Sony. It is generally less expensive than Macintosh and certainly more widely supported. What might be originally available only for the Apple operating system will eventually become available for Windows. However, the inverse is not true. Most software discussed in this book is available for Macintosh and PC computers, but not all. The very widely used CAD application, AutoCad, is only available for Windows PCs. This is also true for 3-D Studio Max, a high-end 3-D modeling application for PC. As an educator I insist on using and teaching software available to both platforms. The ability to share work is essential and such single-platform software may cause problems for some users.

Computer Power and Speed

Digital drawing requires great power and capacity in the primary computer functions: data processing, data storage, and memory. A digital artist needs very powerful processing combined with additional graphics support and enormous storage space to work effectively. In others words, a digital artist needs as much power, speed, and storage as he can afford.

The processor (actually microprocessor) is the most critical component of a computer. The power of a processor is determined by particular variables. The principal ones are the processor speed itself, the speed at which data is moved in and out of the processor (bus speed), and the amount of data that can move through the processor at the stated speed (bandwidth). Processor speed, also known as core or clock speed, is easily stated and is one of the distinctive statistics of a computer much like the horsepower of a car engine. The processor speed is expressed as a frequency rate: 300 MHz (one million cycles per second), 2 GHz (one billion cycles per second or roughly the pedaling speed of Lance Armstrong climbing L'Alpe d'Huez), and so on. Faster speed executes data instruction faster.

The bus speed is another very important factor that determines overall processor performance. The bus speed determines how quickly data is moved to the processor from the main memory. A processor may have a tremendously high clock speed, but if the data cannot get to it or back from it, the speed may be rendered useless. Low bus speed results in data bottlenecks, like driving into Los Angeles on a Monday morning. You may wish for a 24-lane, 120 mile-per-hour freeway thus increasing the bus speed and bandwidth at the same time. Bus speed is measured like processor speed as a frequency rate such as 400 MHz or 1.25 GHz. High bus speed coupled with high processor speed are the cornerstones of a powerful computer. However, how much data is processed or transferred at the stated speed is also critical and many not be as clearly stated. That is called bandwidth and this component of computer performance has evolved less rapidly than the speed factors. Most processors and applications utilize 32-bit bandwidth and 64-bit bandwidth is just beginning to become widely available. 64-bit bandwidth requires that the application is capable of utilizing that feature. The computer user should be aware that high bandwidth may not be supported by all software.

There are other elements that affect the performance of a processor and the overall computing power like processor caches (L2 and L3 Cache), which permit data to be buffered in ultra-fast memory devices. This buffering can smooth out data bottlenecks.

Graphics Accelerators

Graphics accelerators are a necessary addition to a computer used for drawing and painting. A graphics accelerator is a card that is added to the primary processing board (motherboard). It can be purchased with the computer and installed by the manufacturer or easily added on after purchase. A graphics accelerator includes an additional processor and memory, both of which are dedicated to support the display (monitor). It is designed to process only graphics information whereas a computer's main processor is designed to address a much wider variety of computing tasks. A graphics accelerator speeds up screen re-drawing and frees up the primary processor for other tasks.

Graphics accelerators are measured by their memory in VRAM (video RAM), type of video bus (PCI is now standard), and data width measured in bits. 128-bit accelerators are now common, but will probably be outstripped in the near future.

It is hard to be a bad or useless computer. Even entry-level machines are equipped with very fast processors and reasonably good bus speed and bandwidth. A graphics accelerator is essential for digital drawing, so make sure a computer purchased for this work has one or it can be added later. You may need to attach several peripherals (printer, scanner, external hard drive, etc.) to any computer used for digital drawing, so be aware of how many ports or inputs a computer has. This is where inexpensive computers can fall short. Inexpensive computers may also be limited to the amount of additional memory they can hold.

Memory

Computer memory (random access memory, RAM) allows the overall computing system to temporarily store the data in use. A large digital file is normally stored on the hard drive of the computer until it is put to use. Then it is moved to the RAM while work is being done. Every time you save the work a new copy is written on to the hard drive. When you save a large file, it may take several seconds or more to execute the save as the data is moved to the hard drive from the RAM at a much slower speed than data moving from the RAM to the processor. That is why a save command takes longer than making a paintbrush stroke. The brush stroke instructions are executed between the processor and the RAM and moved to the hard drive only when you save it. If you had no RAM and worked only from the hard drive, you would age significantly just cropping a high-resolution digital photo. RAM is much less expensive now than it was a few years ago. Buy as much as you can and try to plan for expansion if your computer architecture allows it.

Data Storage

Digital files generated on a computer require large amounts of data storage space. Fortunately this is easily the least expensive critical aspect of computing capability. Current hard drive sizes are generously large and have increased in storage capacity while decreasing in cost much more rapidly than any other piece of the computer.

But the largest standard hard drive may not be enough. Fortunately adding a second hard drive internally or externally is simple and very inexpensive. External drives are very handy as a means to make very large files very portable. Make sure you have lots of storage space. It is preferable to have duplicates of important files on separate drives or storage media for safe-keeping. It is very helpful to have a large capacity portable hard drive to easily transport very large files or vast numbers of files from one computer to another—like between work and home. A USB flash drive is a very handy and cheap way to safely carry up to a gigabyte of data.

Be aware that data storage technology changes over time. The basic idea of a hard drive has remained as a component of computers for decades. Portable data storage has changed many times from floppy discs, to optical discs, Zip and Jaz discs, flash drives, CD-RW, and DVD. Invest in an inexpensive, reliable, and common data storage format, and do not forget that you may need to replace your data storage system at some time in the future. "Permanent" storage is not truly possible.

Computer Monitors

A computer monitor shows your digital work in progress. Monitors come in a range of sizes. They distinctly resemble televisions and their physical format is so similar to televisions that it takes little explanation to understand the fundamental relationship of cost to size: bigger is always better and always more expensive. A big screen allows one to open more palettes and tools, which makes working vastly more efficient.

Monitors are made in one of two fundamental types: a cathode ray tube (CRT) or liquid crystal (LCD). The CRT looks like a big, boxy traditional TV, and they are essentially just that. LCD monitors are significantly flatter, lighter, look better, and use less energy. CRT monitors are rapidly disappearing from the marketplace and are dirt cheap. The choice of monitor type will affect the overall cost of the system and selecting an economical CRT monitor may permit the buyer to put money into processor or memory.

Images appear crisper on an LCD monitor due to the pixel architecture of the screen. Some users feel CRT monitors have capabilities in reproducing subtle color shades and tones superior to LCD monitors. LCD monitors reduce eye strain and glare for the user, thus the health and safety factors give LCD an edge. CRT monitors can be viewed at a wider angle from the viewer. Some LCD monitors accept digital input called digital video interface (DVI). That means the LCD monitor reads information directly from the digital output of a graphics card without being translated into analog data. Most users of DVI LCD monitors feel the image on screen is more accurate. What you see is indeed what you get with a DVI LCD.

Both monitor types, CRT and LCD, have outstanding ability to render color accurately. There is little difference from one monitor brand to another because the essential components of monitors are fabricated by a very limited number of manufacturers. Most monitors made now have excellent color capabilities. A computer's operating system is what controls color and resolution on the screen, and it should be capable of configuring the monitor to adapt to differences in ambient light through the operating system. If you work at home in a room with a lot of windows, the ambient light is very different from a windowless office with fluorescent lighting. One should be able to configure the monitor so that white is displayed as white, not blue or yellow. This is known as setting the white point. Operating system monitor set-up software should allow the user to adjust contrast, brightness, and color balance in addition to the white point.

Monitor size is the diagonal measurement of the screen. The usual options are 15″ (36 cm), 17″ (42 cm), or 20″ (55 cm). Of course, larger is always better. Monitors also have resolution that is a measurement of image quality. Monitor resolution is expressed by stating the number of pixels displayed on the screen horizontally and vertically. A pixel is a single point on the screen itself and the smallest unique element of an image. Pixels are arranged in horizontal rows on a screen from the bottom to the top; 800 × 640 is a common resolution, though extremely low. It uses exactly 640 horizontal lines consisting of 800 pixels each totaling a field of about half a million pixels. The resolution remains constant despite the screen size. This means 800 × 640 looks acceptable on a small 15″ screen but noticeably worse on a larger 20″ screen. A higher number is always preferable for graphics display; 1280 × 1024 display uses almost three times the amount of pixels than a display set at 800 × 640 thus requiring a significant increase in processing power simply to draw the screen. Of course, 1280 × 1024 resolution will render far more detail.

Monitors often make work look considerably better than the printed output for a number of reasons. Monitors can display colors that printers cannot create. This phenomenon is principally due to the fact that a monitor mixes color additively (toward white) and printers mix color subtractively (mixing toward black).

Input Equipment

A mouse and keyboard is the standard input tool for a computer. Most artists believe that a mouse is an inadequate drawing tool. Try writing your name with a mouse and see if you like the results. A digitized tablet is a hard, flat pad on which the user draws to directly input drawing to a computer. A digitized tablet is much more like traditional drawing and many artists would never consider using anything else. Try writing your name on a digitized tablet and pen to compare with the performance of a mouse. Write your name with a pencil and you will understand that computers still have a way to go to refine the interface between what the hand can do and how the computer translates gesture.

A mouse is a poor drawing tool but a digitized tablet is a clumsy "click and drag" tool, so there is

no perfect solution. A trackball is a reasonable alternative to a mouse for some, but is not a particularly good tool with which to paint. Both the mouse and trackball devices need regular cleaning. Any dirt or lint in the device will render it frustratingly erratic for drawing.

Many digitized tablets come with a wireless mouse as well as a pen for these two different types of input. Digitized tablets also have a variety of pen styles to choose from including ones geared just for painting such as a digital airbrush. Digitized tablets and pens can be individualized to respond to personal characteristics like hand pressure and brush speed.

The only significant negative aspect to a digitized tablet is the size to price ratio. Entry-level digitized tablets are quite small at 4 × 5 or 6 × 8 inches. Larger tablets are much more expensive. However, even a small tablet is an extremely useful tool and should be a part of a digital toolkit.

A flatbed scanner is another essential input device. A scanner has physical similarities to a copy machine in that they are principally a flat glass platen over a scanning device. Any flat or low-profile document can be scanned and converted into a digital file by a scanner. It is a rapid and accurate tool for getting drawings, photographs, paintings or any other image into a digital file for use on the computer. Scanners can often scan transparent originals as well as slides and film. They can be set to scan at different image resolutions from very low (72 pixels per inch, PPI) to extremely high (4000 and higher PPI), which permits the user to effectively control image quality from the outset. There are many reputable manufacturers of scanners making very accurate and affordable equipment.

Printers and Large-Format Printing

A printer is an essential piece of equipment if you need to make actual paper copy of your work. Printing technology now permits an individual to print excellent quality artwork at home for a relatively low investment or cost per print. Printers are manufactured in a wide variety of sizes, resolution capabilities, and printing processes. Printers have the greatest range of costs of any of the equipment discussed here. Printers can be extremely inexpensive or very expensive to purchase. In either case printers are costly to maintain due to the ink or toner required.

Inkjet Printers

Inkjet printers are the most common and affordable printers available. Inkjet (also known as bubble jet by some manufacturers) printing technology permits manufacturers to provide extremely low-cost equipment to the consumer with very good color imaging. Inkjet printers operate by spraying very small droplets of ink on the paper to form an image. The printer uses a four-color ink system (cyan-magenta-yellow-black; CMYK) and groups several droplets to form a single pixel of color. Printing resolution is close to 300 PPI but may be measured by actual dots of ink instead of the pixels (which will be a much higher number). The larger expense of most small-format inkjet printers is the ink. Two refills of the ink cartridges might exceed the cost of the printer.

The actual paper utilized in an ink jet printer will have a profound affect on print quality. Plain copier paper is highly absorbent and will tend to blur the image and dull color slightly. Coated or glossy paper will give a crisper and brighter image.

Inkjet printer technology permits a wide range of printer sizes; $8^1/_2 \times 11$ or 14 inch is the base size for most home printers. Desktop inkjet printers capable of 19- or 24-inch widths are available at a reasonable cost. Stand-alone wide-format printers are available up to 42 inches in width and provide very good quality graphics on a wide range of paper, vinyl, or fabric.

Laser Printers

Laser printers fuse heated toner on to the page without actually touching the paper surface as inkjet printers do. Laser printers are initially more expensive than inkjet printers; however, laser printers do not use the large quantity of ink that inkjet printers do and are less expensive over a large amount of printing. Laser printers are also faster than inkjet printers. The quality difference between color laser and color inkjet printing is not great. Inkjet printers do tend toward more vivid color than do laser printers. Laser printers are not available in wide formats.

Dye-Sublimation Printers

Dye-sublimation printers work by transferring layers of transparent dye on to paper using the same CMYK color system common to laser and ink jet printers. The dye is heated and deposited on the paper surface. Color is applied in three individual passes of the paper through the printer, one pass for each of the colors with black. Dye-sublimation printing produces extremely high quality, photo-quality color images with either glossy or matte surface finish. Color rendition by dye-sublimation is excellent and subtle tonality is successfully rendered. Dye-sublimation printers are available for home use but are considerably more expensive than inkjet printers. Dye-sublimation printing is limited to $8^1/_2 \times 11$ or 14-inch paper size and requires that a print leave a substantial white border on the paper edge for paper handling in the printer. Dye sublimation printing is quite slow compared to laser and inkjet printers.

Thermal Wax Printers

Thermal wax printers also use a heat transfer process. Thermal wax printing produces excellent color results that may not be as subtle as dye-sublimation. Thermal wax printers are more affordable than dye-sublimation printers both in initial investment and in maintenance. Thermal wax requires a unique paper type and is limited to the same size formats like a dye-sublimation system.

Commercial Printing Systems

There are printing systems available at commercial printing houses that produce excellent color results in a wide range of sizes. The Iris printing system is one such type of printing technology. Iris was developed to create long-lasting museum-quality prints. The Fiery system produces extremely high quality color prints and is capable of rendering excellent subtle colors and tonality. Both Iris and Fiery systems are not affordable for most consumers.

DIGITAL IMAGE PARAMETERS

A digital artist needs to understand the basic technical parameters that determine physical size and resolution (image quality) of their work. It is an area of knowledge where many students and professionals both fall a bit short. Understanding the basics of resolution is critical if you want to share or print your work.

Image Resolution

All digital images are made of pixels. A pixel is the smallest possible component of a digital image such as a dot or point. Individual pixels are what Adobe Photoshop and other painting applications manipulate. It is tempting to describe pixels as "dots," but using these terms interchangeably can create confusion. Image resolution is the fundamental measure of digital images. It expresses the size of a digital image measured in pixels. Figure 16.1 is a digital photo of a French marketplace. It is a very high resolution image made of 3000×2250 pixels, making a total bed of almost 6,750,000 pixels. The image is displayed in Photoshop at 400 PPI. That makes the picture 7.5×5.625 inches large.

Figure 16.2 is a close-up of a tiny area of the same photo showing the individual pixels. This close-up displays only 1200×900 pixels of the original image. The resolution measured in PPI is identical.

A more extreme close-up of the same image in Figure 16.3 is kept to the same 4×3 inch physical size. It is now reduced to only 72 PPI and contains only 288×216, or 62,208 pixels.

The same full image at low resolution (72 PPI) is seen in Figure 16.4. It requires only 540×405, or 218,700, pixels for an image the same physical size as the original.

The close-up seen in Figure 16.5 is exactly the same dimension and resolution of Figure 16.3. It is 72 PPI and contains only 288×216, or 62,208 pixels. It looks different because it started from a much lower resolution image, so 288×216 pixels of the low-resolution image is a larger area.

Digital images do not have any physical size until they are printed. They are simply a mass of digital information of color and the placement of the colors. This digital information can be made into almost any physical size desired. A digital photograph has no physical size either. Digital cameras are measured in units known as megapixels (one million pixels). This means a 4-megapixel camera makes a digital image containing 4,000,000 pixels. A digital camera will also format the proportion of the images to a 4:3 ratio or some other common format; thus,

Figure 16.2 Close-up of French marketplace image at 400 PPI. Photo by Sarah Louise Galbraith.

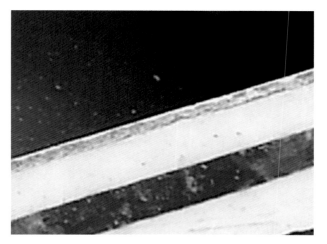

Figure 16.3 Extreme close-up of French marketplace image at 72 PPI. Photo by Sarah Louise Galbraith.

Figure 16.1 400 PPI image of a French marketplace. Photo by Sarah Louise Galbraith.

Figure 16.4 Full image of French marketplace at 72 PPI. Photo by Sarah Louise Galbraith.

Figure 16.5 Close-up of 72 PPI image of French marketplace. Photo by Sarah Louise Galbraith.

The common term for resolution is PPI. It is actually pixels per inch, but the word dot seems much more pervasive than pixel. Only printed images and printer capabilities can truly be measured in PPI. As stated above, digital images have pixel dimensions that will result in different PPI depending on the physical size. The close-up of the French market tomatoes illustrated here is a good example of that. The image only has about 72 × 48 pixels if it were displayed at 1 inch by $^5/_8$ of an inch. It would have a resolution of 72 PPI. Enlarge that image and the resolution (measured as PPI) must go lower and shrink the image making the resolution higher.

Resolution

Image resolution describes image quality on screen or in print. The term resolution is used to measure both equipment and artwork. It is important to understand the relationship between the resolution (image quality) of a document you are working with and the resolution of a screen or a printer with which you see or print your work. Digital images are most often measured in pixel dimensions that do not necessarily imply a specific physical size.

A monitor has an absolutely fixed number of dots on it that emit light in either red, green, or blue at various intensities to display an image. Those dots do not change size in any way. What those dots display are pixels of information as instructed by the software through the computer. A single pixel of information from a document will require several dots in a cluster on the screen for display. The first step in determining overall screen resolution is its own resolution setting. A setting of 640 × 580 on your monitor (which is extremely low) will display only that number of pixels that is 640 × 580. Open a document in any application that uses a ruler. Set your monitor at the lowest resolution. Measure a displayed inch on your monitor with a real ruler. It may measure much closer to an inch and a half at low resolution. Set your monitor to a high resolution like 1280 × 1024 and the "inch" will measure at less than three-quarters of an inch. This phenomenon is why many people are shocked when they print a picture in Photoshop and it is bigger than what they see on the screen.

Printers and images that are printed are best measured in true PPI. If a printer is capable of print-

spreading out the 4,000,000 pixels in a 4:3 format. This gives the photographer an image measuring 2400 × 1800 pixels using just over 4,000,000 pixels to fill a 4:3 format image. Digital images are measured by their *pixel dimension* instead of PPI or physical size until they are printed. This image has no PPI defined resolution nor does the camera itself have a PPI resolution. It is up to the user to define its physical size if the image is to be printed. Take a 2400 × 1800 digital image and display it on a monitor as a 4 × 3 inch image and it will be at 600 PPI. Enlarge the same image to 10 × 7.5 and it will be 240 PPI.

ing at 1400 PPI, then it will render 1400 individual points of ink or dye per linear inch of an image or 1,960,000 per square inch. The same is true for a printed image. This does not necessarily mean that a printer will print one dot per pixel. Normally a high-quality printer will use many dots of ink to describe a pixel.

Resolution quality is highly subjective. In some instance 300 PPI may be excellent, in others it may be inadequate. It depends on the quality of the printer and its own characteristics, how close the viewer is to the image, and the paper or media on which it is printed.

DIGITAL DRAWING AND PAINTING SOFTWARE

Software, or applications for drawing and painting, break into two fundamental types: drawing and painting. A more precise technical definition of these two types is bitmapped and vector-based. Generally speaking a painting application is bitmapped and a drawing application is vector-based.

Bitmapped Applications

Most painting software is classified as bitmapped software. These means that the action of drawing and painting creates a complex pattern of pixels in the document itself. Draw a blue circle in a bitmapped application and you have a circle of thousands of individual blue pixels. To later move or change the blue circle you have to select all of those particular pixels, a task that might be simple or very difficult depending on the color of the rest of the pixels around them. Bitmapped images can draw and paint circles easily, but they do not "remember" them as circles. The shape drawn becomes part of the overall pixel bed differentiated by hue or value.

A bitmapped image may be very complex. It can be divided into *layers* so that some elements of the drawing are isolated from each other. Insert text into a Photoshop document and it is automatically placed on its own layer. That makes it possible to easily edit the text by isolating it. The text is in fact a vector object until the layer is merged into the other layers. Photoshop identifies the text as a group of particular editable objects that maintain a specific interrelationship. Merge the text into the whole document

and it becomes nothing more than another part of the pixel bed and is unable to be easily edited.

Bitmapped drawings and paintings behave more like traditional drawings and paintings. Draw a curved line on a sheet of paper. Try to "edit" that line by making it longer or changing the curvature. The method is to erase it and re-draw it. One cannot pick up the line like a piece of string and change it. That is what vector-based applications can do.

Vector-Based Applications

Vector-based applications draw items as objects. These objects can be manipulated at any time after they are made. Draw a circle in a vector-based application and it remains a circle from the point of view of the application. It can be enlarged, flattened, rotated, etc., as an object. Vector-based applications are for more precise drawing and model making. They are lousy painting applications, but a vector-based shape such as a piece of architecture can easily be made into a bitmapped file and painted in a bitmap application. Some vector-based applications allow you to do the reverse, that is to import a bitmapped image and turn it into a vector object.

Choosing Software

Software is selected based on cost and what the software offers. If you want to paint, you buy painting software. There are lots to choose from and there is no need to own the well-known or market-dominant products. If you teach or are learning for professional reasons, then you may need to consider software brands differently. I would not teach a student a software brand that is not commonly used. Students may need to list their skill on a resume and it is best that they know what the majority of the world uses. It is important to use commonly used software if you share your work. You may be perfectly happy painting on an application downloaded for free. But if you send that file to be shared with a client who cannot open your work, you have a problem. If you are working professionally, do not reinvent the wheel. Use widely adopted software.

Drawing and Painting Software

There are dozens of applications available for drawing and painting. The most widely used products include Corel Draw, Corel Painter, Alias SketchBook, Xara, Macromedi Freehand, Adobe Illustrator or Streamline, CSDC Omnigraffle, Gee Three Slick, and many others. There are dozens more available online for free from ArtRage to Zbrush. Most of these are bitmapped with some vector capabilities.

The most widely used application does not even appear on the list above; the Adobe Photoshop image-editing software. Photoshop is the fundamental graphic tool for theater artists because of its versatility and power. It is true that other applications like Corel Painter paint much better than Photoshop. However, Photoshop's tool selections allow an artist to do so much with an existing image. To Photoshop is a verb in itself. It is the backbone of most drawing and re-touching work. Photoshop has vastly improved its brush selection as well so that it paints much better than past versions. For pure painting work, Photoshop is not a good choice. Corel Painter, for example, is far more intuitive and clever at how it emulates a wide variety of art tools and media.

Modeling Software

The choice of which three-dimensional modeling software to purchase is a difficult one to make. The choice of which one to teach is even more difficult. Cost, ease of learning, platform, power, and the software's ranking within the industry are major factors that go into the decision. 3-D Studio Max is considered by many as the industry standard and is only available for PC platform. Maya, a Macintosh-based product, has also received strong industry recognition. Both of these products share one significant factor; they are both very expensive and very difficult to learn, especially if you have no background in digital modeling. The cost and steep learning curve may not make them entirely appropriate for an entry-level class in digital modeling. These are well-suited for an intensive, advanced digital modeling class. A student with strong skills in either of these two applications will be well positioned to enter the job market in digital modeling. This is the software that is used by the industry where quality, power, and flexibility of the software outweigh cost concerns.

There are many less-expensive alternatives to high-end modeling software. One potential source is to focus on the modeling packages that are part of the AutoCad or VectorWorks CAD suites of software. These are very useful and convenient as they have seamless interface with their own drawing capabilities. These can be much easier to learn as well. The characteristics of the modeling software may not be as flexible as desired for stage designers; however, an alternative can be found in relatively low-cost modeling software. Products such as AC3D, Artlantis, Rhinoceros, 3DOM, Strata 3D CX, TrueSpace, and others have tremendous flexibility, can be relatively easy to learn, and produce stunning results.

THE DIGITAL DRAWING PROCESS

Working digitally requires that the artist pay attention to how drawings are started and how they are saved to assure the best results. These are the parameters of a digital drawing and they are often invisible to the artist while working, unlike when working with traditional materials when it is quite clear if one is working on a very large or very small canvas. The artist needs to be in control of the digital working environment.

Setting Up a Document

The drawing set-up includes determining:

- The size of the image which could be measured in pixels, inches, centimeters, or as a ratio
- The resolution of the image
- The file format of the image (Photoshop, JPEG, TIFF, etc.)
- The color type (or mode) of the image (usually a red-green-blue; RGB or a cyan-magenta-yellow-black; CMYK)

You need to determine the ultimate use and output of the image from the beginning. Is the image to be printed? If so, does it need to be a large print like a paint elevation or rendering, or a small print such as one-quarter page illustration? Is the image to be shared electronically only and never printed? Is it meant to be available on the Web or sent by e-mail? In the case of printed images, one wants to have as high a resolution as the printer permits, particularly for the nuances of a rendering. However, posting an image on a Web site requires only low (72 PPI) resolution for the monitor.

Working from Existing Documents

If you are working from an existing document such as a scanned image or a digital photo, then all of the above parameters are already set; however, you may need to change them for the same reasons listed above. Set the image file format, color type or mode, and size and resolution as you need.

DIGITAL DRAWING EXERCISES

These exercises assume the artist has some fundamental knowledge of digital drawing techniques in Adobe Photoshop. The techniques assumed include how to open a new document or an existing one, how to manipulate document size and resolution, how to cut and paste, and how to do basic image correction of color, value, and contrast. Basic knowledge of layers is also assumed.

The Digital Drawing Classroom

It takes time to learn digital drawing skills. Those learning these skills will all acquire skills at a different rate, just as they do with traditional drawing. It is important to establish an atmosphere conducive to learning in any classroom and the digital drawing classroom is no exception.

Students have a universal reaction to learning in front of a computer. They will stare at nothing but the monitor. If the instructor needs to lecture or demonstrate in a manner that demands a student's full attention and note taking, it is highly advised that students turn off their computers. Students are always eager to explore the computer and make the software do something. Demonstrating while the students are able to work on the computer may feel surreal to the instructor, who may feel largely ignored, but it can be very effective. Students do listen to basics—and to each other. Classrooms in which the students can share work and ask each other questions are desirable.

Some things to encourage as good digital drawing practice include:

- Always display the file you are working on as largely as possible on your monitor. You need to see it as well as you can, so do not leave any monitor real estate unused.
- Save your work often. Your computer will crash sometime. That is 100% guaranteed. Save often.
- Back up your work. There are many ways to inexpensively save multiple copies of your work. This helps prevent the loss of your work and will extend your own life.
- Have only the software you need on at any given time. If you are not using Adobe Illustrator, then quit it.
- Do not work directly to a cheap storage unit, especially a USB flash drive. These USB storage devices are marvelous for storage. However, they are terrible as a working drive and they make your computer unstable. Work on the hard drive of your computer and save your finished work to the storage device.
- Set up your desk and chair for comfort and support. Digital drawing can be surprisingly hard on the hands and back. Take time to give yourself a comfortable and safe environment. Be assured that you will spend a lot of time in front of a computer once you start doing digital work. There is no such thing as a 5-minute Photoshop job. It takes time to draw well, and drawing digitally is no exception.

Chapter 17

Digital Drawing Exercise One: Basic Digital Drawing

This exercise uses Adobe Photoshop as a sketching tool to make a monochromatic chalk drawing. The goal of this exercise to is to learn basic drawing set-up and to experience a variety of drawing tools called brushes. It requires a photo of the subject to be drawn. I recommend a simple object like an apple. You will need to know how to change colors and brushes with Photoshop to work this exercise.

Step One—Set the photo of your apple, or an apple close to you so you can refer to it while drawing.

Step Two—Open a new Photoshop file using the NEW command. Make a document 5 × 5 inches at a resolution of 300 PPI as shown in Figure 17.1. Make sure the MODE is set to GRAYSCALE.

Step Three—Begin a freehand drawing of the apple by roughly drawing the outline using a small diameter (3 or 5 pixels) standard brush. Feel free to draw long or short strokes, whichever feels more comfortable for you. For most, drawing digitally for the first time will not feel terribly comfortable or natural, especially if drawing with a mouse. If you draw a line you do not like, just undo or erase it. This is one of the great advantages of working digitally.

You may not like the results of the drawing at this stage. One reason may be the brush itself. The standard brush draws a fairly opaque, hard edge line that may look clumsy to you. I recommend using a CHALK brush at a fairly small size. I used an 8-pixel

diameter whereas the default size for this brush is 36 pixels.

Also, change the OPACITY of the brush itself to 50 percent for a less dense line. No matter which brush you use for the outline, remember that it does not have to be a perfect drawing. Mistakes can easily be erased and re-done at any time.

Step Four—Begin drawing the apple itself. Continue to work with a chalk brush that yields a nice texture, but make the size appropriate to the object drawn. I worked with the same chalk brush in a range of sizes from about 30 to 90 pixels. I recommend that you leave the opacity setting at 50 percent for the duration of the drawing. The chalk brush behaves more like a real drawing instrument in that it layers up and darkens as you draw over an area. I also change color from dark to medium gray as I worked areas of light and dark. Figures 17.5 through 17.7 show the progression of drawing with the chalk brush.

Step Five—Keep working over the apple form with the chalk brush to develop the drawing. Remember the basic drawing guidelines from previous drawing lessons; always move the drawing tool to follow the contour of the object and keep in mind the direction of light and shadow on the object. Draw the larger, lighter areas and keep working over the shape with a smaller, darker brush for the detail and shadowed areas, as shown in Figure 17.8.

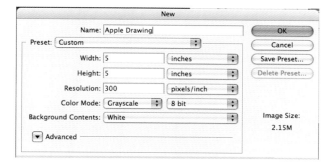

Figure 17.1 Photoshop NEW file window.

Figure 17.2 Digital line drawing of an apple.

Figure 17.3 The chalk brush in the Photoshop default brush palette.

Figure 17.4 Using a chalk brush to draw the apple yields a grainer texture and a more interesting drawing.

Figure 17.5 Begin modeling the form of the apple.

Figure 17.6 Continue modeling the apple with a larger brush size.

Figure 17.7 Use low-opacity brush settings for intermediate tones.

Figure 17.8 Model the apple leaf and intensify shadow with a small brush size.

Step Six—Add a small area of shadow to the ground as you approach the end of the drawing.

Work with the drawing as large as possible on your screen so that you can more easily see the overall light and shadow on the form. Squint at the drawing occasionally to evaluate the light in it. Make your last few strokes with your largest brush size to work over the surface and tie the drawing together.

Figure 17.9 Cast shadow is added to the ground beneath the apple.

Figure 17.10 The finished drawing of the apple.

Chapter 18

Digital Drawing Exercise Two: Basic Digital Painting

This exercise asks the artist to make a painting on a blank canvas. It requires only the computer and software. You should have a working knowledge of trompe l'oeil painting techniques or how light describes physical objects. You should also have a basic understanding of how selections work in Photoshop, how to select colors and brushes, and the basic use of the gradient tool. This exercise will also describe how layers are used in painting.

Step One—Open a new Photoshop document 6 × 8 inches large at 300 PPI with a white background. Make sure it is in the RGB mode. Save the drawing with a name you like.

Step Two—Create a circle using the MARQUEE tool wherever you choose on the canvas. Save the circle selection at this point. This is done by selecting SAVE SELECTION in the SELECTION pull-down menu. Name the circle selection as "circle." Save the drawing.

Saving and re-using selections is an extremely useful Photoshop skill. Once you save a selection as described above, you can re-activate the selection at any time. This is done through the CHANNELS PALETTE where there are the four main channels of an RGB document: RGB combined and the three individual red, green, and blue channels. Below those four channels are the black and white channels of the saved selections. In your case, you should have a selection named circle in your CHANNELS PALETTE. To activate that selection, hold down on

the COMMAND key (Macintosh) or CONTROL key (PC) and click on the box in the CHANNELS PALETTE containing the name of the channel you want to activate, in this case "circle." This activates the selection.

Step Three—Paint the circle any color you prefer. I work in a green hue in this example. Set your foreground color to the color you want for the circle. The easiest way to paint the circle is to fill it by using the FILL TOOL under the EDIT pull-down menu. Save the drawing.

Step Four—Create two new selections to define the upper and lower horizons. Do this by drawing a rectangular selection to describe the lower horizon. I made the horizon below the middle of the canvas. You will not want to include any part of the circle in the lower horizon, so do not cover the circle when you paint the lower horizon. To remove the part of the circle that overlaps the horizon, open the CHANNELS PALETTE and activate the circle selection while simultaneously holding down the OPTION key (Macintosh) or the ALT key (PC). This subtracts the circle from the lower horizon selection. Save the resulting selection as lower horizon. Do the same to create an upper horizon and save that selection. Now paint the two horizons separately. Use colors that will separate them. I made the lower horizon brown and the upper horizon blue. I applied these two steps with the gradient tool going from the selected color to a tint of it toward the horizon line. Save the drawing.

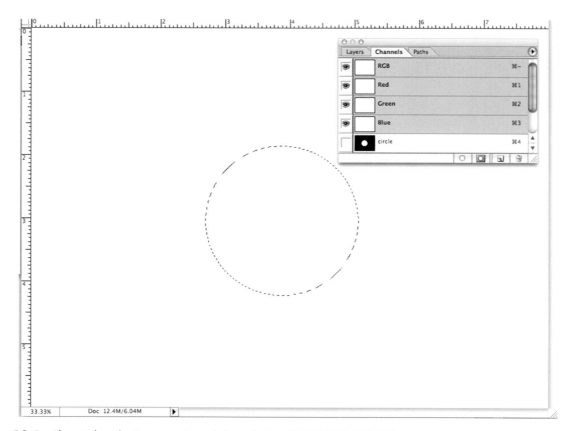

Figure 18.1 The circle selection is activated through the CHANNELS PALETTE.

Figure 18.2 The circle is colored with a green hue using the FILL TOOL.

Figure 18.3 The sky and ground were painted using the GRADIENT tool.

Step Five—Begin to model the circle into a sphere by adding highlight and shadow. Start by activating the circle selection so you do not paint in either of the horizon selections. Modify the base color to make a tint and shade of it and apply those two variants to

the sphere. By sure to establish a light source before you begin to apply light and shade. You can save colors in Photoshop by using the SWATCHES palette to record your colors as you go. I used a very large coarse brush shape and applied color at a low opacity

Figure 18.4 Highlight and shade are applied to the circle over the base coat. The light source is above and to the left of the circle.

Figure 18.5 Texture is applied to the floor using wide broad strokes with the chalk brush.

Figure 18.6 Highlight and shadow are applied to the sphere.

to allow it to build up like charcoal drawing. I also work with coarse strokes to begin to add texture to the drawing. Save the drawing.

Step Six—Paint the floor by activating the lower horizon selection and apply color variants of the base color. I used the same brush from the previous step to apply long strokes of darker brown to the floor. Click once then hold the SHIFT key down and click again to make a straight brush stroke. Save your work.

Use a similar approach to paint the upper horizon. I changed brush shapes to a more cloud-like brush and applied different shades and tint of the blue hues of the sky. Save your work.

Step Seven—Paint the circle to create depth and turn it into a sphere, as shown in Figures 18.7 and 18.8.

Figure 18.7 Shadow and texture applied to the floor.

Figure 18.8 Texture and color are applied to the sky.

I used a large coarse chalk brush at a low to moderate opacity to apply the tint and shade to model the surface. I made lowlight and highlight colors from the tint and shade to further model. I also went in with a very large brush and the original base color to dab back in the original color that created nice texture on the surface. I used a small amount of the light source color, which I imagined to be yellow-amber, as a bounce light. Save your work.

Figure 18.9 Sphere filled with violet before being made into a cast shadow.

Figure 18.11 The finished painting.

Figure 18.10 The completed cast shadow from the sphere onto the ground.

Step Eight—A cast shadow will help complete the image. I made a shadow by copying the entire circle as a separate layer. Then I made a third copy of the same layer. Each of these layers will retain the channels and the saved selections and allow you to easily manipulate the image. On the top copy, I used the inverted circle selection and deleted all but the painted circle. I deleted all but the circle on the middle copy as well. The reason to have two copies of the circle is to use the top copy as the visible painted circle (or sphere), the middle copy as a shadow and the bottom, original layer as the background.

Fill the middle layer circle with a dark violet color to serve as a shadow, as seen in Figure 18.9.

Then use the TRANSFORM control in the EDIT menu to reshape the shadow so it appears to lay down on the ground behind the sphere. The shadow hides perfectly behind the top layer by having the shadow sandwiched between the top and bottom layer. Set the BLENDING MODE to MULTIPLY and adjust the LAYER TRANSPARENCY of the shadow layer for a more convincing shadow. You might add a second cast shadow to indicate a more complex environment. Save your work.

Step Nine—Do some final adjustment of the painting by putting in more dark shadow color on the sphere. Use the same color from the cast shadow with a coarse brush at low transparency. Finally, add some bounce light from the table to the underside of the sphere.

Chapter 19

Digital Drawing Exercise Three: Intermediate Painting

This exercise makes a color image from a monochrome source. It uses layers, selection techniques, and blending modes as well as exploring how to apply color. This exercise requires basic knowledge of painting tools and layers in Photoshop. I take a familiar object from nature such as the sunflower and attempt to transform a black and white portrait of it into one with color. I selected this image because of the boldness and clarity of the subject in it.

This exercise demonstrates clearly the range of painting ability in Photoshop, particularly the use of blending modes. A blending mode is a means to determine how the hue, value, and intensity of each pixel will interact with new colors as they are applied to the canvas. The default blending mode is "normal" and it applies color in a fully opaque manner over all pixels equally. The opacity can be adjusted, but the normal mode will always apply color evenly. There are twenty-five different blending modes and these are available for brushes, the paint bucket, the fill command, and the gradient tool as well as layers interacting with other layers. Not every blending mode is available to every tool under every condition, but there are plenty of blending modes available at all times with these tools to give the artist a wide range of control when painting.

Blending modes sort into several categories of effect: lighten, darken, saturate, dodge, burn, and add light. These categories are further divided by how these effects react to existing light and dark values, hue, and saturation. The definitions below explain each function.

Normal—Edits or paints each pixel to make the result color. This is the default mode.

Dissolve—Edits or paints each pixel to make it the result color. However, the result color is a random replacement of the pixels with the base color or the blend color, depending on the opacity at any pixel location. It yields a grainy overlay effect of the new color dissolving into the existing color.

Behind—Edits or paints only on the transparent part of a layer. This mode works only in layers with LOCK TRANSPARENCY deselected and is analogous to painting on the back of transparent areas in a sheet of acetate. (Available only to brushes, not layers.)

Clear—Edits or paints each pixel and makes it transparent. This mode is available for the Line tool (when fill region FILL PIXELS icon is selected), the Paint Bucket tool, the Brush tool, the Pencil tool, the FILL command, and the STROKE command. You must be in a layer with LOCK TRANSPARENCY deselected to use this mode.

Darken—Looks at the color information in each channel and selects the base or blend color, whichever is darker, as the result color. Pixels lighter than the blend color are replaced, and pixels darker than the blend color do not change.

This is really useful to add shadow color. This will not build up darkness.

Multiply—Looks at the color information in each channel and multiplies the base color by the blend color. The result color is always a darker color. Multiplying any color with black produces black. Multiplying any color with white leaves the color unchanged. When you are painting with a color other than black or white, successive strokes with a painting tool produce progressively darker colors. The effect is similar to drawing on the image with multiple magic markers.

Color Burn—Looks at the color information in each channel and darkens the base color to reflect the blend color by increasing the contrast. Blending with white produces no change.

Linear Burn—Looks at the color information in each channel and darkens the base color to reflect the blend color by decreasing the brightness. Blending with white produces no change.

Lighten—Looks at the color information in each channel and selects the base or blend color, whichever is lighter, as the result color. Pixels darker than the blend color are replaced, and pixels lighter than the blend color do not change.

Screen—Looks at each channel's color information and multiplies the inverse of the blend and base colors. The result color is always a lighter color. Screening with black leaves the color unchanged. Screening with white produces white. The effect is similar to projecting multiple photographic slides on top of each other. Screen is essentially the inverse of multiply.

Color Dodge—Looks at the color information in each channel and brightens the base color to reflect the blend color by decreasing the contrast. Blending with black produces no change.

Linear Dodge—Looks at the color information in each channel and brightens the base color to reflect the blend color by increasing the brightness. Blending with black produces no change.

Overlay—Multiplies or screens the colors, depending on the base color. Patterns or colors overlay the existing pixels while preserving the highlights and shadows of the base color. The base color is not replaced but is mixed with the blend color to reflect the lightness or darkness of the original color.

Overlay is great for adding thin washes, but it has no effect on black or white.

Soft Light—Darkens or lightens the colors, depending on the blend color. The effect is similar to shining a diffused spotlight on the image. If the blend color (light source) is lighter than 50 percent gray, the image is lightened as if it were dodged. If the blend color is darker than 50 percent gray, the image is darkened as if it were burned in. Painting with pure black or white produces a distinctly darker or lighter area but does not result in pure black or white.

Hard Light—Multiplies or screens the colors, depending on the blend color. The effect is similar to shining a harsh spotlight on the image. If the blend color (light source) is lighter than 50 percent gray, the image is lightened, as if it were screened. This is useful for adding highlights to an image. If the blend color is darker than 50 percent gray, the image is darkened, as if it were multiplied. This is useful for adding shadows to an image. Painting with pure black or white results in pure black or white.

Vivid Light—Burns or dodges the colors by increasing or decreasing the contrast, depending on the blend color. If the blend color (light source) is lighter than 50 percent gray, the image is lightened by decreasing the contrast. If the blend color is darker than 50 percent gray, the image is darkened by increasing the contrast.

Linear Light—Burns or dodges the colors by decreasing or increasing the brightness, depending on the blend color. If the blend color (light source) is lighter than 50 percent gray, the image is lightened by increasing the brightness. If the blend color is darker than 50 percent gray, the image is darkened by decreasing the brightness.

Pin Light—Replaces the colors, depending on the blend color. If the blend color (light source) is lighter than 50 percent gray, pixels darker than the blend color are replaced, and pixels lighter than the blend color do not change. If the blend color is darker than 50 percent gray, pixels lighter than the blend color are replaced, and pixels darker than the blend color do not change. This is useful for adding special effects to an image.

Difference—Looks at the color information in each channel and subtracts either the blend color from the base color or the base color from the blend color, depending on which has the greater brightness value. Blending with white inverts the base color values; blending with black produces no change.

Exclusion—Creates an effect similar to but lower in contrast than the DIFFERENCE mode. Blending with white inverts the base color values. Blending with black produces no change.

Hue—Creates a result color with the luminance and saturation of the base color and the hue of the blend color.

Saturation—Creates a result color with the luminance and hue of the base color and the saturation of the blend color. Painting with this mode in an area with no saturation (gray) causes no change.

Color—Creates a result color with the luminance of the base color and the hue and saturation of the blend color. This preserves the gray levels in the image and is useful for coloring monochrome images and for tinting color images.

Luminosity—Creates a result color with the hue and saturation of the base color and the luminance of the blend color. This mode creates an inverse effect from that of the COLOR mode.

These definitions are very useful references; however, you need to use blending modes to get a feel for their range and effectiveness. Keep in mind as well that all blending modes are further modified by the opacity of the mode. Low opacity use of a particular blending mode, such as hard mix, may be very subtle unlike the name of the mode.

Step One—Open the image you wish to paint. It is most likely a grayscale Photoshop file and it must be converted into a color image to add color. To do this, go to the IMAGE MODE pull-down menu and select RBG Color or CMYK Color.

Step Two—This image has two principal elements: the flower petals and the flower head. One should be selected and saved, then inverted and saved so that the two pieces are available at all times. There are a few very dark spots and also a few very light spots in the image. These two additional groups should be selected separately and saved as well.

Step Three—The painting can begin on each of the separate selections. I recommend starting with the largest selection. In this case it is the leaves. The painting begins with an overall fill of this area with a bright yellow color. Activate the selection of the

Figure 19.1 Grayscale image. Photo by Sarah Louise Galbraith.

Figure 19.2 The leaves are colorized using the FILL tool in MULTIPLY mode. Photo by Sarah Louise Galbraith.

leaves and choose the color desired. Add the color by using the EDIT FILL tool, but do not use the standard FILL mode called NORMAL. Instead, use the fill mode called MULTIPLY. This paint mode does not simply cover over the base color, instead it adds to it when the base color is lighter. In this way, the darker parts of the leaves remain darker.

Once the leaf area has an over color you like, modify the darker areas. Use the REPLACE COLOR tool found in the IMAGE ADJUSTMENTS pull-down menu. The REPLACE COLOR tool allows you to select a part of the image based on the current color and change that area only. In this case, choose the darker parts of the tinted leaves and use the hue

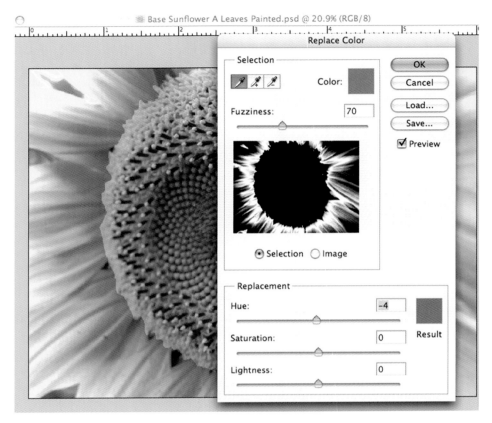

Figure 19.3 Using replace color. Photo by Sarah Louise Galbraith.

Figure 19.4 Increasing saturation using overlay painting mode. Photo by Sarah Louise Galbraith.

Figure 19.5 The flower head is colorized using the FILL tool in HARD MIX mode. Photo by Sarah Louise Galbraith.

Figure 19.6 The light and texture of the background is seen through the negative space between the petals. Photo by Sarah Louise Galbraith.

slider control to change the dark gray to an orange color, as shown in Figures 19.3 and 19.4.

Painting the head of the flower is done in a similar fashion. First, activate the selection for that area. Then select the color you wish to use. I had a slightly more orange version of the leaf color. The color is first applied with the FILL command, but in a different mode. This time I used the HARD MIX blending mode for the FILL command, but at a low opacity of 30 percent. This retains more brightness of the original image. I wanted an even brighter flower head so I painted in a bright orange color with a brush set to airbrush style using the OVERLAY blending mode at a low (35 percent) opacity. This gave the image the saturation and brightness I sought.

Step Four—Paint the two small sections of dark and light areas not yet painted. The light areas are bright light of the background coming through the flower. The dark areas are green leaves of the plant seen through the flower.

Figure 19.7 The finished painting. Photo by Sarah Louise Galbraith.

Step Five—The painting has a few spots where the sharp edge between two selections is obvious, particularly where the green leaves were painted. These can be softened with the BLUR tool set at a low strength, about 30 percent. The tool can be used to soften edges "farther" into the painting so that the closest objects appear most sharp. The final application of a bright yellow color over the entire image appears to add a glow to it. The color is applied with a very large airbrush (400 pixels) using the SOFT LIGHT blending mode at a low opacity (35 percent). This blending mode appears to add light to the image as well as color.

Chapter 20

Digital Drawing Exercise Four: Creating a Multi-Layer Photographic Image

This exercise merges three very different existing photographic images into a single cohesive image. The requirements are to provide three images taken in very different places at different times. In this case, I am using three old photos. The use of light and shadow is one of the critical components of any drawing. Light and shadow are even more critical in digital drawings and compositions where they most often must be consciously manipulated from the existing light or completely revised in the final image. This exercise requires basic knowledge of layers in Photoshop. It will explore color correction techniques, re-scaling, making shadows, and some re-touching.

Step One—Merging several images together requires that the images be made nearly identical in size and resolution before they are merged. The first step is to check image parameters of each image file for consistency. As I am using old photos, they should already be similar in size. Look at each of the images in the IMAGE SIZE command under the IMAGE pull-down menu. You can see the original images in Figures 20.1, 20.2, and 20.3 before they were cropped and slightly re-sized.

Each image is now set to be exactly 5 inches wide, or high in the case of the Man on Bridge, and

Figure 20.1 Original scanned photograph, Man on Bridge. Photo by author.

Figure 20.2 Original scanned photograph, Parked Car. Photo by author.

Figure 20.3 Original scanned photograph of Palladio's Villa Rotunda. Photo by author.

Figure 20.4 Cropped and re-sized Man on Bridge. Photo by author.

Figure 20.5 Cropped and re-sized Parked Car. Photo by author.

Figure 20.6 Cropped and re-sized Palladio's Villa Rotunda. Photo by author.

Figure 20.7 Color-corrected Man on Bridge. Photo by author.

all are 600 PPI resolution. Each of the cropped images is saved as a Photoshop file with a name different from the one it had when it was scanned. Save your work.

You will need to decide which of the three images is the intended target or background image to which the other two will be added. In this exercise, the image of Palladio's Villa Rotunda in Vicenza, Italy, will serve as the target, or background image. The plan is to add the Man on Bridge and the Parked Car to the Villa.

Step Two—This is the point in the process to clean up any faults in each of the three images and to correct value and color balance between them. Look carefully for any spots and scratches in the images and correct those with the rubber stamp tool. There are very few of these flaws, though I find the Man on Bridge a bit fuzzy so I sharpened it. I look at each image for the distribution of value across the

gray scale by using the LEVELS tool found under the IMAGE ADJUSTMENTS pull-down menu. These three files have fairly good value distribution and needed only a little white added to the somewhat dark man on Bridge and Parked Car. The difference in color between the three images is obvious. The Villa Rotunda is slightly yellow, the Man on Bridge is very reddish, and the Parked Car is bluer than the other two. I used the EYEDROPPER tool in Photoshop to more accurately compare the color of the three images. I did this by setting the eyedropper tool to read a 5 × 5 pixel average and have it read similar areas of each images. In this case, I examine the pale, hazy skies of each image. I open the INFO PALETTE to see a numerical readout of the color content of the area examined by the eyedropper tool. This shows me that the Man on Bridge is higher in red and green than it is blue. The Villa Rotunda is also higher in red and green, but to a lesser degree. The Parked Car

Figure 20.8 Color-corrected Parked Car. Photo by author.

is slightly higher in blue than red and green. I can now adjust each of the images to add or subtract the appropriate amount of color. With the color corrected on all of the images, it is time to merge them together. Save your work.

Step Three—The automobile from the Parked Car and the man from the photo Man on the Bridge are to be inserted into the drive leading to Villa Rotunda. Begin by selecting the man. The selection is carefully made with the LASSO tool. Drag the selection into the target image to place it as a new layer. Do the same process with the automobile by selecting it and placing it into the target image. The result is a single image file (Villa) with two new layers. Save your work.

Step Four—Now adjust the scale of the two new layers. Use the SCALE tool under the EDIT TRANS-FORM pull-down menu. The automobile is obviously too large for the drive so it is reduced then placed farther into the background. The man is moved to the foreground where the scale looks correct. Save your work.

Step Five—The two new layers are in the correct place. It is time to make a shadow for each. The direction and color of the shadow is based on what the target layer tells us about the lighting conditions. The wall on the left is in sun and the wall on the right is in shade. Thus the sun is coming from right to left. The shadow of the Cyprus tree and the porch of the villa appear to be falling closer to us indicating that the sun is slightly behind them. The shadow of the man and the automobile must fall forward and to the left.

Start the shadow-making process by duplicating the entire layer of the object lacking shadow. Duplicate the layer with the man. Make sure the copy layer is behind the original layer, or below it in the layer stack. Select the shadow of man layer. Choose a dark

Figure 20.9 Color-corrected Palladio's Villa Rotunda. Photo by author.

shaded area in the target layer and pick a color from it to serve as the shadow color. I took a shadow color from the deep shaded area of the front of the villa. SELECT ALL on the shadow of the man layer and fill the object with the shadow color. Use the FILL command or the PAINT BUCKET to do this. Use the EDIT TRANSFORM SKEW or DISTORT commands to make the shadow flat on the ground in the direction of the light. Make the shadow roughly parallel to an existing shadow in the background. Once the shadow placement looks correct, adjust the opacity and blending mode of the shadow layer to make a transparent shadow. I used the blending mode MULTIPLY and set the transparency to roughly 60 percent.

Repeat the process on the automobile by making a shadow and laying that shadow on the ground. It may require two shadows, one to lie directly below the vehicle as well.

Step Six—Finish the overall integration of the layers with a small amount of color taken from the background and added to the other layers. Select a color from the gravel path of the Villa with the EYE-DROPPER tool. Choose a broad, coarse brush like a dry brush and set it to a fairly large size, about 100 pixels. Set the brush opacity to 25 percent and brush some color lightly on the back of the car and the legs of the man, as if dust from the path has settled there. You may wish to adjust the overall color of the man or car layer to fit the overall image.

Figure 20.10 The man and car are selected from their images and copied into the Villa Rotunda image.

Figure 20.11 The man and car have been scaled to realistic sizes in the Villa Rotunda image.

Figure 20.12 The shadow cast by the man onto the drive of the Villa Rotunda image has been created.

Figure 20.13 Cast shadow from the car is added to the image.

Figure 20.14 The finished composite image.

Chapter 21

Digital Drawing Exercise Five: Painting an Architectural Scenic Elevation from a Line Drawing

This exercise takes a line drawing of a unit of architecture and uses Photoshop to create a scenic paint elevation. It requires a black and white or grayscale line drawing in a digital format. Basic Photoshop brush and selections skills are required knowledge for this exercise. The techniques practiced in this exercise include basic and intermediate painting and multiple selection techniques.

The subject in this exercise is a drawing created in VectorWorks and exported as a Photoshop file. The same techniques described here can easily be applied to another VectorWorks drawing or a drawing made by hand and scanned. The requirement is to bring a high-resolution line drawing to Photoshop, at least 300 PPI. Lesser resolution drawings are much more difficult when you have to make rapid and accurate selections and the line quality will look clumsy when printed.

Step One—Begin with a clean line drawing. This can be a scanned hand drawing or an imported CAD drawing. In either case, the resolution for the drawing must be at least 300 PPI. The example here was created in VectorWorks then exported using the EXPORT EXPORT IMAGE FILE command found under the FILE pull-down menu (Figure 21.2). The resolution for the image file is set at this point, as is the file type. VectorWorks permits files to be exported

in Photoshop format as well as JPEG, PICT, TIFF, Quick Time, and others.

Step Two—The elevation needs to be separated into several channels containing the objects within the elevation that will be painted together. The bricks (window cornice separately), the mortar, the stone blocks, various parts of the window frame, and the glass are all saved as separate channels. This permits these elements to be painted individually. The selections are made by shift-clicking using the MAGIC WAND tool. Click the magic wand within one brick to select it. Then select the next brick while holding down the SHIFT key. Continue to add to the brick selection by clicking on each brick separately until all have been selected.

Step Three—Painting begins when all the selections have been made and saved. The first painting step is to reduce the darkness and opacity of the line drawing itself. This is done using the REPLACE COLOR command found under ADJUSTMENTS in the IMAGE pull-down menu. This command was used in the intermediate digital painting exercise (Chapter 19) in which a black and white image was painted into a color image. The line color (black) is replaced with a medium gray, as shown in Figure 21.5.

Step Four—The mortar selection is activated by clicking on their channel name in the CHANNEL

Figure 21.1 Line drawing created in VectorWorks.

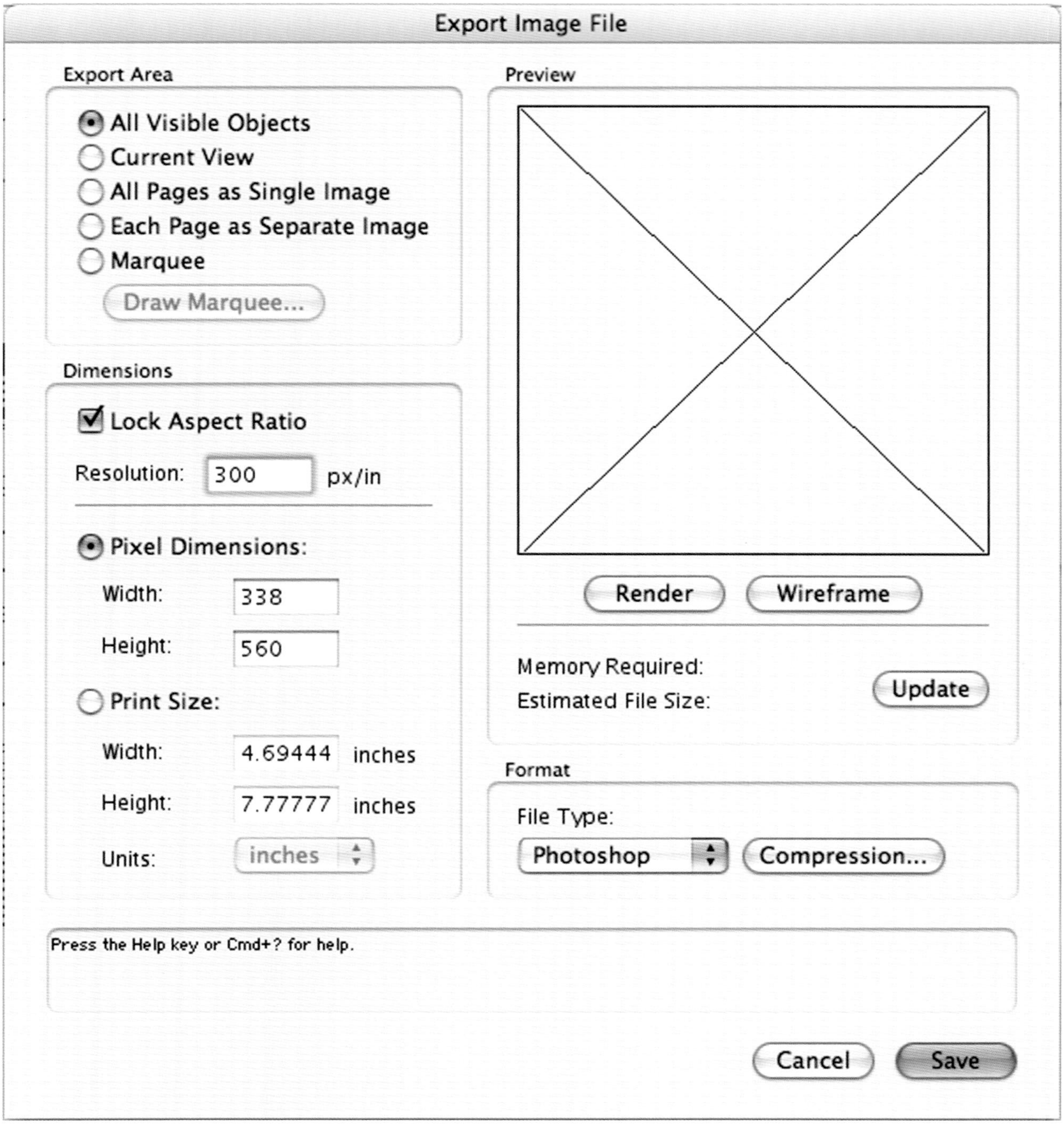

Export Image File

Export Area

- ◉ All Visible Objects
- ○ Current View
- ○ All Pages as Single Image
- ○ Each Page as Separate Image
- ○ Marquee
  - (Draw Marquee...)

Dimensions

☑ Lock Aspect Ratio

Resolution: [300] px/in

- ◉ Pixel Dimensions:
  - Width: [338]
  - Height: [560]
- ○ Print Size:
  - Width: [4.69444] inches
  - Height: [7.77777] inches
  - Units: [inches ▲▼]

Preview

(Render)   (Wireframe)

Memory Required:
Estimated File Size: (Update)

Format

File Type:
[Photoshop ▲▼]   (Compression...)

Press the Help key or Cmd+? for help.

(Cancel)   (Save)

Figure 21.2 VectorWorks IMAGE EXPORT window.

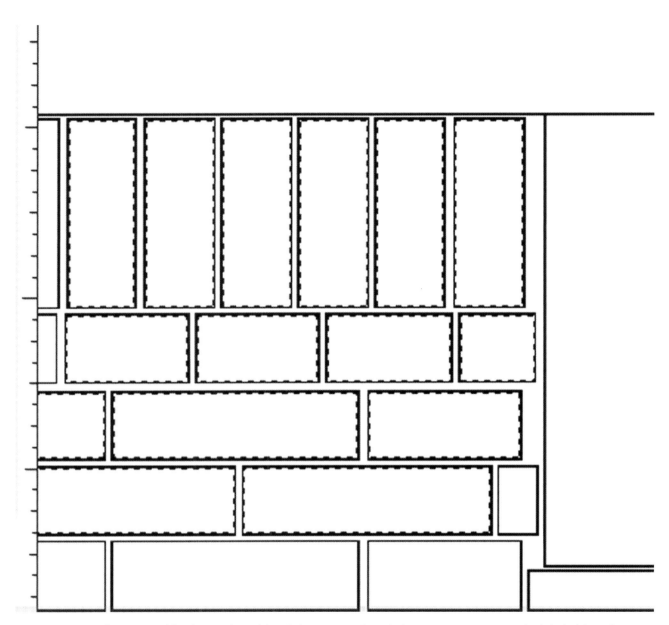

Figure 21.3 The group of bricks is selected by clicking on each with the MAGIC WAND tool while holding down the SHIFT key.

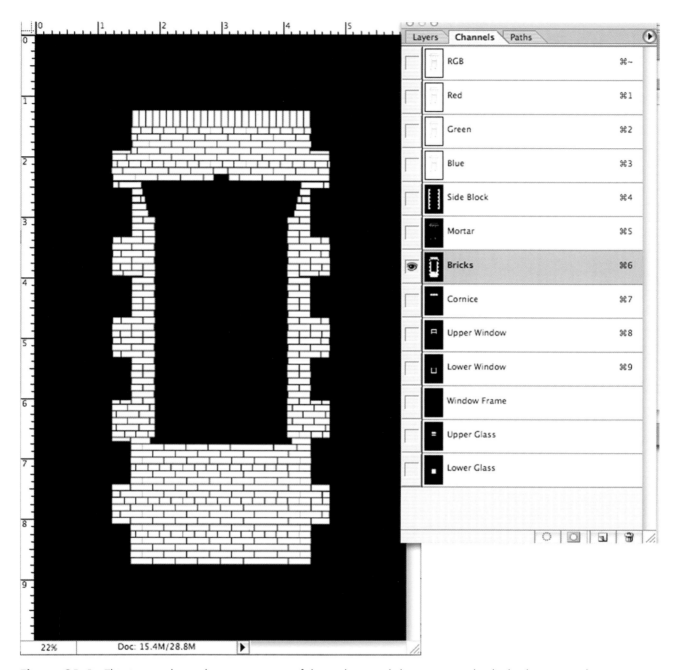

Figure 21.4 This image shows the various parts of the architectural drawing as individual selections in the CHANNELS PALETTE.

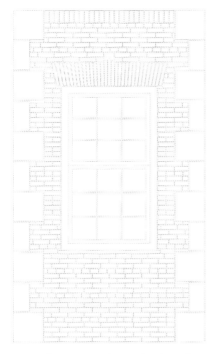

Figure 21.5 This image shows the line drawing medium gray.

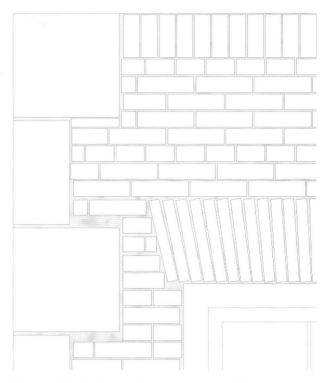

Figure 21.6 The brick mortar is painted first.

PALETTE while holding down the CONTROL key (Macintosh) or ALT key (PC). The mortar is painted a mixture of three colors. A pale olive and a darker cool gray are blended together as one would paint a wet blend. The brush named "spatter" works well for this used at a very large size (about 300 pixels) at 100 percent opacity and at a low flow rate (about 20 percent) in the normal mode. A third color, a very pale burnt sienna, is added using the FILL command at 100 percent opacity but set to the darken mode so that the pale color is only apparent in areas lighter than itself. In this way, it does not affect the previously used darker colors.

The bricks and cornice are made active to paint them as a group. These two channels are made active by clicking on their channel name in the CHANNEL PALETTE while holding down the CONTROL key (Macintosh) or ALT key (PC). Two channels are made active at one time if the SHIFT key is also held down while making the second, or added selection. The bricks are painted in two steps: a wet blend and a spatter. The wet blend begins with a fill of dark red as a base color. Two colors are blended on top of the base using the spatter brush

described above. This brush is one of the brushes in the default brushes in Photoshop. The colors wet-blended onto the base are a tint of the base and a pale green.

The third painting step for the bricks is to use the brush called "dry brush." I modified the brush to a much larger size (200 pixels), at 100 percent opacity with a 40 percent flow rate. Working with short brush strokes produced a good uneven spatter. A very dark warm gray and the original base color were spattered on at this point.

Step Five—The stone blocks located on the right and left side of the wall are painted using a similar technique as the bricks. A base color (pale yellow ochre) is applied using the FILL command at 100 percent opacity and in normal mode. A light and dark color are spattered on the base; a tint of burnt sienna and a chrome green. The application of these colors is at a 40 percent opacity in a darken mode. A third and fourth spatter of chrome yellow and purple are also added. An irregular wash of very low opacity (10 percent) warm gray is added with a large chalk brush using the multiply mode to allow it to build up with brushing.

Figure 21.7 The bricks and cornice are painted with a red base and two-color spatter.

Figure 21.8 A spatter texture is added to the bricks and cornice.

Figure 21.9 The stone blocks are painted a contrasting ochre hue.

Figure 21.10 The window frame, muttons, and mullions are painted a warm green hue, then an ochre spatter texture is added.

Figure 21.11 Highlights and shadows are added to the bricks.

Figure 21.12 Highlight and shadows are added to the stone blocks.

Figure 21.13 Highlight and shadow are added to the window frame.

Figure 21.14 A cloudscape is inserted behind the window.

Figure 21.15 The finished painting.

The windows and frame are selected and given an opaque base coat, then a pale ochre spatter is added.

Step Six—Highlight and shadow are now added to the block and brick. The tool used is a small (5-pixel) standard solid brush at 100 percent opacity and flow using the lighten blending mode. The highlight color is a tint of chrome yellow. The shadow color is a shade of purple applied using the darken blending mode at a lower opacity, about 60 percent. In both cases, the brush tool is made to draw straight lines by using the tool in conjunction with the SHIFT key. Click just once at the start of a straight line, then hold down the SHIFT key and click at the end point of the line. A line the width of the brush will be drawn between the two points. Make certain that the appropriate channel is activated (brick or block) while doing the work. This will save a considerable amount of time as highlights and shadows can be drawn in very long lines across the elevation instead of on each individual piece.

Step Seven—Highlight and shadow are applied to the window with a similar technique used for the block and brick; however a different brush is used. A small diameter (9-pixel) soft airbrush works well for the larger shadow and highlight of the window frame. The highlights and shadows of the window are refined by using progressively smaller brushes to make deeper shadows, cut lines, and sharper highlights. The windowpanes are painted in two steps. First a gradient of gray-purple (gradating to transparent) is added in diagonal swipes partially across each window group. Remember to use the CHANNEL PALETTE to isolate the windowpanes first.

Then a reflected cloudscape is added. It was a sky selected from another image, copied, and inserted into the windowpane channel using the PASTE INTO command instead of the PASTE command. PASTE INTO adds image to the selection as a new layer. The layer is set to the multiply blending mode and the opacity is reduced to 20 percent so the clouds just barely reflect off the glass.

Step Eight—A cast shadow of tree leaves is added in the final step. The leaves, like the clouds, are taken from another image as a MAGIC WAND selection. The selection is pasted into a new layer. The leaves are filled with the same shadow color from the window by using the FILL command. The leaves are scaled and placed on the wall to the appropriate location. The leaves layer is set to a multiply blend mode and the opacity is reduced to approximately 25 percent. Finally, the leaves are blurred slightly by use of a Gaussian Blur filter.

Chapter 22

Digital Drawing Exercise Six: Painting an Existing Digital Model Rendering

This exercise takes an image generated from a digital modeling application and paints it with Photoshop. It requires a pre-existing image from a digital model.

The point of this exercise is to significantly improve an image generated by digital modeling. This exercise uses low-opacity paint between the various elements of the setting, foreground, and background, for example, to enhance focus of the rendering. It uses painting to add costumes to the figures generated in the digital modeling software and to complete the surround of the audience. The initial digital image has a very mechanical appearance.

Step One—Make a copy of the background layer. This assures that you always have the original layer. Add costumes to the two mannequin-like figures. Zoom in closely to see your brushwork as best as possible. Paint in clothes using a fairly small coarse brush such as a chalk brush 10 pixels wide. Use the multiply blending mode to paint dark colors. This allows the quality of light to remain from the original while adding the structure of the fabric to the figure. Light colors are applied using lighten or screen blending mode. The feet can be given much better shape and a clearly defined shadow where they touch the floor by painting the shoes. Model the head by adding hair and enhancing the highlight and shadow of the contour of the face.

Step Two—Suggest the presence of an audience. Paint in a rough suggestion of an audience in dark-

ness around the setting in the empty risers. This step is done roughly and suggestively to deliberately contrast the precise feel of the digital modeling. A coarse spatter brush is used from small (20-pixel) to large (100-pixel) diameters. A few spots of light are added to the mass to suggest faces.

Step Three—Bring focus to the scene on stage. This is a process of diffusing or diminishing the presence of the surround and background and enhancing the presence of the stage area.

The windows are given more presence by adding glass surface to them. A multiple selection is made of the window openings by using the magic wand selector at a tolerance of 32. Select the darkest area within a pane and add to the selection by clicking on any other areas within each pane while holding down the SHIFT key. Select the adjoining pane in the same way while still holding down the SHIFT key. Save the selection when all panes are selected in a window unit by choosing SAVE SELECTION under the SELECT pull-down menu. This process was used in several previous exercises. Activate the two windowpane groups and paint them lightly with a pale reflected light. Use a large airbrush (100-pixel) in screen blending mode at very low opacity (about 15 percent).

Divide the image into two large selections. Draw an outline of the set area and save that selection.

Invert that selection and save it as well. Paint mottled darkness into the area outside the set. Select a color by using the eyedropper tool to pick up a

Figure 22.1 The original digital model. Design by author.

shadow color from the drawing. Use a very large (500-pixel) coarse brush such as a chalk brush. Set it at very low opacity, about 20 percent, with the blend mode at multiply and add darkness to the recesses of the audience area. Inverse the process by adding mottled light to the set. Activate the set area selection. Use a pale color, set the blending mode to screen, and use the same brush parameters. De-select the set and make a new selection of the arch unit behind the set by using the magic wand selection tool and making

multiple selections holding down the SHIFT key. Add some darker texture to the arch unit.

The windows suggest a light source and the presence of that light contributes to the composition. A very pale light coming from the windows is added with a large airbrush (150 pixels). Set the blend mode to screen and the opacity to 20 percent. Click once on the window surface and hold down the SHIFT key. Click a second time where you want the light to fall on the floor and a straight brush stroke is made.

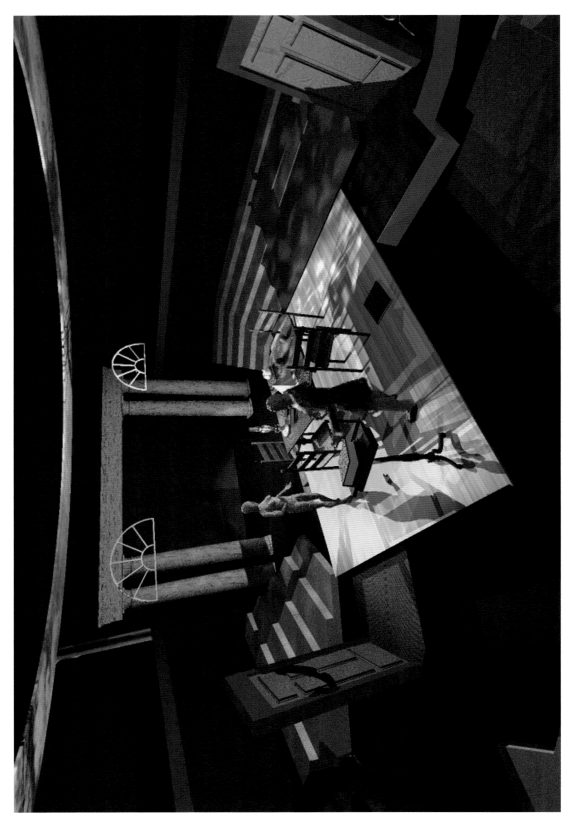

Figure 22.2 Shirt, jacket, trousers, and shoes are painted onto the foreground male figure. Design by author.

Figure 22.3 A dress is added to the female figure as well as hair for both figures.

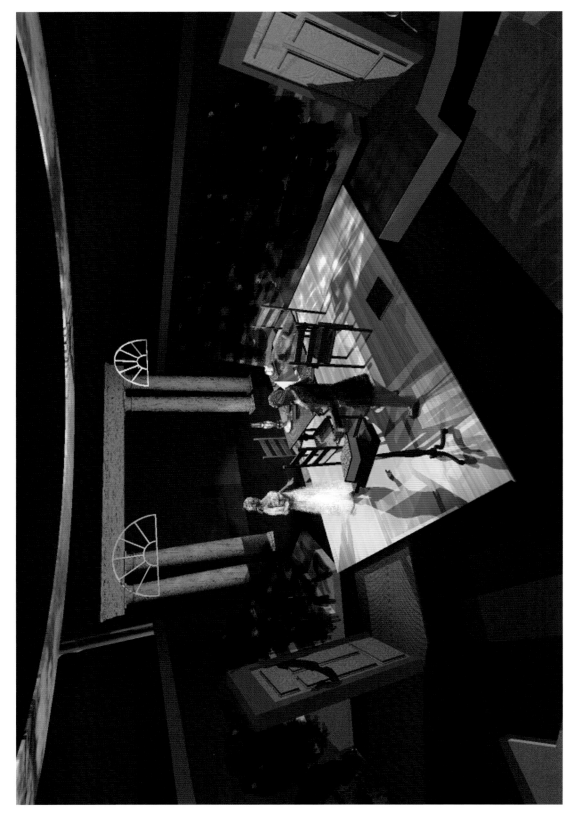

Figure 22.4 The "audience" is added to the seating risers.

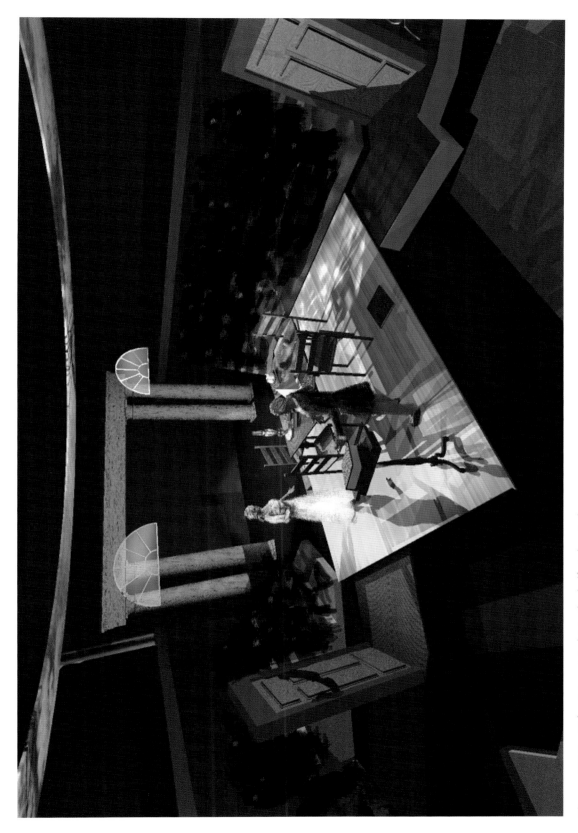

Figure 22.5 "Glass" is painted into the half-circle windows.

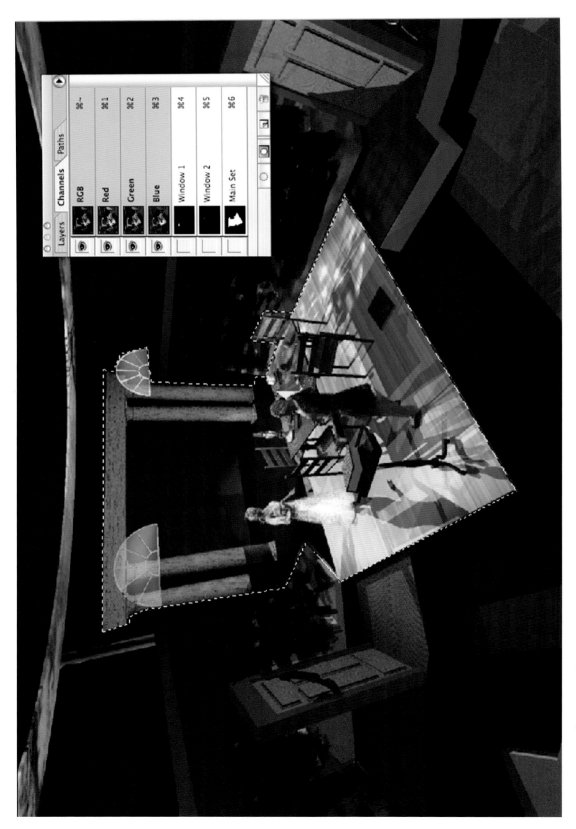

Figure 22.6 This image shows the set as a separate selection.

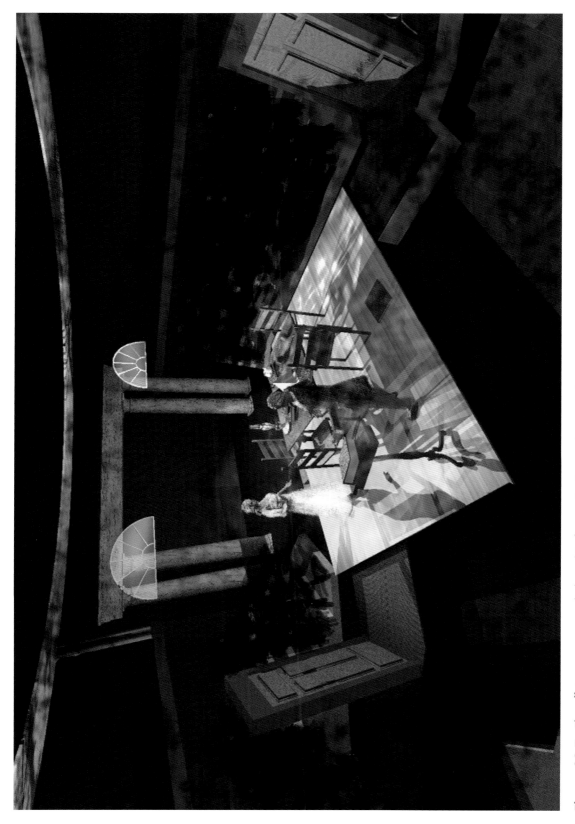

Figure 22.7 The off-stage areas are darkened to focus attention on the set and actors.

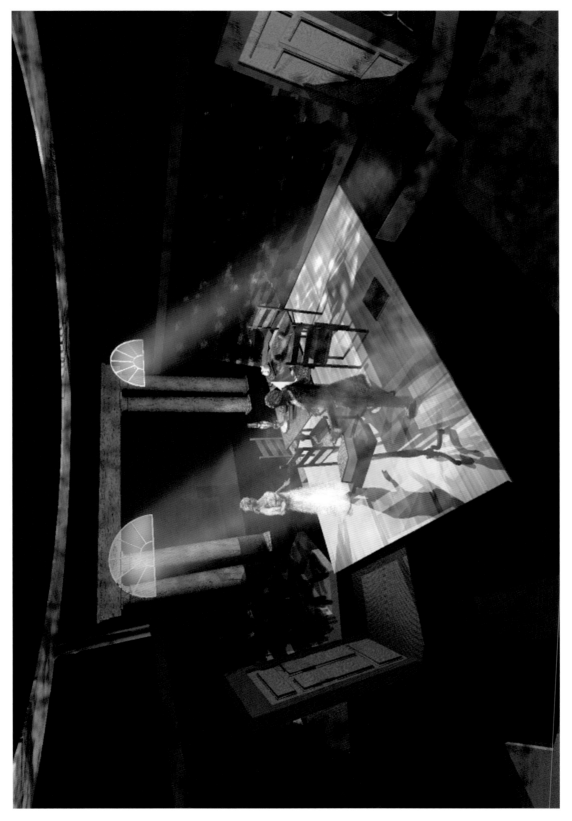

Figure 22.8 Light coming through the windows is added to finish the painting.

Chapter 23

Digital Drawing Exercise Seven: Painting Light into a Scenic Sketch

This exercise takes a bare line drawing of a stage design and adds color and light. It requires a monochromatic sketch of a stage design. The format of the sketch can be either a scanned pencil drawing or a digitally generated drawing. In either case, the drawing must be brought to Photoshop in a reasonably high resolution (300 PPI minimum) file. The example here was digitally generated in VectorWorks.

This exercise builds upon the layering skills covered in Exercise 6 in Chapter 22. The techniques covered in this exercise emphasize the lighting of a scenic image as opposed to painting the scenery in Photoshop. The Photoshop skills required for this exercise include an ability to make and save multiple selections (as in previous exercises), knowledge of brushes and blending modes, and an ability to work with layers and channels.

In this exercise the drawing is divided by layers and channels. Light and dark colors are added to these isolated sections of the drawing. Light is mostly added to this drawing in an additive manner. This is accomplished by adding light in a separate layer set to one of the blending modes that mix to white: LIGHTEN, SCREEN, COLOR DODGE, HARD LIGHT, etc. By painting in additive color to the areas of the drawing that comprise the background, the artist can effectively create a hazy background. Dividing the drawing by layers allows the artist to place light in front of or behind various elements.

Light that falls on the floor is painted in a layer above the layer with the floor. Other layers are used to mask parts of the drawing; for example, the masking and proscenium are used in more than one layer to mask away light that appears in a layer below. This allows the artist to work rapidly.

Step One—Open the drawing to be painted. It is important that this original drawing is of adequately good resolution (300 PPI minimum) so that the lines in the drawing are not blurred. Clean lines will yield much better results when selecting the various elements of the drawing to be painted. Make certain the drawing is RBG or CMYK mode.

Step Two—Select all areas in the drawing that will be lit as a contiguous whole; for example, make a selection of the front of each of the three walls. Their side edges, or reveals, are selected separately. The back wall of this sketch has three principal areas: the wall surface, the reveals of each slotted opening, and the openings themselves. Along with the five selections described above, this drawing also has the floor, proscenium, masking, and a proscenium reveal. Furthermore, the principal wall selections are divided by placement: stage right, center, and left. Save all selections in the CHANNEL menu as described in previous exercises. Save your work.

Step Three—Make a copy of the original drawing layer to conserve the drawing and all the selections. The principal objects are filled with

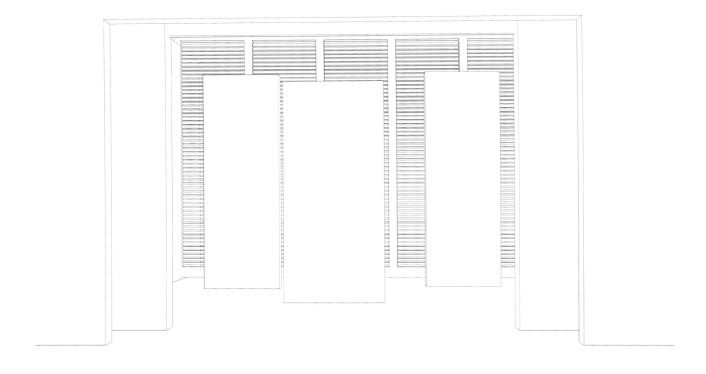

Figure 23.1 VectorWorks drawing to be painted in Photoshop.

various shades of gray in the copy layer. If there is no figure, one should be added on a separate layer.

Step Four—Add light to the stage working from the background to the foreground. Photoshop allows light to layer up toward white (additive color mixing) by using blending modes. The ability to mix toward light can be used in the brush or gradient tools used to apply light or in the blending between layers. Adding shadows and shade (subtractive color mixing) is also possible by using the correct blending mode.

The process described here makes use of the established channels to light the surfaces of the design. This exercise also uses intermediate layers to add light and shadow between elements of the setting.

Light the three elements of the back wall: the wall surface, the reveals or edges of the openings, and the openings themselves. Blue light will come through openings of the wall assuming there is a cyclorama behind. Select the wall openings and fill with a blue color. The reveals of these openings are painted by filling with a lavender sidelight. The channel of the wall surface is activated and painted with a very large airbrush. Dark lavender is applied

with a large airbrush (600 pixels) in a normal blending mode followed by a few slashes of amber with the same brush in an overlay blending mode at 50 percent opacity.

The three main walls are painted with light. Lavender is applied first in diagonal swipes using a very large airbrush (600 pixels), leaving a few uncovered lines. The blending mode is normal and the opacity 100 percent. Amber is applied in diagonal strokes with the same brush but using an overlay blending mode and 40 percent opacity. The wall reveals are painted with the amber light with a normal blending mode at 100 percent opacity.

The floor channel is activated and painted with a gradient. The radial gradient type is selected and the color is set to gradate from amber to blue. The gradient begins at the feet of the figure to the stage left edge of the stage.

Step Five—Light the figure with back, side, and front light. This requires that separate channels are drawn and saved for the areas where the light falls in the stage space. Draw a cone shape for each of the light beams from their source location (stage right, left of back center) with the lasso tool. You may wish

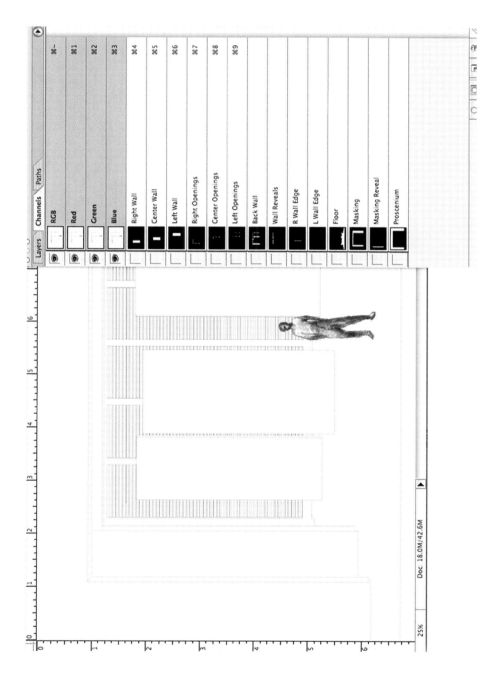

Figure 23.2 Individual selections are saved in the CHANNELS PALETTE.

Figure 23.3 In a copy layer of the image, selections are painted shades of gray, and a human figure is added.

Figure 23.4 The back wall, opening reveals, and the openings in the wall are illuminated with lavender "light."

to feather the selection, then save each of them. Next, create a layer for the light beams and a copy of the figure layer. Place the light layer between the two figure layers. Activate one of the light beam selections, for example, the stage right sidelight. This selection will be painted with the light of that sidelight, in this case an amber light. Paint the light only on the empty layer between the figures. Apply the light with a very large airbrush as used with the other light. Use the screen blending mode for the brush as this will allow the three lights to blend to white on that layer. Set the layer containing the light to hard light blending mode. This allows the light in that layer to react with a luminescent glow to the darker colors behind it.

Paint in all three selections separately using three colors you choose for side and backlight. This example uses amber and blue side light with a yellow-green backlight. Adjust the opacity of the brush applying the light and the light layer itself as you

Figure 23.5 The three main walls of the set are lit with lavender and amber.

paint to achieve the appropriate effect. This example sets the layer at 100 percent opacity and the brush at 50 percent opacity.

Create three shadows of the figure, one for each of the light sources. Copy the figure again three times. Fill in each of these three figures with a shadow color and distort them to lie on the ground. Set the blending mode to multiply and reduce the opacity. Brush onto the shadow some of the color of the light sources that fall on the shadow.

Step Six—The channels previously selected to isolate individual pieces of scenery can be used to create secondary copies of the selection, which can be distorted and made into a shadow, as was done with the figure. To create shadows from the scenery, the background layer needs to be copied once for each piece or group of scenery to be made into a shadow. This rendering used the back wall and the back wall openings as separate shadow layers. The proscenium, proscenium reveal, and masking channels together will serve as another shadow layer.

It is envisioned that light coming through the back wall casts light on the floor, thus the back wall itself creates a shadow. To make this, activate the new layer with the back wall (called Back Wall Shadow). In this active layer, activate the back wall channel. Invert this selection and delete. This will leave nothing in the channel other than the back wall itself. Invert the selection again. At this point the back wall is selected. Fill it with a shadow color, most likely the same color as used for the figure shadows. Fill it in normal mode with 100 percent opacity. Distort the shadow to lay it down on the stage floor radiating from upstage to downstage. Set this layer's blending mode to multiply and adjust the opacity to your liking.

The layer itself containing the back wall shadow should be placed just below the set mask layer in the

Figure 23.6 The floor is painted with an amber-to-blue gradient.

layer stack. It is likely that parts of this new shadow appear to fall on the proscenium and masking itself. Surely this is physically impossible, though very possible in Photoshop. These parts of the cast shadow may be deleted by activating the proscenium and masking channels in the back wall shadow layer and simply deleting them. This makes it appear as if the downstage walls block the shadow coming from upstage.

Create another cast shadow from the proscenium, proscenium reveal, and masking channels in another layer. Delete all but the contents of these three channels from the layer, fill the channels with a shadow color, and distort the selections and adjust blending mode and opacity, as shown in Figure 23.9.

The light coming from the back wall on to the stage floor can be added in a similar fashion. Acti-

vate the layer with the back wall openings, select them, and delete all other contents. Fill the wall openings with the light color seen within the wall openings using VIVID LIGHT blending mode at 100 percent opacity. The vivid light blending mode makes the color used appear to glow against darker colors. As with the shadow, distort the wall light to make it appear to lie on the floor. Set the blending mode of this layer to lighten and adjust the opacity to the desired effect.

Step Seven—Three final layers are added to this image to tone the light intensity and increase focus on the figure. These layers, called light, shadow, and haze, are made as empty layers and placed just below the top layer (figure) in the layer stack. The light layer will be used to add brightness, and the shadow layer used to add shade to the overall drawing. The haze layer is used to diffuse the back wall with haze.

Figure 23.7 The figure is illuminated with three light sources.

Figure 23.8 Light coming through the back wall of the set casts shadows from the walls on the floor.

Set the light layer to lighten blending mode, the shadow layer to darken blending mode, and the haze layer to normal blending mode. Set all of these layers to approximately 50 percent opacity.

The light layer is used to paint in light around the figure. Use the gradient tool set to a lighten blending mode at 50 percent opacity to make a radial gradient from light to transparent from the figure outward. This subtly emphasizes the lightness of the area and makes the light beams more pronounced. Use a shadow color in the shadow layer and set the blending mode to multiply at 50 percent opacity. Make linear gradients from shadow color to transparent from the far edges of the image toward the center.

The haze layer is where the final painting step takes place. A considerable layer stack is amassed by this time and the drawing has become a fairly large

file. It is helpful to flatten the layers when all the painting is finished so the final file is more easily shared.

The haze added in this layer diffuses the back wall, particularly around the edges by the proscenium opening. Haze is painted in using a large airbrush paint tool. The tool is set to a low opacity, about 30 percent, and used with the hard light blending mode to produce a reflective haze. It is painted over the surface of the back wall in the most visible areas of the wall. Paint will cover other areas like the proscenium and the three main walls. This can by deleted by activating those channels and simply deleting.

The back wall has receded considerably by this point. A slightly higher contrast light from within the wall could be added to the image. The back wall reveals are activated in this haze layer and orange

Figure 23.9 Cast shadow from the wall is added to the floor.

light is added in the hope that a warm color would bring some contrast there. The orange light is added to this selection using the FILL command set to a very bright blending mode and vivid light at 50 percent opacity.

Step Eight—Adding projection is an alternative method of adding light to this drawing. To demonstrate this, a projection will be added to the three main walls as a separate layer within an existing layer.

Open the new file with the image to be used as a projection and execute a COPY command. Go to the file you have been lighting and select the set mask layer. Within that layer, activate the three channels that are the three main walls behind the actor. Use the PASTE INTO command to insert the copied image. The new image will be added as a new layer. The added image can be moved and re-sized as desired in its own layer and will appear only through the three active selections of the set mask layer. The blending mode of this new layer remains normal and the opacity is set to 50 percent.

The image has been successfully transformed from a monochromatic drawing to a dynamic representation of stage light. The use of layers to separate areas and channels to isolate surfaces helps the artist have control over the placement of light in a manner similar to the process of stage lighting. The use of blending modes effectively represents the natural process of additive blending of color in light.

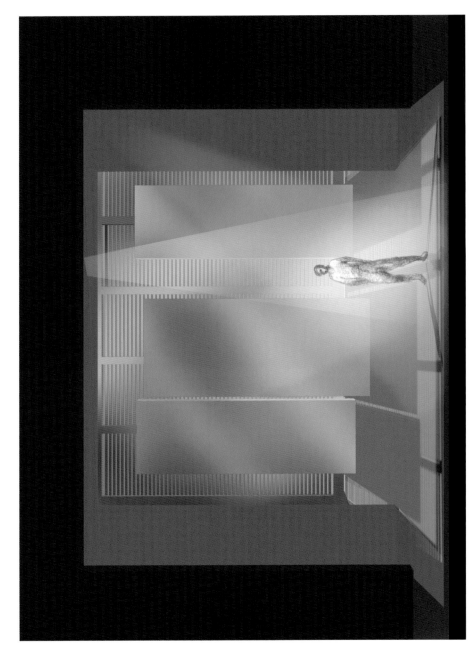

Figure 23.10 Light from the back wall illuminates the floor.

Figure 23.11 A light layer is added to increase focus on the figure.

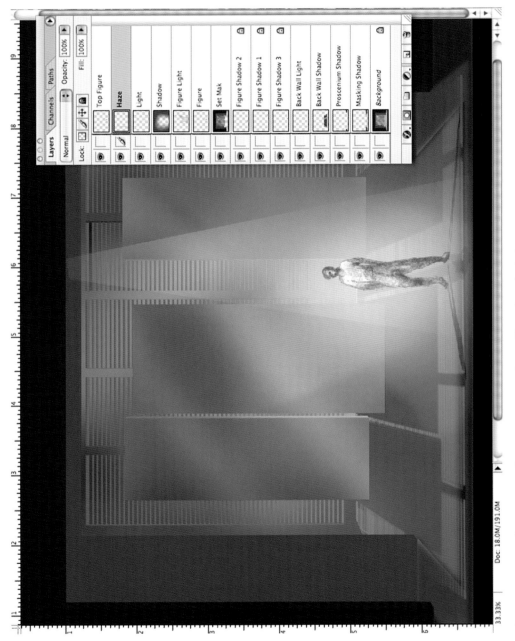

Figure 23.12 The image to this point is a very large file with multiple layers.

Figure 23.13 The back wall recedes after a layer of haze is added.

Figure 23.14 Imported images representing projections are added to the three main walls to finish the rendering.

Index